INTRODUCTION TO

RISK AND INSURANCE

INTRODUCTION TO

RISK AND INSURANCE

Ralph H. Blanchard

BeardBooks

Washington, D.C.

ISBN 1-58798-100-9

Reprinted by arrangement with the University of Nebraska Press.

Reprinted 2001 by Beard Books, Washington, D.C.

Printed in the United States of America.

Preface

There is nothing new in the present volume; it is a collection of papers presented by the writer in various forms and at various times during his forty-five years' study and teaching of insurance. When their publication was originally suggested by Edwin J. Faulkner, it brought to mind an incident that occurred in 1936. After a brilliant address by Ernest Palmer, in which he discussed numerous problems of the insurance business in thoroughly up-to-date fashion, he said, "What I have said I thought was good doctrine twenty-one years ago when I expressed these identical views to another insurance gathering. . . ."

It is hoped that these papers may contain ideas that have been valid over the years. They appear here as they were originally except for some amendments in language. Occasional comments are added in the form of footnotes; they are followed by "(1964)."

Since these papers are not designed to present a continuous story, there is some duplication, which may serve as emphasis rather than surplusage.

The writer is happy to acknowledge the cooperation of publishers who have freely consented to reproduction of papers; their sources are indicated in footnotes.

RALPH H. BLANCHARD

Plympton, Massachusetts
July 31, 1964

Contents

Preface		v
1.	Risk and Insurance	1
2.	The Insurance Mechanism	19
3.	Insurance in the Depression	27
4.	Fire Hazards	34
5.	Prevention	40
6.	Ratios	45
7.	Research	51
8.	Changing Times and the Insurance Agent	55
9.	Public Relations	61
10.	Constructive Competition	64
11.	Automobile Insurance and the Traffic Problem	69
12.	Insularity in Insurance	75
13.	The Casualty Actuary and Social Insurance	79
14.	The Lawyer and Insurance	84
15.	Losses, Expenses, and Profit	92
16.	Health Insurance and the Insured	98
17.	Education	104
18.	Risk as a Special Subject of Study	110
19.	The Education of an Adjuster	116
20.	College and Company Education	119
21.	Reserves	123
22.	Unearned-Premium Reserves	128
23.	Investments of Insurers	133
24.	Coinsurance	138

25. Fire Loss Adjustment   144
26. Apportionment of Loss in Fire Insurance   151
27. The Basis of Premium Rates   159
28. Purchasing Insurance   164
29. Deductible Average   169
30. Description of Property in the Fire Insurance Contract   172
31. The Insurance Buyer Looks Ahead, Personal Insurance   177
32. Insurance and Government   183
33. Revision of the New York Standard Fire Insurance Policy   190
34. A Proposal for State Regulation of Rates   196
35. Insurance Terminology   199

Index   206

RISK AND INSURANCE

1. Risk and Insurance*

Knight says that "Uncertainty is one of the fundamental facts of life."[1]
And like certain other "facts of life" it helps to make life interesting. Out
of uncertainty spring discussion, hope, planning, accomplishment,
progress. But it also gives rise to dispute, fear, defensive tactics, failure,
retrogression. Uncertainty is at its greatest height when, of two possibilities,
each is equally probable—consciousness of uncertainty is greatest when
one *believes* that either of two possibilities is equally probable.

This distinction between fact and belief is important. We *know* nothing
of what the future will bring, but we act on a belief in the future, based
mostly on our experience of the past, whether or not we are conscious of
the past in making judgments for the future. If we have observed or
learned of events constantly recurring in relatively fixed patterns, we
achieve a feeling approaching certainty that these events will recur in the
same patterns in the future. The greater the number of instances and the
less the variability of the pattern, the greater one's feeling of certainty that
the events will continue to recur in the same way in the future. Whether
the events are peculiar to one's personal life, or are phenomena of the
universe, the tendency to believe is much the same. One expects weariness
to follow effort as darkness follows light.

In some cases one feels certain that events will recur but is uncertain
about the pattern. There will be adequate rainfall over a period, but its
distribution by days and months may vary. In other cases one feels
uncertain about both; for example, whether one will be ill and, if ill, at
what stage of life, how long, and how severely.

Our beliefs, our feelings of certainty and uncertainty, while related to
the facts of experience, are subject to the bias of self-interest. "Why be a
hypocrite when it is so easy to deceive one's self?" One is sure that a
program of higher taxation will have disastrous effects on business
enterprise. And inaccuracy of observation may have a similar effect. One

---

* From Bryson, Lyman (ed.), *Facing the Future's Risks* (New York: Harper and Brothers,
1953). Used by permission.
[1] Knight, Frank H., *Risk, Uncertainty and Profit* (Boston: Houghton Mifflin Co., 1921),
p. 347.

is more intensely conscious of the danger of disability from violent accident than from illness, though illness causes much the greater amount of disability. And there are cases where the strength of one's desire is so great that experience, observation, or statistical data have little influence. Examples will occur to the reader.

So far, this paper has considered the more or less automatic production of beliefs by the facts, real or fancied, of one's situation and experience, conscious beliefs produced by an unconscious process. But, in the affairs of the individual, and still more in the affairs of corporate business and of government, there are beliefs, and actions based on those beliefs, that are thought of as resulting from the careful application of reason to ascertained facts. For example, one gathers and classifies data on the traffic over a given section of roadway, and plans and constructs a new highway, allowing a margin of extra capacity for changes in density. If this work is done by an engineer who has no personal interest in the particular program, it is almost a mechanical process, but even here the enthusiasm of the engineer for planning and construction may introduce a tinge of bias.

The significance of all this is that, in accordance with our beliefs or our emotions, we react to the uncertainty of situations in which we find ourselves, and also plan for the future. It is in planning for the future that we calculate, however loosely, the probabilities of various lines of action or inaction, to the extent that we have a choice.

It may be said that everyone hopes to profit from his situation, his activities, or his decisions, using "profit" in the broad sense of achieving satisfaction. Part of his purpose is negative, minimization of dissatisfaction. The fact that a person is alive makes him subject to uncertainties of health. He had no choice in respect of the situation of being alive, but he may choose how to conduct himself in that situation. Many, if not most, of his decisions will be simple reactions to desires; others will be based on reasoned conclusions from experience, his own or that of others. In the usual development, the former class will tend to contract, the latter to expand as he grows older. The latter may be emphasized by misfortune in the shape of early illness from disease or traumatic injury.

Existence in the world of men also means opportunity, by positive action, to seek satisfactions; of comfort, power, wealth, or what not. And it is here that the concept of probability of gain or loss enters. Will a certain line of conduct lead to the satisfactions that this particular person desires? A young man decides to study medicine, to forego immediate satisfactions in pursuit of opportunity for scientific study, respect, financial return. He reasons that he probably will attain these things by investing money, time, and effort in his education. He knows that the results are not certain, that degrees of success vary all the way from flunking out to becoming a famous and highly paid authority, but he "takes the risk." Often he does not reason but only follows a path that attracts him because of his immediate interest in the subject, or because his family will finance his study, while he would otherwise be on his own.

Another man goes (or drifts) into business. He seeks profits in the economic sense, crudely, a return of greater income than he has expense. But he also seeks power, prestige, and the specific things that his money will buy. As he makes his business decisions he is constantly weighing probabilities, consciously when he adds up the figures and observes statistical trends, unconsciously when he relies on "business judgment." He never *knows* what is going to happen but he takes the risks involved in conducting his business in the conviction that the probabilities are in his favor.

Early in the development of civilization the only weapons that man had to ward off untoward occurrences would now be classified broadly under the head of *prevention*, including avoidance of risk. He might wield a superior club, roll a stone before the entrance to his cave, or seek a place to live where he would be safe from flood. These means were largely individual. He also learned to cooperate to some ends, particularly for protection against other cooperators.

The form of cooperation that seems to have been one of the first to have in it the seeds of insurance was the adoption of the principle of *general average*, under which sacrifices of individual interests to preserve an entire venture at sea were borne ratably by all the interests concerned in the venture, in accordance with well established rules.

The first conscious transfer of risk, of responsibility for bearing the financial results of chance loss, as a business was between individuals. Who took the initiative, "insurer" or "insured," is not known, but transfer there was, under a contract nullifying the "insured's" obligation to pay a loan, if a specified ship or cargo failed to arrive safely at its destination. The prime concern of the individuals was the loan; the "insurance" was incidental.

The next important step was the separation of the insurance from the loan, an individual agreeing, in return for a consideration, to make good a loss in whole or in part. Often the total of the insurance was the sum of the amounts subscribed or "underwritten" by several individuals. In this manner the insurance business was carried on at the London coffee houses, of which the most famous was Lloyd's, before incorporated insurers were known. These early underwriters were often, if not usually, merchants who wrote insurance as a side line.

Aside from the development of insurance in connection with commerce, some rudimentary steps were taken in the early days in the direction of life and health insurance.

Modern insurance in Great Britain and the United States had its definite beginnings in the eighteenth century. Several dates are worthy of mention as posts from which this modern system developed. The Sun Insurance Office, Ltd. of London is the oldest insurance company in the world; it was founded in 1710. The Royal Exchange Assurance and The London Assurance were established in 1720 by royal charter granting them a monopoly of *organized* marine insurance but saving the rights of "private or particular persons" such as the individuals who conducted their underwriting business at the coffee houses and elsewhere. The Society for Equitable Assurances on Lives and Survivorships (now the Equitable Life Assurance Society) was founded under a deed of settlement dated September 7, 1762. In 1771, individual underwriters, feeling the need of a central meeting place for the transaction of their business, founded Lloyd's, London. The Railway Passengers Assurance Company, pioneer in personal accident insurance, was completely registered on March 22, 1849. The Employers' Liability Assurance Corporation, Ltd., organized in 1880, was the first insurer to write liability insurance.

In the United States, the first organized attempt to provide insurance was the formation, in 1735, of the Friendly Society in Charles-Town (now Charleston), South Carolina, of whose history and demise in 1741 only scattered details are available. In 1752, the Philadelphia Contributionship for the Insurance of Houses from Loss by Fire, the oldest insurer in the country, was founded, to be followed shortly, in 1759, by the Presbyterian Ministers' Fund, the oldest life insurer. The oldest stock insurer, the Insurance Company of North America, was established in 1792. Two companies must be mentioned as the pioneers of modern life insurance, the New England Mutual Life Insurance Company, which was incorporated in 1835 but did not commence business until December 1, 1843, and The Mutual Life Insurance Company of New York, which was incorporated in 1842 and began business February 1, 1843. Other significant years of incorporation are 1835, Manufacturers Mutual Fire Insurance Company, the first of the factory mutuals; 1863, The Travelers Insurance Company, the oldest accident insurer; and 1887, American Mutual Liability Insurance Company, the first insurer organized to write liability insurance.

Both in Great Britain and in the United States, the first insurances were written by individuals, to be followed by organizations, some for the cooperative insuring of their members, others for the cooperative management of insurance enterprises designed to profit by writing insurance. In this country the writing of insurance by individuals (with the exception of the business done by Lloyd's underwriters in Illinois and Kentucky) is not now permitted. The premium income of the various types of insurer in the United States amounted, in 1950, to approximately $15,000,000,000.[2]

Why did insurance originate and why has it developed to occupy its present outstanding position in the business world? Basically, because individuals and organizations have found themselves, or expected to be, subject to risks of loss that they were unwilling to bear themselves, to the extent of being willing to pay others to take those risks. That unwillingness may be expressed through legislation requiring insurance primarily for the benefit of third parties, as in the case of workmen's compensation and of liability for damages due to motor-vehicle accidents. Insurance is often a condition of entering into business relations, as in the placing of mortgages or the making of contracts for construction or other work. And many enterprises would not be undertaken, were it not possible to eliminate in whole or in part certain of the risks inherent in them.

To say that all insurance is rationally negotiated to serve a demonstrated need, or that persons in general carefully analyze the risks to which they are subject and transfer to insurers all but those that they choose to bear would be to state that Utopia, insurancewise, is here. Insurance is sold by advertising, salesmen, packaging, development of attractive products, and other devices that appeal both to the rational and emotional sides of human nature. No exception is to be taken to the satisfaction of an emotional need through insurance, for such satisfaction may be highly rational; it is only when emotional appeal replaces or deadens judgment that one might question its propriety.

The immediate "effect of insurance is to . . . convert the contingency into a fixed cost."[3] The individual, whether dealing with his personal affairs, with matters of business, or with activities that come under neither head, is constantly deciding what he or his organization shall do for himself or itself and what others shall be employed to do. His decision will be based on his taste or distaste for various functions, on his estimates of ability, on possible or probable financial results, including the comparative rewards to the specialist and the "general practitioner," and on various considerations of general business policy. In dealing with insurance, he will have the opportunity to determine whether he will do best to bear a particular risk himself or, applying the principle of division of labor, to transfer it, at a price, to a specialist in risk bearing, the *insurer*.

This is not to imply that *any* individual or organization can transfer any

[2] In 1962, approximately $41,000,000,000. (1964)
[3] Knight, *op. cit.*, p. 213.

risk it chooses. Insurance is not available to that extent nor, probably, will it ever be so available. When insurance was first written, the motive of the insured was to transfer the most evident risk, the results of which might be serious. He was thoroughly conscious of the risk of loss from such causes as fire and the "perils of the sea." He transferred these risks to another who hoped, by combining many risks and by careful choice and estimate, to make a profit, to take in more in premiums than he paid out in losses and expenses. Or the insured might transfer his risk to a mutual organization of which he became a part, substituting the smaller risk of being a member of an insuring group for the larger one to which he was subject. In either case he converted a contingency into a fixed, or approximately fixed, cost. That is, he did so to the extent that the insurer was so conducted as to be able to meet its losses — the insured is always subject to the risk of failure of the insurer.

As business and personal situations have developed over the centuries the risks to which man is subject have developed *pari passu*. Insurers have widened and deepened their knowledge of risks and have added steadily to the variety and extent of risks that they have been willing to accept; or indeed have sought by intensive methods of promotion. And insureds have come increasingly to realize the existence and importance of the risk element in their personal and business lives and to use insurance as a means of solving the risk problem.

Within the memory of my generation one who insured his physical property against loss by fire was considered to have done all that a prudent man should do; mortgagees felt that they were sufficiently protected against loss of their security by requiring fire insurance. Men bought life insurance more as an "anchor to windward" than as a means of creating and passing on an estate. In special situations liability or workmen's compensation insurance might be carried, the latter often only because it was required by law. Only in the marine field, particularly in ocean marine, was practically complete coverage against fortuitous loss the rule. Other forms of insurance were bought (and sold) in hit-or-miss fashion.

Today, the attitude is becoming quite different, although relatively few have yet learned to think intelligently on problems of risk and insurance. Perhaps it may be said that people now recognize pretty generally a wide variety of risks against which they need protection, and that they are willing to pay for such protection, but that they still have little knowledge and less understanding of insurance. Nor do they evidence the same interest in increasing their knowledge and understanding as in other fields. Many shrewd business men who probe far into the implications of their other problems abdicate when insurance comes up for consideration. The individual dealing with his personal problems may accumulate insurance but usually has no carefully thought-out plan of insurance.

In the marine field, this general statement does not apply. Shipowners, ship operators, and shippers are highly conscious of insurance, understand its functioning, and make insurance arrangements on the basis of careful and efficient planning.

It has seemed to me that the apathy of the general public stems largely from the esoteric nature of the business of insurance. It has a language of its own; it often avoids commonly understood expressions to substitute technical or semi-technical wording, to say nothing of the necessarily technical language that has grown up in connection with so many of its intricate operations. The public, even that segment that uses insurance extensively, has little contact with the operation of the business; dealings are with middlemen, often competent, thoughtful, and bent on protecting their clients' interests, but in too many cases having none of these characteristics. And risk problems do not have the immediacy of today's and tomorrow's operations.

The increased attention given to *programming* is doing much to acquaint the business executive and the man of means with risk problems and particularly with the uses of insurance in meeting such problems.

While the term "programming" is most frequently heard in connection with life insurance, its significance is by no means limited to that field. In its broadest connotation, it means analysis of the risks to which a person or organization is exposed, determination of the available means for meeting those risks, and adoption of a program designed to meet them most effectively and economically. It means far more than "buying insurance," though insurance may well constitute a large, even a major part, of the program.

Consider a large manufacturing corporation turning out a product by a series of processes of varying degrees of hazard; some highly hazardous by reason of inflammable or explosive materials and of operations that may ignite or detonate these materials, others having neither of these hazards; some involving extreme danger of accident to employees, others relatively safe. The corporation operates warehouses, offices, factories, and vehicles; it receives and ships its materials and products; it installs its products under contract; it maintains a large sales force. Adequate analysis of the risks to which such a concern is subject would reveal an amazing and perhaps frightening array.

Not only would the analysis result in a statement of specific perils and hazards but it would develop significant interrelations. The processes giving rise to fire hazard might be housed in inflammable buildings so built as to facilitate rather than control the spread of fire. The employees working on dangerous machines might have that danger enhanced by improper lighting. Stocks of finished goods might be stored in quarters adjacent to stocks of inflammable raw material. And so on indefinitely.

Analysis of the individual's personal risks would develop in a small way the same sort of showing in terms of his property and activities; his house, domestic employees and equipment, automobile, sports. But he would be concerned with the financial results of death, particularly early death, and disability. To what risks are he and his family subject because of their dependence on his life and activity?

An analysis of the risk problem having been made (and here it has been possible only to suggest the scope of such an analysis), the next question is what to do about it. And, with varying degrees of emphasis, the logical attack is direct. What can be done to eliminate, avoid, or decrease the risk? Noninflammable materials may be substituted for inflammable; machines may be redesigned to prevent contact of operators with dangerous points; processes involving explosion hazards may be isolated; equipment and trained staff may be provided to minimize the untoward results of accidents. Even the individual may do much by keeping his house in repair and by fencing danger spots. The objective test of the desirability of measures of these sorts is whether they "pay"; whether the results in decrease of hazard are worth the cost. At times this test can be applied by use of statistical or accounting techniques; often the answer comes from judgment.

After whatever is practical has been done to attack risk at the source, the next consideration is of resources to bear the remaining risk; more accurately, to bear its financial results. Perhaps the first question now to ask one's self is, "To what extent are these results in my (or our) case predictable?" If they may be approximately forecast, they may be directly compared with existing resources, or plans may be considered to provide resources if not already available. The management of a department store may maintain a fund to offset losses from bad debts or may charge as a cost of doing business the small percentage of sales that those losses average over the years. In any business there is a multitude of small losses too insignificant to be taken into account; they are merged without recognition into operating costs. In many cases the question is not whether a type of loss can be borne in its entirety but whether it can be borne up to a point. Even the individual is in a position to bear the occasional visits to the doctor for dressing a cut or treating a cold, though he would be unable, or embarrassed, to meet the cost of a protracted illness. A business may well be able to pay indemnity and give medical care for the run of accidental injury or disease under the provisions of a workmen's compensation law but find itself in difficulties in the face of a catastrophe.

The individual may have a personal fortune, or funds may have been left in trust for the education of his children. He may own the material resources of a home and its accoutrements. Insofar as these will meet his needs or those of his family he need not create other financial resources. But he and the business man must think of the financial needs that his present and reasonably certain future resources will not meet, as well as the possibility of loss of the resources themselves.

And now the programmer comes to insurance, to the question of transferring risk to an insurer in order to approximate certainty for the insured. What principles should he apply? Here he must first consider *possibilities* rather than *probabilities*. Insurance should be taken against losses that, if incurred, would be financially embarrassing. For example, a factory that is the sole or an important unit of a firm's business should be covered by insurance. But if a loss would be a matter of indifference or even, in effect, a gain, insurance is not indicated. It is wasteful to cover a building that is of no present or prospective use, or one that is to be razed at some expense to the owner. And it is to be remembered that, if premium rates are accurate, the odds are against the insured who "takes a chance" on insuring such a building, for the insurer must collect more in premiums than it expects to pay out in losses, in order to meet the expense of operating the insurance business.

It follows that the man who buys insurance on the principle of insuring against the loss most likely to happen (most probable) is on unsound ground.

When it comes to determining the kinds and amounts of insurance to purchase the prospective insured encounters many difficulties, not the least of which is the fact that the insurance business is not organized to meet in full and in detail his particular needs. He will often not be able to retain the risk of small losses, transferring the excess to an insurer. He will find that certain kinds of conceivable insurance are not written or are written only in very restricted fashion. He may exhaust the market before covering the entire amount of the possible loss, the risk of which he desires to transfer. And he will frequently learn that laws, rules, or the insurer's judgment will deny him the exact contract provisions that he desires.

Not the least of his troubles will be the determination of how much money he is willing to spend for insurance. There is no unassailable formula for solving this problem, though perhaps a more "reasonable" answer may be achieved in dealing with business problems than with personal affairs. In fact, it may be taken as an axiom that, except in very rare cases, complete coverage, within the area of available insurance is beyond the means of the individual. If he sets up a complete program as an ideal, he will be faced with the necessity of trimming it down in accordance with his sense of duty, his desires, and his judgment.

Two outstanding developments of recent years have contributed to giving the insured more carefully tailored insurance protection, by both (1) analyzing his risks and fitting insurance into its proper place and (2) arranging his insurance coverage effectively and economically.

One of these developments is the progress in training the representatives of the insurance business—agents, brokers, and insurers' employees—to consider risk problems from the client's point of view; to take a quasi-professional attitude as adviser as well as salesman. This is not to say that insurance men have generally achieved a status equivalent to the doctor or lawyer, but they have made considerable advances in that direction. Both insurers and organizations supported by insurers and middlemen have done, and are continuing to do, good work in promoting and in implementing this movement.

The other principal development is the rise of the insurance manager, or, I prefer to say, the "risk manager." In his most effective role he is in charge of all aspects of the risk problems of his employer, with adequate authority to secure information, and to prescribe and administer solutions. In his least effective, he is a clerk who keeps track of the insurance carried. In too many cases he is actually only what his popular title indicates, an "insurance buyer." The line of evolution of the position is from the clerk (the embryo) to the manager. And, fortunately, that evolution is going on apace; sometimes by improvement in the ability and status of the embryo, often by the introduction of already skilled personnel. The adequately equipped risk manager sees his problem as a whole and in its related parts. He is an expert and, as such, able to deal on a plane of equality with insurers and other experts whose superior knowledge has in the past often baffled the business executive. The efficient risk and insurance programs of those concerns employing such a manager may be happily contrasted with the frequently haphazard methods of the past.

For the business concern that is not able to employ a full-time manager, there are competent consultants who render similar services.

None of these groups should be thought of as replacing the others. The best results seem to be attained by harmonious interchange of advice, facilities, and service.

During all these years of growth and evolution, insurance has not been permitted to go its own sweet way—government has taken an interest in its activities and condition. This interest has been expressed, and the resulting regulation of the business carried out, by state insurance officials (usually "commissioners" or "superintendents") administering state insurance laws and exercising a considerable extra-legal influence on the conduct of the business.

Until 1944 it was generally felt, though by no means unquestioned, that regulation of insurance in the several states was not within the power of the federal government, since the Supreme Court of the United States had repeatedly declared that insurance was not commerce. On June 5th of that year the Court reversed itself, declared insurance to be commerce and therefore subject to federal regulation to the extent that it was interstate in character or effect. All members of the Court who took part in the case agreed that insurance was subject to federal regulation under the commerce clause of the Constitution, but there was sharp disagreement between the majority, who decided that the Sherman Act, as then on the statute books, applied to insurance, and the minority who took the opposite position. This latter question was of particular importance, since, under the Sherman Act, the making of prices in concert is, *ipso facto*, illegal, and since the making of prices (premium rates) in concert is fundamental to the operation of most kinds of insurance.

The Congress showed no disposition to favor taking over regulation of insurance by the federal government and enacted Public Law 15 (79th Congress), the net effect of which has been largely to exempt insurance from federal regulation to the extent that it is regulated by state law. To provide the regulation of premium rates that would exempt them from the impact of the Sherman Act, state laws were enacted almost universally. The present position is that insurance is still subject to state regulation, modified and intensified to keep that activity within the domain of the state government.

The prime object of governmental regulation has been, and is, solvency —ability of insurers to meet their obligations to insureds. But the standard of solvency for insurers is considerably higher than for the usual run of business, which is that of ability to meet financial obligations as they mature. An insurer must not only be able to meet maturing obligations but must be in condition to meet obligations that it has *incurred*, regardless of when they may mature. What that condition is in a particular case is determined by statutory rules and by the calculations and judgments of the state insurance department. For example, an insurer must set up a reserve (liability) for the total calculated or estimated probable costs of all claims made against it that have not finally been satisfied, even though the time of payment may run into the indefinite future. It must have sufficient admitted (state-approved) assets to cover its liabilities and its capital, if any. In practice, it must have a reasonable surplus. Of late years there has been evident a tendency to require contributions by insurers to funds administered by the state out of which deficiencies of insolvent insurers are to be met. Laws to this effect applicable to certain key lines of insurance have been enacted.

The National Association of Insurance Commissioners, an unofficial but influential organization of the state regulatory officers, has largely standardized the forms of annual statement required to be filed by insurers. This statement, which accounts in detail for the condition and operations of the insurer, is audited by the state insurance department of each state in which the insurer is admitted to do business. In addition, complete periodical examinations are made of the books and methods of each insurer by the insurance department of its home state, usually with the cooperation of the departments of one or more other states in which it is admitted. Special reports and special examinations may supplement the regularly scheduled statements and examinations.

After solvency, governmental regulation is most concerned with practices, especially as they affect the insured. Except in life insurance, where premium rates are set by individual insurers, and where competition, the writing of insurance on a participating basis, and well recognized minimum financial requirements govern their level, rates for the principal lines of insurance are generally made by *bureaus*. These bureaus are organizations of insurers; their purposes are the gathering of data, calculation of rates, filing of rates with state authorities on behalf of their members, promulgation of rates (usually only on approval by the insurance department), and, in many cases, policing the application of rates. Both the rates and the operation of the bureaus are subject to state regulation, as are the rates used by independent insurers who are not part of the bureau organization.

Three generally recognized criteria are applied in determining the propriety of the general level of rates for a line of insurance and of the rate to be charged in respect of a particular class of thing or insured, or indeed of an individual subject of insurance. They are *adequacy*, *reasonableness*, and *nondiscrimination*.

By "adequacy" is meant the quality of being sufficiently high to enable the "average" insurer to meet its losses and expenses of doing business. The requirement that rates be adequate is enforced in the interest of solvency. If an insurer persists in charging lower than adequate rates, it will sooner or later be unable to fulfill its promises of protection or service to the insured.

"Reasonableness" places an upper limit on rates. They must not be so high as greatly to exceed adequacy—only high enough to yield the insurer a reasonable profit. What is a reasonable profit has been much discussed. Though agreement has been reached among insurers, and between insurers and state insurance departments, on what percentage of premiums is reasonable, that agreement has varied from 0 to 5 per cent, depending on the line of insurance under discussion and the locale of the agreement. Valid, precise determination or formulas seem to be chimerical—actual determination simmers down to the results of judgment and compromise. That profit is justified that is sufficient to serve as a basis for continuing the insurance institution and for stimulating its development in the public interest.

Both of the preceding criteria may be met if the aggregate charges of insurers conform to them, but adequacy and reasonableness in the case of the individual insured or class of insured is a matter of "nondiscrimination" or of the rates not being "unfairly discriminatory." While these words are in current use, I prefer to say that rates should *fairly discriminate* between insureds. In other words, the rates paid by A and B, whose probabilities of loss or expense assumed by the insurer vary, should similarly vary. Otherwise, one of these insureds will be contributing too much, and the other too little, to the financial pool managed by the insurer.

The states have as yet done little in the field of competence, though beginnings have been made in the regulation of practices of intermediaries between insurer and insured. New York has been most active, requiring aspirant brokers to qualify for examination by insurance experience or by education in insurance and to pass a written examination before being granted a license. Significant beginnings have also been made in setting up qualification requirements for agents, public adjusters, and independent adjusters.

There are, perhaps, three special reasons for extensive and intensive regulation of the insurance business: (1) the value of an insurance contract rests entirely on the ability and willingness of the insurer to fulfill the promises embodied in the contract, after it has been made; (2) much insurance is written for the benefit of third parties; and (3) insurance is a technical subject to deal adequately with which requires technical knowledge and skill.

A life-insurance contract may, conceivably, be in force for some 85 years; the typical contract runs for several years. Even if the insurer is sound and honestly and competently managed at the time the contract is made, its entire condition and management could, in the absence of safeguards, change during the currency of the contract. In large measure its continued soundness depends on the quality of its investments. In less degree, other types of insurer must be held to courses that will continuously enable them to meet their contingent promises of future action. Just as there is great temptation for the individual to purchase means of immediate enjoyment rather than insurance, so managements of insurers are subject to temptation to achieve present apparent success in the hope that it will not jeopardize future solvency. These facts indicate the necessity of statutory rules and constant supervisory vigilance to preserve insurance institutions through changing times and personnel.

Life insurance is typically written for the benefit of third parties; workmen's compensation insurance is required by law to insure the carrying out of the provisions of workmen's compensation acts; liability insurance is required of motor-vehicle owners or operators, under certain conditions, to insure financial responsibility for the payment of damages; in practice, or by law, other sorts of insurance are required in order to guarantee fulfillment of duties or contracts. The third parties often have little or no direct voice in the choice of insurers or contracts; their positions must be protected by the state.

Insurance is difficult to understand and the operations of insurers distant, complicated, and highly specialized. State insurance departments, particularly in the more progressive states, act as the expert representatives of the public to penetrate this maze and, so far as may be, see to it that technical processes are employed to proper ends.

What has been said of the purposes and methods of state regulation should not be taken to mean that such regulation is perfect. But it has succeeded in maintaining a high level of solvency and has done much to protect the public from schemes that might, in its absence, have been little more than rackets wearing an insurance mask. Events before the days of strict regulation are evidence enough of such possibilities.

A weakness of present-day regulation is the variation in standards and abilities as between states. This weakness is considerably alleviated by the requirement that an insurer, as to all significant aspects of its entire business, must live up to the standards and be subject to the supervision of the most exacting state in which it does business. And the bulk of the insurance business is done by insurers entered in states with high standards.

The conventional analysis of the experience of insurers into losses, expenses, and profit, while serviceable for calculating premium rates, has obscured the purposes of insurers' expenditures and the benefits received by insureds in exchange for their premium payments. Reports in the popular press have created the impression at times that the difference between premiums received and losses paid represents profit to the insurer.

A more instructive analysis would classify disbursements of insurers as follows:

I. Direct benefits to insureds
   A. Loss payments
   B. Adjustment expenses (to the extent that they represent service to insureds)
   C. Expenses for prevention of losses
   D. Expenses for other service to insureds
   E. Surplus returned to insureds
II. General administrative expenses
III. Selling expense, as such

The difference between the total of these items and the premiums charged to cover them would represent surplus earnings.

Perhaps the conventional item most generally misinterpreted is that usually labeled "acquisition expense," the amount expended in the process of selling insurance, carrying on the necessary incidental negotiations, and putting the insurance coverage in proper order. A part of this amount, often a large part, covers the expense of service for the direct benefit of the insured, as distinguished from reward to the salesman for making the sale. In the suggested analysis such service expenses would be classified under I, D; the payment for making the sale, under III.

While it is evident that society is content to bear the net cost of maintaining the insurance institution, it is not often realized that this net cost is not the difference between premiums and losses, but the sum of the general administrative expenses, pure selling expense, surplus earnings, and such investment earnings as accrue to the insurer from funds advanced by insureds; a considerably smaller amount. And it is in return for this net cost that the broader benefits of insurance are received: knowledge of the existence of perils and hazards, their measurement, elimination of risk; all of which do their part in making possible modern business organization and operation, and contribute to personal and family security.

What of the future? What might be done to make insurance a better tool used more efficiently? I suggest that the basic need is a clear understanding on the part of the public that insurance is a financial tool, of varying designs for varying purposes, to be used to the extent that it serves a purpose and in the way best suited to the particular purpose. Truisms hardly worth setting down were it not that they are so much disregarded. Too few buyers of insurance think first of what they want to accomplish; too many are attracted by, and act on, unsound motives.

Buyers want insurance that may be expected to "pay off," an attitude that often results in insuring against small losses and disregarding the possibility of large ones. The deductible principle, so soundly applied in marine insurance, is unpopular elsewhere; premiums are paid to cover what is largely maintenance or losses that would be no serious burden to the insured. And yet under-insurance is notorious. At the other extreme insurance that offers large sums for small premiums attracts customers; witness the popularity of the slot machines at airports and of "double indemnity."

Users of insurance should address their thinking to determining what perils and hazards they are subject to; the possible losses to which they might give rise; the extent to which they can, without embarrassment, bear the losses themselves; the financial situation in which the occurrence of any possible loss would leave them or their families; the relative importance of each such situation; and the amount and manner of payment of premiums to which they are willing to obligate themselves. All of which would involve no technical knowledge of insurance, only a reasonable ability to assess their own needs and resources.

At this point they would be ready to use the services of insurance; to set their specifications before the insurance man as they would hand their blueprints to the contractor. He might well have useful suggestions that would lead to amendments, and the available insurance would probably not be exactly tailored to the specifications. But such procedure would lead to a better functioning of present insurance facilities and, if generally adopted, might well lead to improvement in the available facilities.

One of the common answers to proposals for new forms or methods of insurance is, "there is no demand for it." Aside from the fact that this plea in avoidance is often not true, it puts the insurer in the position of arguing that insurance facilities should not be improved on the initiative of insurers but only on that of the customers. More widespread literacy in matters of risk might well stimulate insurers to greater interest in improved facilities.

Legislative policy has long expressed itself in statutes limiting the kinds of insurance that an insurer may write. Until recently the statutes had divided insurers, with some overlapping, into three groups; life, fire and marine, and casualty. Now, on satisfying certain requirements, each of the latter two may write practically all permitted lines of insurance, other than life. The purpose of restricting insurers to permitted lines is to prevent their embarking on unsafe ventures. At the same time, it limits their ability to serve the insuring public. There seems now to be no good reason why insurers, other than life, should not be allowed to write any sort of insurance "not contrary to public policy." There is no more danger that underwriters will use bad judgment in writing unsound varieties of insurance than that they will conduct their business improvidently within the permitted areas.

Coincident with the broadening of insurers' powers there has taken place a considerable and praiseworthy advance in the direction of the "all-risks" contract. The term "all-risks" is not so absolute as it sounds. In insurance against loss of physical property it means that the contract initially covers all fortuitous loss to which the property may be subject. There are, however, always exclusions that modify the all-inclusive insuring clause—and presumably always will be. But the contract includes a complete statement of what is covered and what is not. It is to be contrasted with the "named-perils" contract that, no matter how many causes of loss may be named or covered, omits coverage, without specification, of any that are not named. From the insured's point of view there is an undesirable indefiniteness in the latter form of contract. It is to be hoped and, I believe, expected, that the all-risks tendency will persist.

Life-insurance and marine-insurance contracts have long followed the all-risks pattern; disability contracts, in large measure; and liability contracts have more lately adopted it.

As already noted, most types of insurance contract cover, uneconomically, small losses that the insured might well bear himself. Such coverage is uneconomical on two counts: (1) paying losses through insurance involves not only the losses but the additional expense of operating the insurer; (2) the cost of handling very small losses is out of all proportion to their amounts. And it is the insured who pays, since, in the long run, insurers must collect sufficient premiums to cover losses *and* expenses. Use of the *deductible clause*, provided for payment only of that part of losses in excess of a specified amount, would meet this situation and enable the insured to apply his premiums where they are most needed, in purchase of insurance against serious losses.

Deductibles have long been accepted practice in marine insurance, motor-vehicle collision insurance, and health insurance, and have recently been introduced, sometimes rather tentatively, elsewhere. Granted that they have no place in life insurance, that they may be impractical in a large part of liability insurance, and that they introduce some difficulties, it is believed that their use, adjusted to the problems of each kind of insurance and of each insured, would do much to enhance the efficiency of insurance and perhaps would improve loss figures by interesting insureds in preventing losses and in suppressing petty and improper claims.

Probably a great deal could be done to simplify insurance contracts; in length, manner of expression, and arrangement. Worthy beginnings have been made, but much remains to be done. Further development of the all-risks contract would help here, for a considerable part of the intricate verbiage of these contracts is made necessary by efforts to draw fine lines between different covers; sometimes to conform to law, often to preserve traditional demarcations.

The changes that are going on in the insurance business, and the changes that might well eventuate, should be mutually contributory. They would be assisted by an attitude of seeking what is good in the new rather than regarding a proposed change as a challenge to one's ability to "kill" it. The burden of proof is properly on the proponent of change, but the proof offered should be given full consideration, and change should not be held to be, in itself, bad. It is believed that the two things that can do most to bring about progressive change are greater understanding on the part of the public and cooperation with the public in setting up sound programs for meeting their risks.

The insurance business has accomplished great things over the two centuries during which it has had its principal development. It is well to note these things, especially the extent to which it has achieved its prime purpose of providing security. But it is also well to consider what it may accomplish in the future, with its past as a foundation. Its possibilities may lie more in its incidental services and in the more efficient application of its security function than in further assurance of its safety.

2. The Insurance Mechanism*

The preceding chapter has dealt with the theory of insurance and with prevention. The present chapter has to do with the mechanism of insurance —its component parts and their interrelations. While, broadly speaking, the same theory underlies the operation of all types of insurance, and the same general mechanism is used to implement the theory, there is the utmost variation in practice.

Classes of Insurance. *Life* insurance—insurance against loss due to the contingencies of living or dying (*life contingencies*)—constitutes one broad class of insurance; insurance *other than life*, the other. Between these two classes certain broad distinctions may be drawn; within them are further classes, distinguished one from the other by increasingly fine distinctions as they are broken down, until one becomes more impressed by the diversity than by the unity of the insurance institution.

Insurance other than life is traditionally classified as *fire, marine,* and *casualty.* Fire insurance is insurance against loss caused by hostile fire and, in practice, carries with it insurance against loss by lightning. Traditionally, fire insurers also write certain *allied lines,* insuring against loss by such causes as wind, hail, rain, collision, riot and civil commotion, explosion, water damage, and earthquake. Marine insurers cover principally losses due to the perils of transportation. Casualty insurers cover a wide variety of causes of loss; their field is principally liability under the law of negligence and under workmen's compensation acts, but they also write many other kinds of insurance such as accident and sickness [health]; glass; boiler and machinery; and burglary, theft, and robbery. Surety bonds are written by casualty insurers, some of which specialize in that field.

There is much overlapping; life insurers write a large and rapidly increasing volume of accident and sickness insurance; the marine-insurance business is largely written by combined fire-and-marine insurers; and there is a marked movement toward multiple-line underwriting (the writing of all kinds of insurance other than life), by insurers other than life.

Insurance Language. The student should beware the pitfalls of insurance

---

* Mowbray, Albert H., and Blanchard, Ralph H., *Insurance* (5th ed.; New York: McGraw-Hill Book Co., 1961), Chap. 5.

19

language, both official and colloquial. The same word may have different meanings in connection with different types of insurance, and the same thing may be described by different words. Words having commonly accepted meanings elsewhere may have other meanings in insurance, and insurance words are often used loosely, even by insurance men. In this text it is intended to make clear the meaning of terms necessary to an understanding of the subjects discussed. Occasionally the authors will use their own terminology, but mostly the usage will be that of the insurance community.

What Is Insurance? For the practical purpose of presenting the mechanism that gives effect to insurance, it may be said that *insurance* is a promise by an *insurer* to an *insured* of *protection* and/or *service*. By "protection" is meant making good financial loss; and by "service," rendering aid of various sorts in connection with the promise of protection. The promise is made only to the extent that the loss may be caused by fortuitous events, and, with certain exceptions, promised protection is legally enforceable only to the extent of actual loss. The insurer is the person or organization making the promise, the insured the person or organization subject to loss to whom it is made.

As a single example, consider an owner of a motor vehicle. He is subject to the risk of claims for damages alleging injury to persons or property; he is also subject to the danger of damage to, or destruction of, his car. He, as insured, may arrange with an insurer that the latter will, within limits, make good any financial loss due to these causes and also serve him in investigating accidents, negotiating settlements, and defending suits.

Consideration. The insurer is not operating a charitable institution; it requires a consideration for its promise. The principal consideration is the *premium* or price that it charges. This premium is determined, in any given case, by the application of a *premium rate* to a unit. What unit is used depends on its suitability as a measure of the risk of loss. Examples are $100 of insurance, $1,000 of insurance, $100 of annual payroll, 1 motor car, 100 square feet of area, 1 linear foot of frontage.

A second sort of consideration, which may occasionally be of even greater value than the premium, is the *stipulation*, an agreement by the insured that certain acts, omissions, or situations are conditions affecting enforcement of the insurer's promise. A fire insurer is not liable to the insured, according to the usual terms of its promise, "while a described building . . . is vacant or unoccupied beyond a period of sixty consecutive days," or unless the insured "shall give immediate written notice . . . of any loss."

The insurer's promise and the detailed agreements affecting it are embodied in the *policy contract*, ordinarily referred to as the "policy."

It is out of this contract that flow all the activities and problems of insurance.

The Insurance Mechanism. As a basis for detailed discussion of the various facets of insurance in later chapters, there will here be presented an outline of the mechanism of insurance. It will include certain necessary definitions of basic terms, and indication of the functions and interrelations of the component parts of the mechanism, but no attempt will be made to achieve completeness or to draw fine distinctions. Each of the broad subjects here explained briefly will, in later chapters, be broken down and discussed in detail; the purpose of this chapter is to present the background into which each subject fits and to prepare the reader to understand the general relationship of each subject to the whole. Before studying any specialized chapter or group of chapters, it is suggested that the diagram on page 25 be reviewed.

Contact. The first essential to making a contract is contact between the parties, direct or by representative.

Direct Contact. The simplest form of contact is direct meeting of insurer and insured, but it is the least practiced. Under the head of "direct" come meetings effected by mail, by the insured calling at the office of the insurer, or by a salaried employee of the insurer calling on the insured. Often a first meeting is effected by a personal call, and the relationship continued by mail; in some cases other combinations of these several methods are used; in others mail is the only means of contact. Insurers using any of these means are *direct-writing* insurers. Occasionally a direct-writing insurer combines representation by intermediaries with direct contact.

Intermediaries. By far the greater part of insurance is negotiated through intermediaries, and the *agent* is the usual intermediary between insurer and insured. The insurance agent is the agent of the insurer. While acting as such, and within the scope of his apparent authority, his acts, omissions, and knowledge are those of the insurer. His authority, his rights, and his obligations are defined by the *agency contract* with the insurer and by law. He may be authorized to make insurance contracts; or he may negotiate with the insured, subject to final action by the insurer. In general, it is his function to induce the insured to buy insurance, to assist the insured in planning his insurance program, and to serve as a continuing means of communication between the parties to the policy contract. The insurer pays him *commissions*, usually a percentage of the premiums on the insurance effected through him, but sometimes a fixed fee, and in some cases also bearing a relation to the quality of the insurance in terms of its profitableness to the insurer or other characteristics. The agent operates his agency as an independent business man, with or without staff as the nature and extent of his business dictate.

The insurance *broker* is the representative (in general parlance, the "agent") of the insured. It is his function to advise the insured and to negotiate insurance contracts for him on the most advantageous terms with the insurers best suited to serve him. He has no contract, though he may have an account, with the insurer and is paid by commissions which he ordinarily deducts from the premium transmitted by him from the insured to the insurer. His rate of commission is regularly somewhat less than that of the agent. He may place insurance direct with the insurer or through an agent of the insurer. If the insurance is placed through an agent the latter's remuneration is the difference between the commissions at the two rates. Brokers operate principally in certain of the larger cities and are not recognized under the laws of certain states. While they may place insurance for anyone, they are particularly concerned with insureds having extensive interests. While the broker is primarily the representative of the insured, he may, under the laws of certain states, be the representative of the insurer for the collection of the premium or the delivery of the policy.

An individual (or organization) may be an agent for certain insurers with which he has agency contracts and, at the same time, be authorized to act as a broker, in which case he is a *broker-agent*. He may not, however, act in both capacities in the same insurance transaction. It is ordinarily to his interest to place insurance with the insurers with which he has agency contracts, but he may find it necessary to deal with other insurers. A risk may be unacceptable to any of his principals; it may be beyond their capacity to insure; or the insured may direct him to place the risk with an insurer for which he is not an agent.

The Inspector. The function of the *inspector* is a universal part of the insurance mechanism, but the manner of its performance and the title of the functionary vary between classes of insurance. Here it is necessary only to indicate that the insurer needs, by some means, and to some extent, to have knowledge concerning the insured and the subject of the insurance. In life insurance they are the same; in most kinds of insurance they are a person (or organization) and a thing. Inspection determines the acceptability of a proposal for insurance, the price, and the terms of the policy contract. It may be the detailed and intimate examination by a physician and the probing of a special investigator into the habits and other activities of an applicant for a large amount of life insurance. Or it may be the classification by an insurers' organization of a small frame house in a rural environment as one of many of the same type that will be covered for small amounts of insurance and that can be treated en masse.

By whatever name he goes, inspector, medical examiner, rater, or credit man, his function must be performed. Its importance and method depend on the kind of insurance and the circumstances of the individual case.

The Adjuster. The *adjuster* serves in the settlement of claims against insurers. His function, therefore, needs to be performed when a claim is made or where the possibility of a claim demands action to ward it off or to prepare for it. The difficulty and complexity of his assignment vary greatly between classes ˚of insurance and individual claims. Very little difficulty is attached to settling a claim for $1,000 under a life-insurance contract if the insured and payee are clearly identified and death took place while the insured was under the care of a physician in his home where he had lived for years. In contrast, consider a claim for loss of $500,000 in profits and continuing expenses due to fire, in a period of decreasing business activity, by a corporation manufacturing a commodity subject to highly elastic demand, and under insurance with several insurers whose contracts expired one hour after the asserted time of origin of the fire.

The adjuster's prime object should be so to settle claims that the obligation of the insurer, as expressed in the policy contract, is met. But he should also seek to do what he reasonably can to leave insureds and the public generally with a favorable impression of insurance. He should strike a balance between protecting the interest of the insurer and satisfying insureds and claimants. And incidentally he should help the insurer in acquiring knowledge of risks at the point where hazards are most vividly and accurately exemplified.

The specializing adjuster is a representative of the insurer, though, to some extent, *public adjusters* represent insureds. And it should be noted that the adjusting function may be performed by persons not labeled "adjusters." An insured may be represented by his lawyer or his broker. The insurer may, particularly in the case of small claims, authorize an agent, an employee not designated as an adjuster, or a lawyer to represent it, either to conduct the adjustment up to a specified point or to make final settlement. The insurance agent is, in effect, though not technically, more often the representative of the insured than of the insurer.

The Contract. The basic rights and obligations of the parties to the insurance agreement are stated in the insurance contract, and the activities and relations of the parts of the insurance mechanism that have been explained flow out of those rights and obligations. It is an essential part of the mechanism in every case.

Insurance contracts are largely standardized—by statute, administrative control, agreement among insurers, or custom. Much the same fire-insurance contract is in use in all jurisdictions; in most, the basic form is required to be used by regulation or by statute. Life-insurance contracts and accident-and-sickness-insurance contracts are required to contain certain standard provisions; aside from these provisions competition and agreement have produced a high degree of standardization. In other fields of insurance, the tendency to standardization is clear; the older the field, the greater the tendency. The basic form may be adapted to particular cases by endorsements, many of which are themselves in considerable degree standardized.

But if one turns to the contract for a complete statement or explanation of the relations, rights, and obligations of the parties one will be disappointed. For the contract is what it means, and what it means is determined by custom, negotiation, court interpretation, and statutes. The contract may require the insured to submit a detailed inventory of property damaged or destroyed, but, in certain types of loss, the requirement may customarily not be enforced. Negotiation may lead the insured to accept a compromise settlement of a claim of doubtful validity, or lead the insurer to pay where technically it is not liable. The court may say that knowledge of the loss acquired otherwise by the insurer excuses the insured's failure to give notice. And a statute may provide that, although the contract requires the insured to file a form of proof of loss on his own initiative, the insurer, if it requires such proof, must demand it and furnish a blank form for filing it.

Reinsurance. Insurers often find it necessary or at least advantageous to *reinsure*, in whole or in part, risks that they insure. The reasons for reinsurance are various and will be dealt with elsewhere. It is sufficient here to note that *reinsurance* is a device for the protection of the original insurer, both in special cases and as a routine part of coping with the problems of insuring the public. The insured's contractual relationship is wholly with the original insurer—his only interest in reinsurance is in its function of contributing to the strength of the insurer by taking over a part of its burden of risk.

Reinsurance is written under contracts largely standardized by custom, and to some small extent by agreement and governmental regulation, but subject to negotiation between reinsurer and reinsured. Insurers may also write reinsurance, and there are many specializing reinsurers who write only reinsurance. Much reinsurance is placed abroad with alien reinsurers, particularly with the underwriters at Lloyd's, London.

Governmental Regulation. While the federal government has the power, under the commerce clause of the Constitution of the United States, to regulate most insurance activities, Congress has not seen fit to exercise that power. It rests almost entirely with the several states, the possessions, and

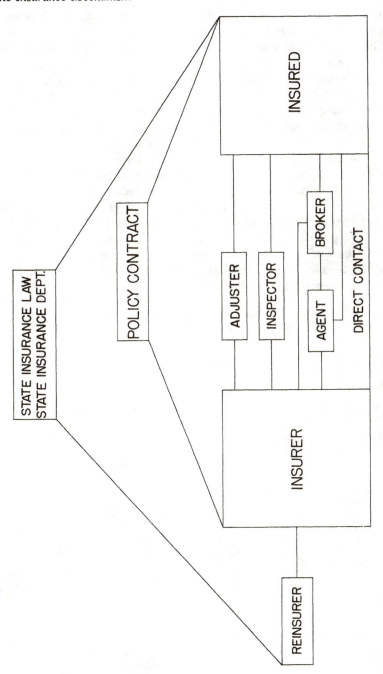

The insurance mechanism.

the District of Columbia, though Congress may change the situation by broadening the scope of federal regulation.

Each state has enacted insurance regulatory laws and has assigned to a state official, or official body, the administration of the laws. The official is usually called the *insurance commissioner*, though formal titles vary. The group of persons concerned with the administration of the law—the commissioner and his subordinates—constitute the *insurance department*.

The general purpose of governmental regulation of insurance is to protect insureds and, to some extent, third parties for whose benefit insurance is written. Its principal and most important aim is to require insurers to maintain their solvency, on which rests their ability to perform the promises made in insurance contracts. Secondary to this aim, but likewise of great importance, is the regulation of practices of insurers and other parts of the insurance mechanism to the end that they deal equitably with the public. A third aim that is relatively new and undeveloped is competence of personnel, particularly of agents, brokers, and adjusters.

With the preceding explanation in mind the reader may find helpful the accompanying diagram of the insurance mechanism.

3. Insurance in the Depression*

To understand the situation of insurance in the present depression, one must understand its fundamental characteristics, its differences from, and relations to, other business.

Variations in nature and methods among the various lines of insurance make generalization difficult. Statements that may be true of most lines are inapplicable to special cases; influences that adversely affect one line are favorable to another. Subject to the reservation that exceptions and qualifications would be necessary to a complete and detailed statement, certain general characteristics of the business of insurance, all of which have a definite bearing on present conditions, may be pointed out.

1. Insurers are financial institutions engaged principally in receiving and disbursing money, and relying for their stability on investments in securities which are expected to guarantee their obligations and to yield a conservative money income. They are, therefore, particularly sensitive to all influences affecting the value of securities, the rate of return on investments, and the value of money.

2. Insurance is a business of prophecy, often of prophecy extended to the remote future. All business, of course, rests on prophecy, but elsewhere there is greater opportunity for adjustment to conditions after the fact. Insurance sets its price, and gives its guarantee, on the basis of probable future occurrences.

3. Valuation, both of assets and of liabilities, is regulated by law and by administrative action. Assets are valued at conservative, and liabilities at high, perhaps excessive, figures.

4. An insurer may be declared insolvent and be taken over for liquidation long before it ceases to be able to meet its current obligations. Its ability to make a statement showing sufficient assets to meet all liabilities (including capital, if any) is the criterion of solvency.

5. Insurers have no funded debts, and consequently no fixed interest charges, except in cases where funds are held to earn such charges.

6. An insurer's plant and personnel, and hence its overhead, are relatively inflexible. In other words, a given combination of offices,

* From *Journal of American Insurance*, April, 1933. Used by permission.

equipment, and men can handle a widely varying volume of business.

7. In the case of insurers selling through agents, expenses for acquisition of business are almost directly proportional to the amount of business done, the cost varying in almost the same ratio as the volume of premiums, since the largest item is in the form of percentage commissions.

8. Premium rates, which determine the income of insurers, are becoming more and more subject to state regulation, either mandatory or persuasive. Such regulation adds another step to the rate-making process and makes for less responsiveness of rates to changing conditions. In addition, state regulatory authorities are naturally more friendly to proposals to decrease rates than to those embodying increases.

An adequate study of the effects of the depression on insurance must await the end of the depression. In the present article it is intended to point out certain broad results of the current economic situation, without attempting to evaluate them with precision, or to treat them exhaustively.

Perhaps the first and most noticeable effect of reduced economic activity appears in the reduction of the volume of insurance written. Decreases occur in stocks of merchandise and other goods, in the unit values of goods, in the volume of contracts for construction work, in the value of goods in transit, in payrolls, in the value of fixed assets, and in numerous other directions.

Both directly and indirectly such reductions have their effect on the volume of insurance. To the extent that volume depends on amounts and values, which are themselves a measure of economic activity, there is a direct relationship. If the merchant reduces his stock in trade, he requires less fire insurance; if the manufacturer's payroll is cut down, it is immediately reflected in his liability premium; lessened building activity means a smaller demand for contract bonds. Examples might be multiplied.

Indirectly, volume is affected by the inability or unwillingness of insureds to purchase insurance as liberally as previously. The insurance bill is scrutinized carefully, and only the absolute essentials are approved; often a chance is taken on the future, and insurance that would ordinarily be regarded as essential is not carried. Where large unearned premiums can be realized by cancellation, such action is sometimes taken, "cheaper" contracts being substituted. Life, and other forms of personal insurance that do not have a direct bearing on the insured's business activity, also suffer from any general scarcity of funds.

The following figures will serve to show the effect of the depression on volume in three major departments of the business:[1]

---

[1] Figures used in this article have been drawn principally from the publications of the Alfred M. Best Co., The Spectator Co., and the Association of Life Insurance Presidents.

Year	New Paid-for Business: U.S. Legal Reserve Life Companies	Index Number (1929 = 100)	Net Premiums Written: Fire & Marine Ins.	Index Number (1929 = 100)	Net Prem. Written: Casualty Ins.	Index Number (1929 = 100)
1928	$18,673,574,996	97	$1,183,174,203	96	$1,096,123,253	97
1929	19,267,332,211	100	1,227,429,472	100	1,126,194,578	100
1930	19,019,790,453	99	1,115,399,838	91	1,070,439,763	95
1931	17,226,248,427[2]	89	965,603,670[2]	79	975,206,499[2]	87

While these decreases in volume are considerable, they are, of course, much less than in many other types of business. The relatively small decrease in volume may be due to the fact that much insurance is written in spite of depressed conditions; property must be protected even though it is temporarily inactive; life insurance will be taken out because the protection is particularly vital when other financial provision has depreciated.

Another reason may be found in the inelasticity of insurance. An automobile which would be replaced in times of prosperity may be continued in use another year. But the owner's liability policy is completely exhausted at the end of its term and can be continued only on incurring the obligation to pay an additional year's premium.

Even a small percentage decrease in premium volume requires careful attention to expense ratios. Stock insurance companies work on a narrow margin between income and outgo, and mutuals are loath to decrease their scales of dividends to insureds. Heavy overhead and inelasticity of organization tend to increase the expense ratio; only careful planning will keep it within control.

Depressions also have a marked effect on loss ratios in many lines, though it is often difficult to separate such effects from those due to other causes which might have been operative even had normal or super-normal conditions prevailed.

In the matter of losses, the bonding business has probably experienced the most adverse results. The results of dishonesty during prosperous times have come to light when the employees concerned could no longer make sufficient profits to cover their speculations. Widespread bank failures have involved the bonding companies in enormous losses on depositary bonds.

Most of the principal lines written by casualty insurers showed a loss ratio in 1931 higher, and often much higher, than the average for the last seven years. This situation is due, at least in considerable measure, to the depression. Beneficiaries of accident and health policies seem to be more easily hurt and to recover less rapidly; workmen injured in industrial

[2] It is estimated that new paid-for life insurance business for 1932 amounted to $14,700,000,000 which would produce an index number of 76. Business in other lines has decreased further during 1932 but figures are not yet available.

accidents have less incentive to return to work; reduced wage scales call for a higher proportion of wages to be paid as compensation benefits; automobile liability settlements are a possible substitute for reduced or vanished earnings. But steam boiler, engine and machinery, and sprinkler leakage insurance show lower loss ratios, due possibly in part to decreased activity. Mercantile open stock burglary losses show a decrease because there is little market for merchandise.

Increases in premium rates to meet increased losses are difficult. Where rates are regulated, time is necessary to secure approval of increases, and approval is usually reluctantly given. The agency force and the public are inclined to be resentful of increases in rates, especially since other prices are being drastically reduced. In some lines, particularly automobile liability, workmen's compensation, and depositary bonding, considerable increases have been imperative and have been promulgated.

During the years 1924 to 1929 the capital and surplus of fire and marine stock companies increased 109 per cent. That this increase was not based on increased demand for their services is shown by the much smaller increase of 18 per cent in net premiums written by such companies. Provision was being made for business which did not exist, even in prosperous times. Such investment was founded on hopes, necessarily disappointed.

It has been pointed out that insurers are built on a basis of invested assets, represented largely by stocks, bonds, collateral loans, and mortgages. These invested assets, whatever the type of insurer, are relied upon to balance the liabilities and show a surplus. Any marked decrease in the value of such assets is a matter of great concern.

Normally such values are determined as of December 31 of each year and are, in the case of stocks and bonds, owned by insurers other than life, the market values on those dates. The enormous depreciation in market values of securities during 1930 and 1931, particularly the latter year, if applied in making up annual statements as of December 31, 1931, would have had a sickening and, in many cases, a fatal effect on surpluses.

The insurance commissioners of most states, believing that market values had declined considerably beyond the decrease in intrinsic values, and that insurers were not likely to be called upon to liquidate securities to any great extent, permitted the valuation of stocks and bonds at the market prices obtaining on the preceding June 30.

For statements made as of December 31, 1932, the National Convention of Insurance Commissioners has recommended that casualty and fire and marine insurers adopt amortized values for bonds not in default, and that, with certain modifications, they continue to use the values of June 30,

1931, for stocks. It was further recommended that the companies set up voluntary "contingency reserves," and gradually absorb the difference between actual market values and "Convention values." These recommendations have been followed by most states, and the 1932 statements which have thus far appeared indicate a general acceptance of the contingency-reserve idea, though it is not clear on what basis the amount of such reserves has been determined.

Even with these concessions, the effect on surplus has been considerable, and when combined with abnormal losses, as particularly in the case of casualty insurers, has been serious. Mergers, liquidations, and contribution of new capital have been the result.

During 1928 and 1929, 133 fire and marine insurers of all types were licensed, while 69 discontinued business, either by way of merger, reinsurance, or liquidation, a net increase of 64. During 1930 and 1931, 52 were licensed, and 152 discontinued, a net *decrease* of 100. During 1932 only 8 new companies were added, while 62 retired, a net decrease of 54.

Similar data for casualty insurance (omitting assessment associations) show 79 new insurers for 1928–1929, and 60 retirements, a net increase of 19; for 1930–1931 the figures were 69 and 109, a net decrease of 40; for 1932, 16 and 44, a net decrease of 28. The tendency is the same, though the proportions differ.

Life insurers, with their assets invested principally in bonds and mortgages, have been less concerned with the deflation of security prices. They are permitted to carry mortgages at face value, and bonds on an amortized basis, provided they are well secured. In general, current income has been sufficiently large to cover all current disbursements, even though the demand for policy loans has caused an increase in that form of investment from 12 per cent of assets at the end of 1926 to approximately 18 per cent as of December 31, 1932. So long as the interest and principal payments are secure, life insurers are not concerned with market prices.

Figures for 48 life insurers holding 86.4 per cent of the admitted assets of all United States legal-reserve companies show that in cash payments to living policyholders and on death claims, during the years 1930–1932 inclusive, they paid a total of $6,169,009,000. Their cash income during the same years from premiums, interest, dividends, and rent was $9,781,198,000, an excess of $3,612,189,000, much more than ample to cover cash disbursements for expenses.[3]

[3] Based on Hardin, John R., "Three Years of Performance," *Proceedings* of the Thirty-Sixth Annual Convention of the Association of Life Insurance Presidents, pp. 81–116. Figures for the last quarter of 1932 are estimated.

Some insurers did not see fit to take advantage of the June 30 values for 1931 and certain states have not permitted the use of these values. Some have set up reserves representing all or a part of the difference between market prices as of June 30 and as of December 31. The result is unfortunately diverse standards of valuation which make statements incomparable with each other, and unintelligible to one who reads them, unless they are fully explained, or reduced to a uniform basis.

The further enormous declines in market prices of securities following December 31, 1931, led to uneasiness among regulatory officials, but the recovery of the market during the latter part of 1932 was to some extent reassuring. Nineteen hundred thirty-two has been marked by reductions in, and passing of, dividends of stockholders and insureds, and by wholesale reductions in the capital of stock companies. During the year capital reductions of fire and marine companies resulted in the transfer of over $87,000,000 to surplus and of casualty companies, over $40,000,000.

In spite of these difficulties, and others, insurance has made an excellent record so far during the depression. There has been no widespread epidemic of failures, and relatively little uneasiness among insureds and creditors. The owners of stock companies have suffered through reduction in the values of their stocks, and through reduced dividends, and mutuals have been obliged to reduce dividends, but the insurance-using public has had little ground for complaint. Such retirements of insurers as have been necessary have in many cases been effectuated by merger or reinsurance with stronger institutions.

Why has insurance achieved these enviable results, in a time of almost unprecedented economic strain? It seems to the writer that there are three outstanding reasons—concentration of the business in powerful and competent hands, conservative regulation of assets and liabilities, and consequently of solvency, and the fact that, even in abnormal times, current obligations can usually be met out of current income.

It is not contended that insurance managements have been all-wise. Far from it. Serious mistakes, due largely to inflationary psychology, have been made. But the larger insurers and groups have been sufficiently well financed to absorb the adverse effects of deflation, and their executives and directors have been among the most competent to guide them in adverse times. Unlike the banking system, which includes a multitude of local small banks, each a complete unit in itself, and administered by poorly trained "bankers", the insurance business is concentrated in large units, which are often in turn a part of larger groups, under the administration of relatively well-trained executives. Their local business is handled by specialized representatives, while the essential control of their condition is exercised in the home office.

State requirements of a high standard of solvency, one which at times may have seemed unreasonably high, demonstrate their wisdom in a time of depression. If insurance is to hold its high place, it must be so conservatively financed that it will be able to withstand the most adverse economic conditions. Preparation must be made, not only for the normal, but also for the sub-normal; not only the *probable*, but also the *possible*, future should be foreseen and provided against.

Insurance men should have learned much during the current era of deflation, particularly the desirability of seeking profits from underwriting rather than investments. Since they are human, the lessons may lose some of their present force, but there is every reason to believe that the institution of insurance will go on giving an increasingly creditable account of itself in the future.

4. Fire Hazards*

Hazards are the raw material of the insurance business. Fire hazards are the underlying causes of the occurrence of fire and consequently of the need for insurance and of the payment of losses by insurers.

Fire hazards may be divided into two broad classes, physical and moral. Physical hazards are those concrete things evident to the senses which may give rise to fire or contribute to its spread. Moral hazards are the intangible human qualities which may have the same results.

Physical hazards are further divided into common hazards and special hazards.

Common hazards are those which are found in greater or less degree in all sorts of risks, such as lighting, power generation, power transmission, heating, inflammable liquids, explosives, matches, smoking, and ventilating systems. These are the fundamental and elementary operations or objects, knowledge of which is necessary as a foundation for operating successfully the fire-insurance business.

Special hazards are those which are peculiar to special classes of risks such as engine testing in automobile factories, operation of kilns in brick making, compounding of chemicals in drug plants, disposal of sawdust in woodworking plants, storage of jute stock in cordage works, accumulation of dust in flour mills, and drying of materials in laundries.

These common and special hazards are all susceptible of inspection and study. Exact evaluation of their importance as causes of fire is impossible, but estimates sufficiently accurate for practical purposes may be made on the basis of records of fire causes and the experience of insurance inspectors. Measures for their control have followed an accumulation of knowledge of their nature and importance. Elimination or diminution of hazards are two important results of their study for insurance purposes.

Moral hazards may likewise be divided into two classes, voluntary and involuntary.

Voluntary hazards include the purposeful causing or increasing of fire losses, failure to take measures of extinguishing or preventing the spread of fires, and defrauding insurers by exaggerating losses. Measurement of

* From *Journal of American Insurance*, April, 1937. Used by permission.

losses from these hazards is impossible, since it would involve an accurate appraisal of human intentions. But proved cases of voluntary moral hazards have been sufficiently numerous and important to show its danger to the insurance business. Incendiarism and arson have been considered of such importance as causes of loss that the National Board of Fire Underwriters has long maintained a special department devoted to their detection and to the prosecution of their authors. The 1936 report of the Board shows that, during the last eight years, they have caused 8,095 arrests to be made, as a result of which 3,506 convictions have been obtained. The extent to which crime and fraud have gone undetected or unpunished is a matter for speculation. Much care is taken to avoid granting insurance protection to persons who have had suspicious fires or whose claims for losses have been questionable.[1]

Involuntary moral hazards are those intangible elements in human character and skill which do not reflect on the honesty of the persons involved but which are nevertheless potent in their effect on fire losses. Carelessness, incompetent management, lack of interest; all of these are reflected in the volume of losses paid by insurance companies. To some extent these qualities are indicated by tangible evidence. Inspection of a risk soon shows whether the owner is careless in the disposal of dangerous substances, whether means of preventing fire are kept in good order, and in general what his attitude is toward practices having a bearing on the occurrence and spread of fire. Inspection of his financial statement, and knowledge of general conditions in his business may likewise give the insurance man a notion of whether the occurrence of a fire would be a solution of business difficulties. For a man may relax his interest in fire prevention without any conscious purpose to bring about a fire loss.

Varying degrees of moral hazard are known to be characteristics of types of business, localities, and nationalities. Such factors in fire hazard are not capable of exact measurement, could perhaps not be proved in court, but they are none the less important in the conduct of the business.

These various hazards caused losses of $293,000,000[2] in 1936. The largest aggregate loss occurred in 1926 when $562,000,000 of value was destroyed. Losses rose steadily from the 1920 figure of $448,000,000 to the 1926 peak, decreased to $459,000,000 in 1929, increased to $502,000,000 in 1930, and then rapidly decreased to $259,000,000 in 1935. The burning ratio (per cent losses paid to risks written) experienced by stock

[1] Two extremely interesting reports of the operations of arson rings are to be found in Kaplan, A. and Berger, S. A., *The Dachis Case* (New York: Davidson Press, 1930), and in Dearden, Harold, *The Fire Raisers* (London: William Heinemann, Ltd., 1934).

[2] Round figures will be used for purposes of clarity; they are based on estimates of the National Board of Fire Underwriters.

companies[3] followed much the same trends although its highest point, .61, was reached in 1921. Commencing at .54 in 1924, it gradually dropped to .41 in 1929, peaked at .48 in 1930, and then dropped precipitously to .24 in 1935.[4] The following chart shows the relationship of these two sets of figures from year to year.

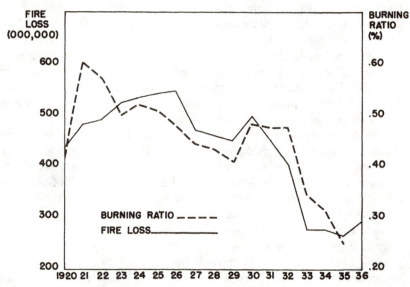

The changes in aggregate losses might be explained in some measure by shifts in the amount of property exposed to loss, but the variations in the burning ratio are indicative of changes in hazards. They are not precise indications since they deal only with insured property, and since they are not based on strictly comparable figures, but they may be accepted as approximately correct.

Insurance men are particularly interested in long-term results. Low losses often reflect temporary conditions, and increases may be expected after a very low point has been reached. But some among them, like the speculators of 1929, seek reasons for believing that we are in a new era, that the combination of circumstances which has resulted in an unprecedentedly low ratio is permanent. They bring to bear arguments based on improved construction, better fire departments, more lenient laws permitting reorganizations to avoid old-fashioned bankruptcies. In rebuttal it is pointed out that burning ratios have decreased before, that in the most recent years incentives to moral-hazard fires have been less

[3] From *Fire Insurance by States* (The Spectator Company).
[4] The ratio for 1936 is not available.

effective, that industrial activity has been at a low ebb, and that a reversal of form may be expected if general recovery continues. The increase in aggregate losses in 1936 to the largest figure since 1932 may be the first sign of that reversal.

Accurate prophecy of fire losses is made extremely difficult by the varied and changing nature of the hazards involved, and by the conflagration hazard, which, while not of the same importance as formerly, is still to be reckoned with. It seems fairly clear that the tendency of the burning ratio is downward but it is also clear that the steep slope of the 1930–1935 section of the curve is abnormal.

It is often not realized to how great an extent the fire hazard is related to other hazards. It has been stated that the fire loss in Cincinnati during the recent flood equalled its total loss for the preceding five years. Oil tanks were dislodged, floating oil presented a serious menace, the water supply for automatic sprinklers was cut off, and operations of the fire department were hampered. Explosions, riots, and earthquakes carry with them serious fire hazards and like floods interfere with the proper operation of devices for fire extinguishment.

New processes and new materials frequently bring increased fire hazard with them. The development of pyroxylin lacquers was accompanied by a serious hazard; it was responsible for one Detroit fire which resulted in a loss of considerably over $2,000,000. Certain methods of protection against termites involve the use of inflammable liquids which are injected into the framework of a building. Oil burners for domestic heating present new possibilities of combustion. To be sure, methods of prevention are rapidly devised to offset these new hazards, but often the need for prevention is realized only after a serious fire has occurred.

Much satisfaction is felt in the progress of "fire-proof," more properly called "fire-resistive," construction. Great advances have been made, but no construction has been devised that is immune to damage by fire. There are many materials that are not inflammable, but the value of which may be wholly or partially destroyed by intense heat. In 1929 the wooden scaffolding being used in the construction of the Riverside Church in New York was destroyed by fire. Its value was relatively small, but the intense heat generated destroyed the value of expensive ornamental stonework through cracking and spalling and weakened steel framework, necessitating repairs which carried the loss to over $1,800,000. In 1934 a fire broke out in a department store in Birmingham, consisting of two communicating sections, one of fire-resistive construction, the other of brick joisted construction. The basement was common to both sections. The entire store was destroyed with a loss of about $1,000,000.

The inflammable contents of "fire-proof" structures are often, when ignited, in greater danger than they would be elsewhere. The fire will be confined and access to it made difficult by the construction which itself resists attack from fire. The extreme heat generated by contents fires may result in turn in serious damage to the building.

One frequently finds examples of inadequate insurance based on the conviction of owners that only a certain percentage of the value of their property is subject to loss by fire. In 1929 a plant manufacturing metal products by nonhazardous processes and valued at approximately $400,000 was practically destroyed by fire, the loss being placed at $385,000. Only $200,000 of insurance was carried on the theory, stated by the President, that he could not conceive of any loss to exceed that amount. The Harahan Bridge, a steel structure carrying vehicular and railroad traffic across the Mississippi, was built in 1916 at a cost of approximately $3,500,000, and insured for $125,000. The only inflammable material consisted of flooring and ties. A fire which occurred in 1928 damaged the railroad section alone to the extent of some $200,000, a figure, which takes no account of loss due to interruption of traffic.

The fire hazard to which a building is subject is not determinable by consideration merely of the risk by itself. Surrounding circumstances, permanent and transient, are important. One of the contributing causes to the spread of the Coney Island conflagration of 1932 was interference with the work of the fire department by parked automobiles and by street traffic. Exposure fires may damage the best-constructed of buildings. The Birmingham fire cited above spread through open windows and even closed wire-glass windows, and caused heavy damage to the interiors of adjacent fire-resistive buildings. Fire underwriters in New York were worried in 1922 by the coal shortage. It was feared that property owners would use makeshift and hazardous methods of heating, and that in inadequately heated buildings sprinkler systems might freeze or be turned off to prevent freezing.

Complete treatment of the subject of fire hazard is impossible in the space here available but it is hoped that enough has been said to indicate its importance in the economic scheme, and to show that practically no property may be considered free from fire danger.

In spite of the diverse and unforeseen causes of fire and the complicated conditions which may foster its origin and spread, the loss over a considerable period of time and over a wide area is sufficiently predictable to make insurance against it a practicable enterprise. But it is practicable only if ample surplus is accumulated to care for years of unusually large losses. The accumulation of such surplus rests in turn on collection of rates which are adequate to cover the average losses of a period of, say, ten years. One of the greatest dangers to the business of fire insurance is a period of abnormally low losses resulting in pressure for reduced rates and speculative underwriting.

5. Prevention*

Insurance, as such, is not concerned with the prevention of loss. Its primary purposes are determination of the amount of loss which may be expected to occur under given circumstances, distribution of that loss among insureds through the medium of premium payments, and making good the *financial* effects of such loss as may occur to the individual insureds.

Owners of property and others subject to loss, whether as individuals or as parts of society, are directly and intimately concerned with prevention. Everyone is subject to risk of loss in some degree, which he may meet, either by preventing the loss, by insuring himself against its consequences, or by carrying the risk himself and shouldering such results as may come to him.

Considering only the economic problem, the perfectly rational and fully informed person would apply the financial test to each of these possibilities and expend effort and money in each way to the extent that it might be profitable. He would adopt measures of prevention so long as the losses prevented amounted to more than the cost of preventing them; he would insure to the extent that relief from possible losses not economically preventable seemed to him necessary or desirable; he would carry himself such risks as he could safely predict or bear without undue strain.

But the "perfectly rational and fully informed person" is a myth. Everyone relies, to a greater or less degree, on the services and stimuli provided by individual experts or organizations. And it is one of the functions of insurers to supply expert knowledge and stimulus in the field of prevention.

Self-interest on the part of stockholders expressing itself through stock companies, or of insureds through mutuals, leads to general activity in prevention. Rates of premium are based on the past; if disbursements can be kept below the level on which rates have been predicted, the result is a larger underwriting gain. Or possibly it may be thought necessary to retard a tendency for losses to reach higher levels than were contemplated in the rates charged; here the prevention of losses to insureds may in turn prevent a decrease in underwriting gains or minimize an underwriting

* From *Journal of American Insurance*, July, 1932. Used by permission.

loss.[1] Such motives prompt the interest and activity of insurers in general safety campaigns, such as "fire-prevention week" and the "Save-A-Life" campaigns of the National Bureau of Casualty and Surety Underwriters.

To the hope for definite loss-reducing results from these campaigns, one must add the favorable advertising given to the institution of insurance. Prevention of losses is a public service which will be increasingly important as time goes on. Performance of such service by private insurance tends to justify the continuance and expansion of that business. Far-sighted insurance men undoubtedly have this thought in mind. However, it is the specific case which has most interested insurers, and in connection with which they have made their greatest contributions to preventive work. The competitive appeal of individual insurers or groups of insurers for the specific risk has resulted in enormous savings to insureds and to the public at large. And it is here that the insurer functions most efficiently both as expert and as stimulus. For it can offer the insured an evaluation of the effect of given preventive measures, and a reward in the shape of a reduction of premium cost, present or prospective.

There are various schemes of merit rating, under which reductions in the risk of loss are made the basis for reduced insurance cost. In fire insurance, for example, most business risks are rated under a schedule providing credits for good points and charges for bad. The installation of an automatic-sprinkler system will call for a definite credit, or reduction in rate. So great are the reductions, in many cases, that the installation of the sprinkler system will be financed by an organization in return for the rate savings over a few years, after which they accrue to the insured who has only the maintenance charges to bear, the capital cost having been financed by the savings.

In workmen's compensation insurance the value of certain physical improvements in a risk can be measured in advance (schedule rating), and the probable savings credited to the insured as a reduction in rate. Adverse conditions lead to an increase in rate. The cost of improvements can be compared with the rate reduction, and a financial test of their practicability thus applied. Contracting risks, and others which have no fixed physical plant, cannot be so rated; instead, all but the smallest risks are "experience rated," i.e., a record of their losses is kept, and their rates raised or lowered in accordance with that experience. Here the connection between particular safety measures and cost of insurance may be more difficult to demonstrate to the insured, but the effect on his pocketbook of favorable or adverse

[1] Much recent publicity has been directed to the end of convincing the public that the whole problem of rate level for automobile liability insurance is in its hands; that individual and group efforts for prevention will bear fruit in lower rates.

experience will be no less clear. The combined use of schedule and experience rating, particularly on larger risks, brings both types of pressure to bear.[2]

More might well be done to impress insureds with the fact that prevention merely of immediate and insurable losses is not the complete aim of preventive work. Damage to a plant by fire, even though covered by ordinary fire insurance and by business interruption insurance, may leave in its trail losses due to disorganization of personnel, loss of customers, and distraction of executives from their work of development of the business, all uninsurable. It has been demonstrated[3] that the "hidden costs" due to industrial accidents are approximately four times the apparent costs of compensation and medical payments. Study of hazards and of means of overcoming them frequently also leads to the discovery of more efficient as well as safer methods of doing work. In one plant, punch presses, controlled by pedals requiring considerable strength to operate, caused many serious injuries to workers' hands. The substitution of dual air trips, easily operated, removed the operator's hands from the danger zone and at the same time enabled the employment of girls at a considerable reduction in wage cost. In the early days of fire prevention, investigation showed that many fires were spread through strata of gas which arose from the lubricating oil used in certain machinery. Substitution of a new sort of oil removed this hazard and provided more efficient lubrication.

In some cases insurers have become primarily prevention-service institutions and provide indemnity only incidentally. Notable examples are found in factory fire insurance and in steam boiler insurance.

The factory mutual insurance system was originated in 1835 by Zachariah Allen, a mill-owner who, having installed apparatus for extinguishing fires, applied for a reduction in his fire insurance rate but was unable to secure it. He then turned his efforts to interesting other mill-owners in the formation of an organization "to study fire prevention, to encourage the use of every effective means of checking and extinguishing fires, and to obtain insurance at actual cost."[4] From that beginning, following the same principle, have developed the Associated Factory Mutual Insurance Companies which had on their books on December 31, 1931, a total amount at risk of over $9,500,000,000. That the prevention efforts of these companies have been effective is shown by the typical experience of the largest of them, which has reduced the average yearly losses per $100 of

[2] Schedule rating in workmen's compensation insurance is obsolescent. (1964)
[3] See Heinrich, H. W., *Industrial Accident Prevention* (New York: McGraw-Hill Book Co., 1931), Chap. 2.
[4] French, Edward V., *Factory Mutual Insurance* (Boston: Arkwright Mutual Fire Insurance Co.), p. 4.

insurance from $0.3341 for the period 1850–1860 inclusive, to $0.0199 for the period 1921–1930 inclusive. Significant of the present emphasis on prevention is the fact that a group of these companies which writes over 30 per cent of the total business expended in 1931 on engineering inspection and prevention work more than was paid out in direct fire losses.

The preventive work of these companies is carried on principally through a central organization which maintains laboratories for testing and experimental work, and an inspection force which is constantly in touch with conditions in individual risks. The stock companies have developed a similar system in their "factory insurance associations" and in the Underwriters' Laboratories.

Even more striking are the figures for steam boiler insurance. The stock companies doing business in New York had losses, for the seven years 1924–1930 inclusive, equal to 14.8 per cent of premiums, and "inspection and bureau" expenses (practically all for preventive work) equal to 38.2 per cent. In other words, their expenses for prevention amounted to more than two and one-half times their losses.

In the case of large risks, such as factories, automobile fleets, and department stores, or where the hazards are definite and serious, as in mines, boiler rooms, and large construction projects, evaluation of the results of preventive work is a comparatively simple problem. The insured can be shown the direct saving to be achieved both in terms of reduced rates, and reduction of losses beyond those covered by his insurance contract. Hence the emphasis on the individual risk.

Much has also been accomplished in the more general but less clearly profitable fields. Standards of construction have been raised through improved building codes, through pressure on manufacturers to produce electrical and other fixtures the fire hazard of which is reduced to a minimum. The National Fire Protection Association devotes itself to educational work and to cooperation with public authorities, and is supported in considerable measure by insurance interests. The value of such work must largely be accepted on faith, but not unreasoning faith. And it must be, and is, supported for the general and ultimate good, rather than for an immediate financial profit to a particular interest.

In the future, as in the past, insurance must be looked to as the principal agency in the advancement of prevention. Measurement of hazards and of reduction of hazards is best achieved through the experience, personal and statistical, of insurance underwriters; the most appealing reward for initiative in prevention is a reduction in insurance rates.

"Insurance develops knowledge of the existence of hazards and indicates their relative importance. It furnishes the best possible basis for approaching the problem of prevention; and, because of the efficacy of prevention in lowering insurance costs, the greatest possible stimulus to preventive work. Further, the effectiveness of the stimulus bears a direct relation to the efficacy of given preventive efforts. In other words, the greater the loss one can prevent by given efforts, the greater the reward in reduced costs, and hence the greater the stimulus to activity.

"Not only does the application of insurance to a particular hazard problem tend to develop preventive work and to put it on the most effective basis, but, to the extent that the preventive work is successful, the cost of insurance and the burden of its requirement is lessened.

"Prevention and insurance are not mutually exclusive nor alternative methods of approach to a problem of hazard; they are complementary and mutually helpful." [5]

---

[5] Discussion by R. H. Blanchard of Albert W. Whitney's paper on "The Place of Conservation in Insurance," *Proceedings* of the Casualty Actuarial Society, XVIII, 199.

6. Ratios*

I expect that your invitation to me to address you on the subject of ratios was suggested by the new Policy Experience Exhibit which your companies are to file this year. The form adopted by the Commissioners calls for the "rate of commission and expense allowance" on each policy and strongly implies that ratios will be calculated from the figures on premiums and losses. In fact, there is little point in requiring these figures unless ratios are to be calculated.

These and other ratios, *properly used*, may be valuable to regulatory authorities, to Conference statisticians, and to insurer managements. In themselves, ratios are meaningless, but they are inherently dangerous because of the tendency of lazy, biased, or poorly equipped minds to make unwarranted inferences from them. To paraphrase Mark Twain: there is something fascinating about ratios; one gets such wholesale returns in conclusions out of such trifling investment of fact. I shall hazard the generalization that a ratio is useful only as a starting point for further research; that it is significant only in terms of the underlying facts that produced it. But again turning to authority, let me quote Justice Holmes: "A generalization is empty so far as it is general. Its value depends on the number of particulars which it calls up to the speaker and the hearer."

It is now incumbent on me to support these assertions, which I believe can best be done by a series of illustrative examples drawn from your business and from other insurance fields.

First, consider the two bases on which experience may be reported and which will produce ratios of either incurred losses to earned premiums or paid losses to written premiums. Some time ago I prepared a table[1] comparing these two ratios for the accident-and-health business for the period 1938 to 1942, inclusive, during which net premiums written increased 78 per cent. For the business as a whole the paid-written ratio was 4 points, or 6 per cent, less than the incurred-earned ratio. For the

---

*Address before the annual meeting of the Health and Accident Underwriters Conference, Chicago, May 17, 1949.

[1] *Survey of Accident and Health Insurance*, Bulletin No. 4, Social Security Administration (Washington, 1946).

45

two classes of business showing the greatest percentage increase in premiums the differences were particularly striking. For hospitalization insurance the paid-written ratio was 54 per cent; the incurred-earned, 59, a difference of 5 points or 9 per cent. For group the figures were, respectively, 62 per cent and 75 per cent; a difference of 13 points, or 18 per cent. With variations in amounts the results were similar in all classes of business. For single years they would presumably have been much greater, since, the longer the period taken, the less the differences tend to become. If you look forward to increasing written premiums from year to year, you should also expect that the paid-written ratio will indicate that the accident-and-health business is doing a less satisfactory job for the public than will the incurred-written ratio. And the latter is the more accurate reflection of the experience.

The same principle applies to an individual company in a single year. The accident-insurance experience of one company chosen at random for 1947 indicated a 42–per cent loss ratio on the paid-written basis, and a 49–per cent ratio on the incurred-earned basis.[2]

The sort of distortion evident in the paid-written overall ratio is emphasized in the long-term noncancellable field. Consider an accident-and-health insurer 92 per cent of whose business is noncancellable; whose written premiums show an increase for 1947 over 1946 of 19 per cent, and an increase for 1947 over 1943 of 82 per cent. Its paid-written ratio[2] for 1947 was 31 per cent; its incurred-earned ratio,[2] 41 per cent. What its loss ratio will finally be on business that has run off the books is conjectural, but its rates have been calculated on the basis of an expected overall loss ratio of over 50 per cent or, with adjustment expenses, of over 55 per cent.

In this case the paid-written ratio is a fact; the incurred-earned ratio is a fact; yet neither is representative of the probable experience of the insurer, and either is of no value in itself. The noncancellable contract is paid for by a level premium, though the probability of loss increases as the long-term contract continues in force. Policies are issued only after medical examination, and, with rapidly increasing premium income, a large proportion of the business is still in the select period. The paid-written ratio takes no account, and the incurred-earned ratio inadequate account, of the higher relative losses to be expected during the later years of these contracts, for which provision is made in determining premium rates.

The heading of one column in the Exhibit, "Rate of Commission and Expense Allowance," is not entirely clear to me, and I understand that no official interpretation is available. Does it call for the allowance for both commissions and expenses used in calculating the premium rate or for the

---

[2] Adjustment expenses included with losses.

rate at which payment is actually made to agents? Of what value is this figure if one does not know its basis? In comparing insurers it would further be essential to know how managerial functions are distributed between agents and home office. An insurer paying commissions strictly for selling might show a much lower rate than one compensating its agents for performing management functions that would otherwise be at the charge of the home office. But the two insurers might actually be incurring expenses at the same rate for selling and management combined.

What of the method of commission payment? Other things being equal, an insurer paying commissions at a level rate for new business and renewals would show a much lower rate of commission in a period of rapidly increasing business than another paying a high first-year commission and low renewal commissions, though the rates of commission to premiums over the full life of the two insurers' contracts might be the same. The higher the proportion of new business to old on the second insurer's books, the higher its apparent rate of commission.

To illustrate this last point, take an example which, though it applies to the life-insurance business, brings out the same thought.[3]

Assume that Company A has:

Business in force, December 31, 1947	$150,000,000
Income in year 1948	
Premium income on old business	7,500,000
Interest income	2,500,000
Premium income on new business	500,000
Total Income	$ 10,500,000

Its expenses are 15 per cent of premiums on old business, and 100 per cent of premiums on new business.

15 per cent of $7,500,000 is	$1,125,000
100 per cent of $ 500,000 is	500,000
Total Expenses	$1,625,000
Ratio of expenses to income	$\frac{\$1,625,000}{\$10,500,000}$, or 15.5 per cent

Assume that smaller and younger Company B has:

Business in force, December 31, 1947	$10,000,000
Income in year 1948	
Premium income on old business	400,000
Interest income	125,000
Premium income on new business	100,000
Total income	$ 625,000

[3] Adapted from Langstaff, M. P., "Facts, Figures, and Fallacies of Life Insurance Canvassing."

Its expenses are 10 per cent of premiums on old business, and 90 per cent of premiums on new business.

10 per cent of $400,000 is	$ 40,000
90 per cent of 100,000 is	90,000
Total Expense	$130,000

Ratio of expenses to income $\frac{\$130,000}{\$625,000}$, or 20.8 per cent

The younger insurer is conducting its business more economically than the older, but the overall ratio indicates the reverse.

Similarly, a comparison of overall ratios may be misleading because of variations in the composition of the business written by the insurers whose experience produces the ratios. Assume that each of two insurers writes $25,000,000 of accident-and-health premiums, that Insurer A has an acquisition-cost ratio of 12 per cent on group and of 35 per cent on commercial, while Insurer B has ratios of 7 per cent and 25 per cent on the two lines. Assume further that Insurer A writes $20,000,000 of group premiums and $5,000,000 of commercial premiums while Insurer B writes $5,000,000 of group and $20,000,000 of commercial. A's overall acquisition-cost ratio will be 16.6 per cent, and B's, 17.4 per cent, although B is doing each class of business at a lower rate of acquisition cost.

Let us wander a bit among other forms of insurance. Recently the following headline appeared in a leading insurance paper: "95% of N. Y. Motorists Insured." Reading the story one finds that "about 95 per cent of drivers *reporting accidents* were insured,"[4] a very different thing. Since the present New York financial responsibility law went into effect, wide publicity has been given to the impression that this and earlier high percentages were applicable to New York motorists as a whole.

You should study the advertised accomplishments of the fire-insurance companies. A recent article bears the complacent title, "Fire Insurance Beats Inflation." It points out that, while living costs about doubled from 1939 to 1949, "$100.00 worth of fire insurance costs about the same." And then, under the heading "Statistics Tell The Story," it is stated that "premium income . . . rose 80.37 per cent in just five years [1942–1947]." The fallacy of comparing a price per $100.00 of insurance with the price of commodities must be evident.

I recall a legislative investigation conducted in New York over twenty-five years ago with Samuel Untermeyer as counsel in which much was made of the excessive profits on liability insurance by selecting classes of business on which there was little exposure and taking the ratios of

[4] Emphasis supplied.

premiums to losses. These ratios ranged from 313 per cent of losses of $47,205 to 6,491 per cent of a loss of $25.00. Mr. Untermeyer got the headlines he sought.

Another comparison is that between the percentage costs of distributing insurance and of distributing commodities. If you select your class of insurance and your class of commodities, it is easy to prove that either the one or the other is being distributed more efficiently—easy if you accept a lower ratio as conclusive evidence of greater efficiency. But the basic question in either case is whether the customer is getting value for his dollar. The ratio in itself is of no significance in either case, except as a taking-off point for determining the facts that produced it. The facts will furnish a basis for judging whether the underlying charges are equitable.

Some twelve states now have statutes under which the insurance commissioner may disapprove an accident-and-health policy form "if the benefits provided therein are unreasonable in relation to the premium charged." I understand that the intent is that nothing in the law should be construed as empowering the commissioner to establish or require a statistical reporting system, or to approve or disapprove premium rates, or to disapprove or withdraw approval from any policy for any reason based on the premium, except that he would have the power to disapprove or withdraw approval of a policy if any rate charged therefore were unduly disparate and incompatible with the coverage provided by the contract.

This is not rate regulation in the usual sense, but with such a provision in the law, it will be best to watch those loss ratios, and to see that they fully reflect the benefits to insureds.

Ratios have, in the past, been principally of service to management in judging trends, in calculating rates, and in determining profits. They have been used largely by persons in a position to interpret them by looking below the surface and by making allowances for any deficiency in their accuracy as indices.

But these ratios are coming increasingly under the eyes of governmental officials and of an interested and potentially critical public. As in the time of Matthew, they seek after a sign—they want a simple indication of what is good and what is bad. Witness the eagerly sought and accepted formulas for determining one's investment or speculative course.

No formula or ratio will give them a sign, but much may be, and should be, done to make recorded ratios as little misleading as possible—beyond that the seeker after light must go to the underlying facts that produced the ratio and decide whether they reveal an acceptable situation or a need for reform. If ratios come to the knowledgeable, discerning, and con-scientious, they will, of course, be properly used. But these fascinating functions, once calculated and recorded, may come to, or be dug up by, persons lacking one or more of these qualities. Hence the need of making them as little susceptible of misinterpretation as possible, and the need of directing attention to the fundamental facts rather than to the superficial results.

May I close with an adaptation of a statement which I once made in another connection and which seems to me still to have validity: It should be borne in mind that ratios of loss or of expense mean little unless interpreted in the light of all the facts. A high loss ratio may mean adequate reserves, excessive reserves, poor risks, or lavish loss settlements; a low loss ratio may mean inadequate reserves, careful selection of risks, an efficient claim department, or extraordinary good fortune. A high expense ratio may be the result of inefficient management, careful provision for the future, or unusually good service to insureds; a low expense ratio, the result of efficient management, unwise retrenchments, or inferior service. Large dividends may reflect real savings or speculative management; low dividends, a policy of thorough-going preparation for the future or managerial incompetence. These forces and others lie back of the bare figures, and it is especially important to consider them until sufficient experience has developed to enable more accurate conclusions to be drawn from simple ratios. Ratios, unless viewed in the light of the causes which have produced them, are never conclusive; they are least valuable when they are the result of limited experience.

7. Research*

The insurance business is based on scientific principles, more or less refined and more or less abused in their application. Often they are ignored or perverted. The business suffers from schizophrenia—it is torn between the desires of the manager, the salesman, and the actuary. The relative effectiveness of the actuary varies enormously. In fire insurance, actuarial theory is applied only in the crudest way with a view to aggregate financial success; in life insurance and workmen's compensation insurance it is an effective and recognized tool.

But in all fields of insurance except life, actuarial science has been used almost entirely as a means to immediate ends. Its extensive development and application in workmen's compensation insurance and its considerable use in other important casualty lines have been brought about largely by the necessity of justifying rates and reserves and by competitive compulsion. In general, insurance practices and, later, theories are adjusted to the world outside insurance by gradual yielding to pressure; one hears much of "meeting competition," and proposals are frequently held to be without merit because "there is no demand." Little has been attempted and less accomplished in the way of investigation for the purpose of learning more about insurance without reference to pressing practical problems.

Misinformation and irresponsible reasoning are used both by those who attack and those who support the present insurance structure, usually in complete conviction of righteousness. "Why be a hypocrite when it is so easy to deceive yourself?" Discussion of major insurance problems proceeds in a cloud of dust with unsatisfactory results. Many very vocal disputants seem to resent the intimation that, whatever one's conclusions may be, one's facts should be accurate. And *post-hoc-propter-hoc* reasoning is accepted as logical demonstration.

In other words, although much is said of insurance as a science, the scientific approach has not been generally accepted. The process of meeting problems with unstudied figures and loose, even if temporarily effective, reasoning means that the same problems are recurrent. They may be forced under cover from time to time but if they are not attacked with

* Presidential address to the Casualty Actuary Society, November 17, 1943.

accurate and full information and with sound reasoning, they are not solved and will appear again to plague us. Aspirin will not cure a headache that results from underlying organic maladjustments.

I suggest that insurance interests would do well to set up a research organization whose function would be to study thought and practice in all phases of insurance and to report facts and conclusions. Such an organization should not be available for the solution of current problems nor for accumulation of ammunition to support preconceived positions. Its spirit should be that of the scientist, rather than that of the executive whose prime interest is in current results. This is not to say that research should be impractical—its only justification would be that of usable results for insurer and insured. My point is that its value should not be tested by immediate practical usefulness nor should it be called upon to support competitive or other controversial activity.

To be practical in the long run—to achieve significance and results in terms of information, thought, and practice—a research organization should concern itself with much that is impractical over the short term. Its only short-term test should be unbiased and competent study of insurance problems. It should be critical in the sense of seeking accurately to evaluate data and conclusions from data. It should be constructive in the sense of being always bent on eliminating the unsound and promoting adoption of the sound. Its primary purpose should be to keep insurance in advance of or at least in tune with the times.

The methods of social science are more applicable to insurance than are those of physical science. Insurance phenomena cannot be isolated and controlled in the laboratory—insurance and the perils on which it is based are constantly changing, and the research student in this field must study trends and the preponderance of the evidence. Most facts will be the result of complicated sets of causes in a state of flux rather than the carefully arranged combinations of the exact scientist. But just as the "impractical" investigations of a Faraday or a Steinmetz have led to highly "practical" applications, so the ruminations and calculations of an insurance research worker should lead to useful improvements in insurance. And just as General Electric and General Motors have the goodwill of the public largely because they anticipate demand, so the insurance business might achieve greater acceptance as a beneficial institution.

But insurance needs something more than merely improvements of its methods and its product; it needs to convey to the public (and its representatives) in understandable terms what it is doing. The term "public relations" is used to cover a vast area and is at the moment in high repute. Public-relations efforts are often only attempts to talk the public into acceptance of an idea or product without too much consideration of the effect of the idea or of the product itself on its long-run acceptability. I believe that research could improve the methods of insurers and their product and develop the analysis which would furnish a basis for making these improvements understandable.

The success of a research organization would depend quite as much on the executive and operating personnel of the insurance business as on the person in direct charge of research. His quasi-autonomous position and his function as an associate rather than as a cog in the machine must be generally recognized. Above all he must be encouraged in independence of investigation and thought, for his carrying out of the principal purpose of his organization should lead him to discover what he believes to be defects in the methods of his employers and of the business generally. Such discoveries or recommendations for change, whether accepted or not, should be received sympathetically rather than antagonistically.

Insurers have built up a magnificent financial structure and have contributed largely to the development and safety of American business and of personal investments. But their very success seems to have bred distrust of change, an almost religious faith in things as they have been. Rightly or wrongly the notion has got abroad that they are possessed of a negative attitude; that they may be depended upon to resist innovations and encroachments. The extent to which opinions rather than facts rule the business is a matter of common observation. It would be the function of research to build up a body of significant statistical data, to study specific problems, to replace impressions with factual conclusions, maintaining at all times a scientifically critical attitude.

Let me outline one problem which might well be assigned to a research organization, that of analysis of disbursements. The present analysis into losses, expenses, and surplus and the breakdown of those items into their component parts is serviceable as a guide to rate determination and to operative policy, but it fails to convey any functional analysis of insurance service. Would it not be desirable to analyze disbursements in terms of (1) payments for the benefit of the insured, which would include losses, adjustment expenses in whole or in part, and expense of services, (2) selling (as distinguished from service) expense, and (3) surplus. The ratios now available are misleading to the uninitiated (and to some of the initiated). It is essential to know what has produced the ratios. Reduction of losses often leads to increase in expense ratios, but with an overall saving to the public. Yet a high expense ratio or its companion, a low loss ratio, is often used as presumably clear evidence of the unworthiness of the insurance institution. A study of the sort I have outlined should provide a basis for sound discrimination between risks and classes of risk in calculating the expense portion of the premium. Graded-rate schemes should provide adequate income to meet the justified expenses of carriers and middlemen. They should not involve "sacrifices" by anyone, other than sacrifice of the advantages of an inaccurate rating system.

Exploration of the possibilities of research in insurance would exhaust my time and your patience. They seem to me to be limitless. I mention a few without elaboration: the financial results of individual exclusion clauses in policy contracts; all-risks insurance on fixed property; bases for selecting agents; new fields for extension of coverage; remuneration of middlemen; the function of government in relation to insurance.

A program of research such as I have suggested should be entered into with the understanding that it may take several years to demonstrate its value. None has yet been organized, though I understand that three research departments are in contemplation. There is no blueprint for it, and it would have to proceed by experimentation. Considerable time would be necessary to develop background and organization, and little in the way of findings should be expected in the near future. Its adoption would, I believe, contribute greatly to the development and perhaps the preservation of the interests sponsoring it.

8. Changing Times and the Insurance Agent*

The theme of your convention indicates that you are conscious of having reached maturity.[1] An individual human being reaches maturity in his twenties and is then ready to take up his problems from the long-range point of view of the remainder of his life. Perhaps a more complex organization, such as yours, made up of over 12,000 individuals, may be expected to come to maturity in the forties.

It is from the long-range point of view that I want to talk to you today. And if I were to choose a text for my "sermon," it would be an observation of Charles Taft's: "The truth is, nothing which concerns this nation of 120,000,000 people can ever be simple again."

I was originally asked to discuss compulsory automobile liability insurance. But as I considered it I became less and less inclined to rehash the pros and cons of that battered subject, and more and more interested in its significance as a symptom of something much broader. The United States has reached maturity, and has found itself in a highly complex situation in which the simple remedies of an earlier and simpler situation are no longer efficacious.

The automobile is a large factor in this complex situation; the seriousness of its effect in terms of suffering and loss of income is not to be questioned. The machinery, legal and otherwise, of an earlier day is inadequate to deal with the newer problem. Compulsory automobile insurance was adopted to remedy one defect in the situation, the inability of some motorists to pay damages for which they are liable. On its worthwhileness for this purpose it should be judged. It is not a complete remedy, since it merely alleviates certain untoward results of a deep-seated disease.

The accidents which gave rise to a demand for financial responsibility are still there; and the creaking and inefficient machinery for compensating their victims, whether by direct settlement or through the courts, is still

* Address before the Annual Convention of the National Association of Insurance Agents, Pittsburgh, October 8, 1936.
[1] "Life Begins at Forty," in commemoration of the fortieth anniversary of the founding of the Association.

functioning. Prevention and adjudication of indemnity are problems demanding thought and action, and there will always be victims of accidents who are entitled to indemnity and who should be in a position to collect it.

Unfortunately, the discussion of compulsory automobile insurance has been obscured by immediate self-interest. In Massachusetts the insurers have been forced to use inadequate rates and to write risks which their underwriting judgment rejected; agents' commissions have been cut; lawyer-legislators have been unwilling to consider fundamental remedies which might interfere with their income from the practice of negligence law; the average citizen has seen only the security of compulsory insurance or the cost of buying it. And each group, motivated by its own interest, has accepted conclusions whose principal virtue was support of preconceived opinions.

Most people like a fight, and the more intense the conflict, the less scrupulous they become in their choice of weapons. After the fight, the winner may feel a certain virtuous satisfaction in the triumph of "right" over the "powers of darkness." But too often the fundamental question which brought on the conflict still remains, to be solved only by careful investigation and disinterested thoughtful cooperation.

You will not solve the problem of automobile accidents and compensation for injuries resulting from them by repealing the Massachusetts law, by whittling down the coverage, by passing laws making insurance compulsory for certain drivers, by safety campaigns. These are partial solutions or temporary expedients. Until you adopt a solution that is reasonably complete and that goes to the fundamentals of the problem, it will continually come back to you for solution.

What is the answer? It may be compulsory automobile insurance with certain objectionable features removed; it may be a plan analogous to workmen's compensation; it may be a substitution of administrative for judicial procedure under the law of negligence; it may be the remedy suggested by Mr. Arthur Goerlich in the September "Broker-Age"; it may be compulsory deductible liability coverage; it may be much more intensive regulation of traffic and licensing of drivers; it may be a combination of these ideas. I do not know. But I am convinced that it is *your* problem. If you do not work out a constructive solution, rather than rest on negative action, someone else will do it, and insurance may not have the voice in the result which it ought to have.

The question of compulsory automobile insurance is only a superficial indication of a deeper problem, and of the wider demand that in one way or another every citizen should be reasonably secure against want, illness, and major accidental losses.

The counterpart of this feeling is found in business in general. While the search for new processes and products and the competition for markets goes on, there is less of the reckless spirit of adventure, and more of a desire to consolidate each gain and to be sure that organizations and assets are protected against calamitous loss. It is no longer easy to replace or rehabilitate a ruined business.

Industrial and merchandizing organizations have had a comparatively free rein in developing from the small single-unit stage to the great multiple-unit corporations of today. Improvement in communications, in statistical and accounting technique, and in the art of management have made possible centralized control of world-wide activities.

Along with these developments have come new processes; huge concentrations of value; new contractual, common-law, and statutory liabilities; new perils. And the clock is not likely to turn back toward simplicity.

If insurance is to maintain its high place in our economic scheme, it must accommodate itself to changed times. In doing so it is hampered by legal restrictions, traditions, and sometimes by a tendency to oppose change as such. It seems to me that in many quarters there is a feeling that the insurance business has certain vested rights in the continuance of things as they are. But insurance is not a sacred institution. It is a practical tool for facilitating individual and corporate activities by eliminating or reducing risk. If these activities change, so must insurance.

This somewhat rambling discussion may seem to be only remotely related to your immediate problems. But I propose, with this introduction, to make a few suggestions, which I hope will be in some small degree helpful to you. I am not of those who feel that the practical work of the world can be directed, or practical difficulties removed overnight, by any amount of academic thinking, writing, or speech-making. At best the academic man can only bring to you what he sees from the side lines, but perhaps he may sense certain tendencies, certain general long-time movements to which the man in the field is too close, in which he is too immediately concerned, to get a clear perspective. And believe me, my sole end is to see insurance conducted on sound lines and serving the most useful possible purposes.

I make two suggestions: first, that you study general and particular tendencies deeply enough to be reasonably well posted on what is going to happen, whether, as agents, you approve it or not; second, that you devote yourselves constructively to adjusting your business to new situations and to taking the initiative in introducing new and more useful practices, without losing sight of what is worthy in the old.

Success in business can, in the long run, come only as a result of constant adjustment and recognition of the inevitable. The carriage maker who might have devoted his energies to fighting the introduction of automobiles and to urging laws to prevent their operation on the highways would long since have given way to his competitor who went into the business of manufacturing bodies for motor cars, or motor cars themselves. The motor-car manufacturers who resisted the introduction of balloon tires and four-wheel brakes were soon forced into line. How many of you remember the prophecies of dire results to come from the use of each of these innovations?

Recently I heard Governor John G. Winant cite the business development of an owner of ice houses on the upper Hudson. He sensed early the decline of the natural-ice business and became a manufacturer of artificial ice in New York City. He is now selling mechanical refrigerators.

And have you observed that automobile manufacturers introduce each year new features which the buyer has not previously heard discussed? They do not wait for a pressing demand to force them to make concessions. They have research departments whose prime business is to be dissatisfied with progress to date, and to see new devices which will make old models obsolete.

I do not mean to imply that the analogy is complete. I should dislike to see insurance advertising new contracts and rates each year which would represent a denial of the virtues of last year's product. But even the automobile is not changing as radically from year to year as its advertising writers would have you believe.

And now with some trepidation I turn to subjects in which you have demonstrated your interest by action. To my mind they divide themselves into two categories: those which represent primarily an attempt to improve the agency system and those which seem to a considerable extent to be motivated by a desire to retain, or acquire, privileges rather than to adjust the system to the world outside it. I fully realize that many measures involve both characteristics, and that necessary defensive action may at times involve one in actions which otherwise would not be taken. So I ask you to assume that if the time were not limited I should introduce many practical if's, and's, but's, and provided's concerning the agency system.

I place at the top of the list of efforts to be commended your campaign for agency qualification. Let it go on until the term "licensed insurance agent" is prima-facie evidence of competence and reliability. Such tests as may be prescribed will not be infallible, any more than the bachelor's degree is infallibly an indication of an educated man. But every sifting process eliminates a group of the unfit, and the remaining group is of higher general caliber. There are incompetent and unethical physicians, but you will stand a reasonably good chance of receiving honest competent advice if you stop at any doctor's office. That situation is a result of rigorous enforcement of high standards in the medical profession and a long-range point of view.

One might almost say that you could concentrate your attention on agency qualification and that other desirable results would eventually flow from the creation and maintenance of highly qualified personnel. But, of course, you must live in the meantime. You see business going to non-agency insurers, commissions on the best risks disappearing in the direction of large brokerage offices, other commissions being whittled down for competitive purposes or by state regulation. It is only natural that you are seeking methods of protecting yourselves against such inroads.

It is in your reaction to these threats of immediate loss that an observer sees danger to your standing. You will not succeed in the long run by erecting legislative fences around a privileged position, nor by attempting to tie up insurers and clients by agreements and business favors which are demonstrations of your power rather than of your ability to serve.

You have given evidence of your awareness of the insurance buyers' movement by inviting prominent buyers to appear on your programs in the past, and particularly by the presence on this program of Mr. Schmidt. In this movement you have an opportunity, individually and collectively, to solve a problem in statesmanlike fashion and to demonstrate the adaptability, permanence, and worth of the American Agency System. For if that system is to survive, it must constantly change. Beware a worshipful attitude toward things as they are and still more toward things as they were. Constant adaptation to circumstances is the rule of survival and increasing success.

The development of a group of specialized insurance managers is the natural outgrowth of the tendencies toward size and complexity of business of which I have already spoken. Such managers do not replace the agent—but they do threaten the business of the incompetent or lazy agent. If you see a tendency to deal with non-agency insurers, to seek direct contact with insurer officers, to self-insure, don't sit in conference and bemoan the times. Develop a service which justifies your commission, show that you know enough about the business to make direct contacts unnecessary, demonstrate that you have something better than self-insurance to offer.

Do not, however, waste your energies fighting the inevitable. When old lines fail, turn to new lines. If you hold business merely for the sake of holding it, as the old-fashioned New England farmer bought land because it "joined" him, you will find yourself "business poor" as he found himself "land poor."

I do not decry self-interest but I urge you to substitute for the pursuit of immediate and evident self-interest that policy of enlightened self-interest which rests on the long-run point of view.

Largely by an aggressive fighting policy you have brought yourselves to maturity. Is it not now in the natural order of things that you should by research and calm deliberation exercise the wisdom of maturity, that you may not waste yourselves on negative action but build positively, constructively?

9. Public Relations*

Much has been said, and written, of the adjuster's opportunity to contribute to good relations between insurers and the public. And much more, perhaps too much, has been said about public relations in general.

What is meant by "public relations?" The term calls up thoughts of courtesy, advertising, speechmaking, rest rooms, and illustrated annual reports. Too seldom is it realized that the only sound basis of good public relations is doing a good job.

True, the additional virtues of doing the job agreeably and of bringing its quality to the attention of the public are to be recommended, but they are not fundamental. Advertising, chrome trim, and courteous service will not create or maintain public acceptance of an automobile once it has a reputation for poor construction. A bare statement of the finances of a consistently profitable corporation is more welcome to stockholders than a three-color, graph-laden explanation of losses.

So, in adjusting, the fundamental necessity of continuing good public relations is doing a good adjusting job, which means accurate determination of existence of liability, of amount of loss, and of extent of liability for payment of loss.

If the insured public were well educated in insurance, and if its insurance programs were well planned, this fundamental requirement would be enough. For in that contrary-to-fact situation most insurable losses would be covered, and the insured would understand the reasons for the adjustment.

But the adjuster has further duties, educational and diplomatic, particularly in the all-too-frequent cases where the insured's loss is not fully covered and where the adjustment brings to the insured the first realization that his insurance is inadequate.

This educational job has two facets. The first is making clear to the often unwilling insured that the facts of his loss and of his insurance coverage together produce the adjustment proposed. These facts may be perfectly clear to the adjuster, and his proposal may be completely in order, but an insured who, for one reason or another, believes that he is being improperly

* From *Our Business*, October, 1950. Used by permission.

61

Risk and Insurance

treated, may well have a "blind spot." A classic example of this situation
is the Lily Cup case. The evidence and the contract provision clearly
indicated that the insurer was not liable for the loss, but a stiff fight to
collect was made in the courts.[1]

Whether the tidal-wave, high-water exception to extended coverage,
which excluded coverage of this loss, was a proper part of the contract is
another question. The adjuster had the job of applying the contract as
written and incidentally of demonstrating to the insured that he was not
covered. The incidental duty was here apparently impossible of fulfillment.

But not all insureds are unreasonable. Some understand with little or
no explanation why a loss is not fully covered; some, in fact, may have
arranged their insurance with a view to bearing a part of their losses
themselves. Others, while not clear as to lack of coverage, may be open-
minded enough to accept a reasonable explanation. It is the adjuster's
business to leave such insureds with the feeling that they have been
treated fairly, giving them whatever demonstration, oral or written, is
necessary to that end.

The second side of the educational job is more indirect but, in its long-
term implications, perhaps more important. It is part of the general
educational job that should concern all departments of the insurance
business, state insurance departments, educational institutions, and the
public generally—developing an understanding of insurance and of its use.

Adjustment problems and unsatisfactory adjustments stem in large
degree from insufficient and poorly arranged insurance protection. Such
protection, in turn, results from lack of knowledge of insurance and
from unwillingness to give the attention that they deserve to insurance
programs. Insureds are stymied by the technical terms and apparently
complex principles of insurance; they do not feel the immediate necessity
of complete detailed preparation for events that seem remote. And, unlike
their calculations of markets, prices, and production, insurance programs
are not constantly checked by results. As long as one has no loss, any
program is adequate. The insured who has no loss has no final check on
his insurance program—it may be only in the exceptional case of serious
loss that the check is thorough.

The public should be taught how to think about insurance and stimulated
to apply their thinking. Since the best educational material is a clear-cut
object lesson, a loss settlement that does not fully cover the insured's
loss is a useful basis for demonstrating the deficiencies of his insurance
program and the method and importance of remedying it. While it is not
the function of the adjuster to plan insurance programs, he would do well

[1] See Lily Tulip Cup Corp. vs. Home Insurance Company, 289 N.Y. 748. See also Kaplan,
Abraham, and Gross, George I., *Report on the Lily-Tulip Cup Case* (New York, 1942). (1964)

to convey to the insured that in making insurance plans one should always "take the point of view of the loss."

Of course, an adjuster who attempts to do a thorough job of education will run into difficulties. There are other parties in interest—agents, brokers, underwriters, and politicians. And there are dishonest insureds and insureds who rely more on fighting or pressure than on planning. So the adjuster, while trying to do a sound job of applying the contract and of education, must also be a diplomat. In this department, the writer has little to offer; he can only mark the necessity of discretion.

One wonders whether the general lack of interest in insurance, as compared with other businesses, is inherent in the human mind or is due to circumstances that are susceptible to change. The indications seem to be that interest is growing but that it is not yet nearly so effective as it should be.

The number of specialized (and competent) insurance managers of large businesses is growing. Organizations appealing to the interest and participation of insureds, such as the Insurance Division of the American Management Association, the Risk Research Institute,[2] and the local buyers' groups, are commanding a wider and more cooperative audience. Insurance questions (often sadly mixed with political considerations) are more often being discussed in the press. Universities and colleges are offering more courses in insurance and are staffing them with instructors who specialize in the subject. State insurance departments are giving more attention to coverage problems.

The focal point of all this growing interest is loss, actual and potential. Losses are the raw material of the insurance business, the reason for its existence and the basis of its whole fabric.

The importance of the adjuster in the insurance scheme has not always been recognized. The times call for recognition. All business, both of insurer and insured, must be content with smaller margins of profit than was once the case. In handling a loss, the adjuster should serve both the insurer and insured and, through his wider influence, help to improve the quality of insurance protection and to extend the operations of the insurance business. The increase in interest in insurance suggests that his functions will be more generally recognized and also that he will be subject to more active scrutiny.

[2] The American Society of Insurance Management, Inc. (1964)

10. Constructive Competition*

The early economists formulated a wages-fund theory which was based on the idea that a certain amount of wealth was assigned each year to the payment of wages. They believed that any increase in the share allotted to one group of workmen would result in an equivalent decrease in the share allotted to others. It seems to me that the insurance business is, to too great an extent, operated on a similar, and equally untenable, theory. And a theory is no less a theory because it happens to be held by "practical" men.

To reduce this statement to more definite terms, competition is too much concerned with taking away business from others, and preventing others from getting business. Much of this sort of activity is sheer waste from the public point of view and inefficient from the point of view of the competitors themselves. The public would be better served, and each group more prosperous, if *constructive competition* were more generally practiced.

I hold no brief for any one of the competitive groups—I should talk to any other group actuated by different principles (a more virtuous sounding word than "theories") much as I shall talk to you, though my practical examples might vary. I am only concerned with contributing in some small measure to the effectiveness of insurance as the servant of the insured and as an instrument of public policy.

It is a fairly easy matter to scare people, to convince them of the dangers of this, that, or the other menace, and to fill them with zeal for fighting *against* an enemy, real or imagined, but it is difficult to get them to put energy and conviction into constructive work, to build carefully and in detail a long-range program which is more concerned with improvement of their own methods than with elimination of their competitors. And this second task is the one which I have set myself, in full consciousness of my own limitations and of the limitations of speechmaking in general.

It would be just as little a contribution to your deliberations to attack direct-writing carriers, self-insurance, or Lloyd's of London as it would be to attack communism before a Roman audience or democracy in Berlin. You would not be one whit further along, although, doubtless, I should be

* Address before the Connecticut Association of Insurance Agents, New Haven, November 3, 1938.

described as having spoken "straight from the shoulder," as though it took courage to tell an audience what it already believes.

Constructive competition goes far beyond merely being *for* your side of the case rather than *against* the other fellow's. It implies constant improvement of the protection and service which you offer. One of the most common objections presented by insurance men to changes in contracts, or to liberalization of laws, is that there is no "demand" for them. This attitude is thoroughly fallacious in many cases. Insurance should not wait for a demand for an improved product. It should create the product and demonstrate to insureds that it is an improvement. Just how the uninformed insured public is to organize and make effective a demand, with sufficient insistence to convince insurers, is beyond me.

It very often happens that insureds become disgusted and meet their needs in ways which are most unwelcome to insurance men who have failed to realize those needs in advance, or who have refused to admit that times change. Take the incident which is generally accepted as responsible for the origin of the factory-mutual idea. A rate reduction for improved construction and preventive devices was refused by the fire-insurance company covering a relatively high-grade risk in Rhode Island, on the ground that "a fire risk is a fire risk." From that refusal to look into the future (a supposed function of insurance experts) developed the direct-writing factory mutuals which date from 1835. In 1890 the Factory Insurance Association was finally organized to perform equivalent services on behalf of stock companies.

Another example. About 1910, the first bankers' blanket bonds were written. There was little interest on the part of American companies in writing this bond until competition from Lloyd's threatened their premium volume. Then they awoke. What had been considered highly impractical became practical, and the former excuse of lack of authority to write such bonds was removed by securing a change in the law. But note that effective effort to supply adequate coverage to banks and brokers came only after the carriers had been goaded by foreign competition.

Examples might be multiplied to illustrate the quite human tendency to resist disturbing changes and to explain gaps in insurance protection by putting the blame on underwriters, law makers, and supervisory officials.

One way of meeting competition is to attempt to disable it by exclusive agreements, by boycotts, or by prohibitory laws. These are defensive tactics and should be used with extreme caution, lest they leave the enemy continuously on the offensive and greatly develop his skill. I have read of controversies between direct-writing companies and agency companies over the question of which spent the most money in hotels, the purpose being to influence the placing of the hotels' insurance business. I suggest that the energy devoted to research along that line might better have been given to improving the coverage offered to hotels. The effect would probably have been more lasting and would have represented a real contribution to the improvement of insurance service. In some communities there has even been a movement to curtail contributions to charitable or religious institutions which do not return them in the form of commissions.

In a recent address, Mr. Walter H. Bennett mentioned two dangerous possibilities in ill-conceived resident-agency laws: using them to attempt to create, in favor of local agents, a monopoly running counter to modern business developments, and giving the public the impression that their only purpose is that of gathering in commissions merely for compliance with a formality. To the extent that such laws embody these purposes, they will react against the best interests of insurance agents.

Some of these practices may meet an immediate situation, but I am convinced that in the long run they are wrong in principle and contrary to the practical dollars-and-cents interest of agents.

I suggest that you, as individuals and as an organization, should devote yourselves to two principal objectives: providing each insured with the most effective possible coverage of the perils to which he is subject, and improving the facilities available to you for that purpose. These needs are complementary but separate.

The time has gone by when it was enough to sell an insured a piece of this coverage and a piece of that, leaving the more remote perils to good luck. The agent should be an expert analyst of the insured's business or personal situation from the point of view of the effect of possible losses. He should, in so far as possible, and with well-considered economy, help the insured so to protect himself as not to suffer financially when accidental losses occur. And if, in the course of his analyses, he finds that coverage which ought to be available is unavailable, he should lend his aid to persuading the insurers to write that coverage. If the laws do not authorize it, he should work to change the laws.

The dinosaur used to wander about the countryside well armed against the perils of his day—but it is said that when the climate changed he had no ideas. Beware of short-run practicality which often consists merely in protecting what you have. Long-run practicality involves looking into the future, forecasting trends, and suiting yourself to them. Lord Bryce once said that one should learn to view the present as though it were the past—a very practical suggestion.

I come to you as an observer and not as one who is faced daily by the problems of collections, of the insured who cannot see the possibility of a total loss or of losses from remote contingencies, or of explaining an inexplicable premium rate. But I appreciate your problems, and I realize that your prime job is making a living. It is precisely because I think that your interests, and the interests of insureds and insurers, are identical *in the long run* that I present these observations. They are not only mine, but reflect what many insureds and insurance men, important and otherwise, are thinking.

If the business of insurance agency is to prosper, its clients must be satisfied that its services are worthwhile, and if you keep your clients in a state of satisfaction with your services, they are not going to be so much concerned with price as is the case where they feel that one kind of insurance is about the same as another.

I have paid my respects to certain practices and tendencies which seem to me to be the opposite of constructive. May I indicate two which seem to me to be definitely constructive?

The first is the agency-qualification law. The high-grade insurance agent has suffered, and still suffers, from the fact that in the past anyone could qualify for an insurance agent's license, and that insurers were willing to appoint almost anyone in order to pick up a few dollars of premium.

The passage of agency-qualification laws and the gradual sifting of agency results by insurers have done something, and might do a great deal more, to raise the general level of the business of insurance agency. All of these efforts, however, should be directed toward the development of competence and character in the agency force. They should in no case be directed merely toward restricting the business to a favored group. Insurance is a business. I see nothing to be gained by calling it a profession, but likewise, I see every reason why the insurance business should work toward what are generally considered to be professional standards. Once the public is able to feel that the designation of "insurance agent" implies a knowledge of insurance and competence to deal with its risk problems, your tasks will be considerably simplified and the public better served. You will be able to devote more time to real service and less to mere salesmanship, but remember that resolutions and new provisions in the insurance laws are only a vehicle for accomplishing these ends. The means they provide must be followed through by all the interested parties.

Another possibility for constructive work is the development of a simplified, comprehensive contract. The present necessity of buying a trunkful of contracts from various classes of insurers in order to get reasonably adequate coverage for a business is a challenge to insurance. I look forward to the time, and I believe it is coming, when artificial walls between carriers will be broken down, and when the listing of perils covered by property-insurance contracts will be obsolete.

The division of the insurance business into major and minor compartments, with rigid and apparently sound-proof walls, is unfortunate. It produces certain ludicrous results, particularly from the point of view of the insured. If I desire to insure my car against accidental damage, I buy a contract covering against all causes of loss. My personal effects, limited to those ordinarily carried in traveling, may likewise be insured against all causes of loss, except in my own home. My house may be insured against a variety of causes listed in the contract, but I bear the losses from any cause not listed. Some companies may write all-risks insurance on some types of property. Others may not write all-risks insurance on anything.

You have had the recent spectacle in New England of insureds recovering losses on their cars, but not on their garages, when the losses arose from the same hazard, at the same location. In some cases they could have insured their houses against windstorm. In others, where the loss was by flood or tidal wave, there was no insurance available. I can see no good reason why insurers, other than life, should not be permitted to write all forms of insurance which are not contrary to public policy, nor why they should not write all-risks coverage on all types of property. Such developments are opposed because they involve realignments and are disturbing. These are not, to my mind, good reasons. I predict that these developments will come, and I suggest that the agents, on behalf of their insureds, would do themselves a good turn by pressing for complete, logical, and satisfying coverage. If you do not do it, others will. Some insureds will be unwilling to pay for adequate coverage—in that case it would be a simple matter to eliminate perils by endorsement, and the whole story would appear on the contract. The insured would not be left uncovered merely by omission, and he would be responsible for the eliminations.

There are many other ways in which competition can be made constructive. It is unnecessary to call them to the attention of this group. I offer these two examples because they seem to me to be fundamental and representative of two directions in which you can most fruitfully work to improve the standing of insurance agents, and to increase the effectiveness of the protection which they offer.

11. Automobile Insurance and the Traffic Problem*

The subject which was originally assigned to me, "Automobile Insurance through Legislation, Is This Necessary to Help Solve the Traffic Problem?" indicated that I was expected to give an authoritative answer to a definite question. My answer would have been "No," and with that word, my talk would have been completed.

I shall make no attempt this evening to give you final answers to the problems suggested by my revised subject. Rather I shall try to define some of the issues which arise from the occurrence of automobile accidents; particularly those relating to prevention and the compensation of victims.

Much is said of the sacredness of human life, of the impossibility of placing a value on life or of compensating for suffering due to injuries. But we know that, regardless of the efforts of engineers, public officials, and the better class of motor-vehicle drivers, traffic accidents occur and will continue to occur. In effect, we say that the convenience and pleasure attributable to the use of motor vehicles is worth more than the loss and misery which they cause. The National Safety Council has estimated the economic loss alone for the year 1937 at $1,700,000,000, of which half was due to personal injuries and half to property damage.[1]

Motor-vehicle accidents give rise to three major problems: how to prevent them, how to distribute their economic consequences, and how to insure the financial responsibility of persons who may be liable to others for damages or compensation. I need not detail for you the extent to which these problems have been the subject of discussion, the laws that have been passed in attempted solution of them, the bills that have been introduced, the commissions that have investigated and reported, the resolutions that have been adopted. You know that these problems constitute together and separately major topics of public interest. Having a common source, they are interrelated but each is worthy of independent

---

* Address before the annual dinner of the Institute of Traffic Engineers, New York, March 27, 1939.

[1] For 1962, the estimate was $7,700,000,000, of which approximately two-thirds was due to personal injuries and one-third to property damage. (1964)

69

consideration. Their interrelations have perhaps been overemphasized. It is unfortunate, too, that so much of the discussion of these problems and so many of the efforts to solve them have reflected the self-interest of influential groups rather than unbiased analysis.

Of the problem of safety on the highways, I shall say very little; I am a layman in the presence of the high priests. But I cannot forbear offering my layman's opinion, for whatever it may be worth, that the safety problem is primarily one of direct action, of traffic and highway engineering, of motor-vehicle laws and their administration, of efficient unhampered police work, of training in the operation of motor vehicles. I have little confidence in ballyhoo and so-called educational campaigns which seem to have as their chief result the personal satisfaction of the organizers.

Nor do I believe that insurance and safety are intimately related in the case of the individual driver. The rewards that can be given and the threats that may be made are not effective. Organized safety work in connection with the operation of fleets of motor vehicles is, of course, a different matter. But I have yet to see figures demonstrating any causal connection between insurance and the occurrence of traffic accidents in which individual owners and operators are concerned.

It is true, however, that if you, the motor-vehicle commissioners, and the police were given an opportunity to pool your efforts in the direction of safety, the compensation of accident victims and the insurance problem would be of no great importance in the aggregate, though it should be remembered that there will always be victims whose cases will be individually of the greatest importance.

At present the economic consequences of motor-vehicle accidents are distributed, in theory, on the basis of fault; in fact, on the basis of chance, trading, and the relative resources of claimants, claimees, and insurers.

The law of negligence, under which liability for these consequences is presumably determined, needs for its just application relatively simple situations. The facts surrounding an accident should be accurately ascertainable, the blame for its occurrence correctly assessable, and the parties equally able to present their cases. Actually, the facts are seldom known with even approximate accuracy, and consequently correct apportionment of blame is impossible. There is no standard for the determination of damages, and such damages as are recovered may be subject to attorneys' fees ranging from 25 to 50 per cent. Court congestion and appeal tactics result in unconscionable delays. Antiquated legal doctrines and sympathetic juries defeat the ends of justice. Reasonably immediate settlement often can be had only at the price of agreeing to inadequate compensation, unless the claimant's injury is a minor one, when he may expect to be overpaid if he deals with a financially responsible person or an insurer. And the negligence system may be made to yield splendid returns to rings of fakers, unethical attorneys, and unscrupulous doctors.

Where settlement is inadequate, the economic consequences are borne by the injured person, tradesmen whose bills he cannot pay, hospitals, doctors, and the community in general.

Two possible solutions for the assessment of the relative shares in these economic consequences present themselves: (1) modification of legal rules and procedures to achieve more accurate and prompter determination of fault and damages, and (2) complete or partial abandonment of the negligence principle in favor of compensation based on the consequences of accidents, regardless of personal fault.

Relatively little has been done to modify the law of negligence or to suit procedure under it to modern conditions, though distinct improvements in the direction of minimizing delay have been made in Boston, Detroit, and Cleveland. Suggestions have been put forward looking toward less formal, extra-judicial procedure which would replace traditional methods, but they have commanded little attention.

It would seem that the issue is fairly sharply drawn between the present system, possibly purged of some of its delays and fraudulent practices, and a system of compensation without regard to fault based on the general principle of workmen's compensation. The basic argument for the present system is that both motorists and accident victims have equal rights to the use of the highways, and that each should bear the untoward results of which he is the cause, judgment in respect of which can be based only on a determination of negligence or the lack of it. The basic argument for compensation is that the use of motor vehicles has as a concomitant the injury, fatal or nonfatal, of members of the public, and that those who benefit by its use should pay the costs to which it gives rise. There are many ancillary arguments, some pertinent and some not, for example, the practical arguments that the negligence system is completely incapable of achieving the ends that it has in view, that it is wasteful, and, on the other side, that a compensation system cannot allow for the widely varying losses of unemployed and executive, that it will encourage malingering, and that it will be prohibitively expensive.

Several schemes have been advanced for a combination of negligence law and compensation, the essence of which is the provision of a small sum to meet medical and hospital expenses regardless of fault, the injured person retaining his right to bring an action for damages beyond that amount.

In making one's choice among these various plans it seems to me that the practical criterion is: which plan will do most to give injured persons adequate care and compensate them for economic loss without accompanying consequences which are worse than the evil it is sought to remedy? It must be remembered that these persons are now receiving care and that the economic loss is being borne. The question is whether the costs can be more equitably allocated and the general public interest be served at the same time.

In making a decision here, it is particularly important to evaluate the arguments which will be advanced on either side in terms of their validity after eliminating the elements of self-interest. Hospital administrators and doctors may be expected to favor the compensation plan; they will see a reliable source of payment of their charges. Social workers will be moved by the provision of funds and care for victims and their dependents. Insurance officials will probably oppose the idea; rigid control of rates and the possibility of state automobile insurance funds will be seen in the offing. Motor interests will perhaps fear added costs which will discourage the purchase of cars. All of them will argue in terms of the very highest principles: Americanism, justice, progress, regard for one's fellow man.

While compensation plans have been proposed and widely publicized, notably that of the Committee to Study Compensation for Automobile Accidents and the later draft law of the Joint Committee to Sponsor the Accident Compensation Plan, this issue is less immediate than that of financial responsibility.

Whatever may be the system of apportioning the economic results of accidents, it will be ineffective to the extent that persons liable for payment of damages or compensation are without funds.

Until recently, the injured person or his dependents who had made claims or carried a claim through to a verdict in their favor were dependent on the financial ability of the motorist to pay or on the chance that he was adequately insured against liability for damages. The carrying of insurance was entirely optional with him. And the least well furnished financially were those least likely to carry insurance.

In general, claimants fare much better in cases where motorists carry liability insurance. The Committee to Study Compensation for Automobile Accidents, after investigating 3400 closed cases of temporary disability, reported as follows:

> Money had been received by the claimants in 86 per cent of the insured cases and in only 27 per cent of the uninsured cases. Enough money was received to cover medical, wage, and property losses in 69 per cent of the insured cases, but in only 11 per cent of the not insured cases.

For 345 fatal cases the following results were reported:

Damages were paid in 88 per cent of the insured cases, but in only 17 per cent of the not insured cases. Of all the 155 not insured cases there were only 5 per cent (8 cases) in which the amount paid exceeded $500, and only 7 per cent (9 cases) in which the payments covered funeral expenses. Among the insured cases, although payments frequently did not cover the full economic loss, damages of over $500 were paid in 73 per cent and funeral expenses were covered in 77 per cent.

Failure in many cases to collect damages due led to agitation for laws that would make financial responsibility, personal or vicarious, a prerequisite of being granted the privilege of putting a motor car on the highway. The first, and the only law in the United States, to make this requirement absolute is that of Massachusetts,[2] which went into effect on January 1, 1927. Since then a majority[3] of the other states have adopted laws requiring evidence of financial responsibility from motorists who have had unsatisfied judgments returned against them, who have been involved in certain defined types of accidents, or who have violated certain laws or regulations. Evidence of financial responsibility has, in practically all cases, meant a liability-insurance policy.

These latter enactments, generally called *financial responsibility laws,* have been largely fathered by the desire to block general compulsory insurance on the Massachusetts pattern, and mothered by the accommodating handmaidens of the powers possessed of that desire.

The war over the Massachusetts principle has been waged on all fronts, and although there are signs of approaching quiet, perhaps from exhaustion, there still pour forth reports, resolutions, speeches, and bills, from both sides of the line.

In considering the *pros* and *cons* of the Massachusetts system, which has become the symbol of compulsory insurance, it is especially necessary to examine the evidence for the Ethiopian of self-interest. Since my particular self-interest is in being impartial, I shall give you examples from both sides.

Every attempt to repeal the law has ended in decisive failure; but the legislature is largely made up of lawyers who may find it highly gratifying to know that motorists have insurance to meet successful claims. Representatives of insurers have argued that the law promotes carelessness and tends to increase accidents; but they are opposed to the law principally because they have lost money under it.

Without passing on the general success or failure of the Massachusetts Act, I shall present my conclusions as to the results of its operations. The

[2] Now New York and North Carolina also have this requirement. (1964)
[3] Now all of the states. (1964)

act has substantially accomplished its aim, that of insuring the financial responsibility of motor-vehicle owners. It has had no measurable effect on the occurrence of accidents. It has resulted in a higher average claim cost per insured car than would have been incurred without it, principally because of increased claim frequency. Whether this increased claim frequency represents proper claims by claimants who might otherwise have had no redress, it is impossible to say. The stock insurance companies have furnished statutory coverage at a net loss, partially because of inadequate rates, partially because of being forced to write risks which they would otherwise have declined. There has been considerable fraud, but whether it has been greater in proportion to the insurance written here than elsewhere cannot be stated. Comparison of rate levels with those of other localities involves factors which make the results invalid as a guide to the effect of the law.

Finally, I shall submit for your consideration certain propositions which may serve as a basis for further thought on the problem of automobile insurance and traffic:

1. It is desirable for all drivers or owners of motor vehicles to be financially responsible for the consequences of accidents.
2. The requirement of insurance will have no appreciable direct effect on safe driving.
3. The present method of assessing damages should be improved either by a more accurate and speedy determination of liability and of the amount of damages, or by a compensation scheme covering a part or all of the damage.
4. Granted that there will always be evasion and interstate and constitutional defects, legal compulsion will go furthest to accomplish general financial responsibility.
5. The enactment of a compulsory insurance plan or of a compensation plan would, in considerable measure, result in a reallocation of costs, which should be distinguished from an increase in costs.
6. A distinction should be made between objectionable results that are inevitable and those that can be eliminated by proper laws and administration.

12. Insularity in Insurance*

The institution of insurance is characterized, in the United States, by minute differentiation of form and function. This differentiation has created separate divisions, each of which carries with it a set of interests more or less at variance with the interests of other divisions.

First, there is the grand partition between the powers of the major types of carriers: life, fire-and-marine, and casualty. The lines of demarcation are a bit fuzzy in spots, but the fields are reasonably distinct.

Little harm, in fact probably much good, arises from the separation of life insurance from other forms of business. The life insurer deals with a well-defined problem which seldom impinges on the programs involving other kinds of insurance. Requirements for safety and consequences of failure are peculiar to that branch. It is generally agreed that the life-insurance business should be separately conducted and specially regulated in the interest of the insuring public.

It is difficult, however, to see any sound fundamental reason for the continuance of the separation between fire-and-marine insurers and casualty insurers. The historical reasons for this separation are clear—but they are not persuasive when one analyzes the functions of these two types of insurer. Were it sought to make a functional division, it might be suggested that, at least, it should not be necessary to purchase insurance from two different types of insurer in order to cover loss of a single piece of property, and that the division should be between non-conflicting forms of insurance, such as insurance against loss of physical property, third-party insurance, bonds, and disability insurance. It is my own belief that this problem should be resolved by doing away with specific powers and permitting authorization of insurers to write any sort of insurance, other than life, not contrary to public policy. I should hope to see insurers making full use of such broadened powers and insureds responding to their opportunity not only to purchase broad coverage but to secure it under a minimum number of contracts without division of responsibility.

A notable development in the fire-insurance business is the practically

* Presidential address before the Casualty Actuarial Society, May 15, 1942. Printed in the Society *Proceedings*, XXVIII, 279.

nationwide provision of extended coverage, an extension by endorsement of the fire contract far in the direction of all-risks coverage, achieved only after much travail and over the dead bodies of assorted separate contracts covering windstorm, explosion, riot, hail, aircraft damage, and such. But certain causes of loss sacred to the casualty insurer are omitted or excluded from the endorsement, although Texas permits it to cover loss due to explosion of steam boilers and related objects "located off the premises insured," if the loss occurs to dwellings or similar specified property. A nurses' home may secure this item of coverage if it is of nonfireproof, but apparently not if it is of fireproof, construction—a very nice distinction. Canada is reckless enough to permit it for any kind of property.

In casualty insurance, coverage has been divided by subject matter of insurance rather than by causes of loss. Liability coverage which has been issued separately for a variety of items is now brought together under comprehensive forms.

The personal property floater is available to insureds in about half the states, and authority for it was written into the early drafts of the New York insurance code, but underwriters achieved its elimination, apparently to protect themselves against their own possible lack of underwriting control, and to avoid any change in the settled lines between fire-and-marine and casualty jurisdiction. They feared that perpetual bugaboo, disturbance of the business.

Oddly enough, opposition to extension of underwriting powers comes principally from those on whom the powers would be conferred. They are in the position of preferring limitation of powers—like old men who shun responsibility and new problems, preferring to cling to past successes rather than to pioneer. I venture to think that much adverse criticism of the insurance business would not arise if its practitioners were as interested in developing new methods as they are in defending what they already have—if they sought as diligently for what is worthy in new proposals as for reasons against their adoption.

Even between the lines written by the same insurers, one finds something of the same attitude. No talk on suretyship is complete without some attempt to demonstrate that bonding is not insurance, and that insurance methods, particularly in the determination of rates, are quite inapplicable to that field. Bonding men have an unwarrantedly high opinion of the mathematical perfection of their insurance colleagues' calculations, and a certain attachment to the pleasures of individual judgment and personal conference which make them allergic to statistical and actuarial practices.

In the fire-and-marine field, the enterprising and strangely named inland-marine departments were finally forced to limit their efforts to write insurance against loss instead of against loss due to this and that individual (and traditionally hallowed) cause of loss. Under the nationwide definition and various strangling statutes the field has been divided among the various types of underwriter, and the fire departments of some insurers have been saved from the encroachments of their own inland-marine departments.

Nowhere does insularity show itself more clearly than in insurance regulation and there particularly clearly in the difficulty experienced with rating and coverage of interstate risks, whether in the casualty or in the fire field. Every sign points to the desirability of coverage and rating systems coextensive with insured business units. But try to write an all-inclusive contract, even for a single line of insurance, and rate it and sell it on a sound basis adapted to a modern nationwide industrial or commercial business. You will find varying contract requirements, resident-agent laws, prohibition and limitation of generally accepted rating methods, no rate regulation in one state and strict regulation in another. Efforts to cut across these difficulties run afoul of the regulatory authorities, who are often torn between local interests, desire to enforce the law, and a realization that interstate activities call for interstate methods.[1]

The weight of authority among students of constitutional law supports the belief that if Congress chose to enact regulatory insurance legislation, it would be sustained by the federal courts. A judge of the Supreme Court of Tennessee has recently said that "it may be conceded that in the prosecution of its insurance business it [a life insurance company] is engaged in interstate commerce."[2] I take no position on the relative desirability of state and federal regulation, but I do suggest that anyone interested in the subject would do well to read chapters 19 and 20 of Van Metre's "Transportation in the United States"[3] to learn how it came about that the "encroachment of federal power upon state power has been such that the states have been compelled virtually to abandon the whole field of railroad regulation." The author points out that the Hepburn Act, providing for drastic federal control, was close to defeat when "some particularly scandalous financial manipulation among the Southeastern railroads became a matter of public knowledge." Note the use that was made in the hearings before the Temporary National Economic Committee of the financial manipulation of relatively unimportant life insurers. And, parenthetically, note the view-with-alarm tactics of certain life-insurance people who gave those hearings wide publicity and, I believe,

[1] See the interesting articles by Clarence W. Hobbs on state regulation of insurance rates, *Proceedings* of the Casualty Actuarial Society, XXVIII, 37–59, 344–470.

[2] Robinson v. Massachusetts Mutual Life Insurance Company, 158 S.W. 2nd 442 (November 29, 1941).

[3] Chicago: Foundation Press, 1939.

gave the investigators ideas that might not otherwise have occurred to them.

Fire- and casualty-insurance interests would do well to put their business in such shape that it will offer little opportunity for the same sort of treatment. Sore spots existed in the life-insurance business and they were dramatized. With the passing of the war emergency, renewed interest in the fire- and casualty-insurance business may be expected. The best way to meet such interest is by eliminating sore spots in these fields.

States and insurance groups, sniping away at each other from their separate islands, might do well to ponder the possibilities of constructive cooperation in the interest of building an improved structure. I prefer to think of representatives of stock and mutual insurers sitting at the conference table to develop a standard automobile contract, rather than appearing before a Congressional committee to discuss their relative contributions to the Treasury.

I might go on indefinitely to cite examples of insularity and to discuss its unfortunate effects. My topics would be experience rating, implementing the war-damage-insurance scheme, graded expense loadings, agency relations, and many more. But it would be foolish to bring these coals to Newcastle. My only purpose is to recall to you their existence, to ask you to consider the broad problems they represent, and to suggest that your jobs as actuarial technicians will be better done if you are guided by an appreciation of their significance.

One last word from my own field. I have long advocated a functional approach to insurance education—basic study of the underlying facts and theory as they cut across the whole insurance institution. It is natural that, with insurance developing along specialized lines, education has followed. I seem to find increasing sympathy for educational synthesis, and I hope that it may contribute something to the growth of a less parochial outlook in the business of insurance than has been in vogue heretofore.

13. The Casualty Actuary
and Social Insurance*

Article II of our constitution states that "The object of the Society shall be the promotion of actuarial and statistical science as applied to the problems of casualty and social insurance. . . ."[1]

While some attention has been given to social insurance in papers and presidential addresses and in the appointment of a Committee on Unemployment Insurance, consideration of that subject has been meager in comparison with discussion of the problems of casualty insurance as a business. Certain of these problems are directly related to social insurance, particularly those of workmen's compensation insurance (without which the Society might not exist). But here the emphasis has been on the technique of the business of implementing workmen's compensation laws rather than on social policy or governmental administration.[2]

I suggest that the casualty actuary, whether motivated by social consciousness or by self-interest, should devote more attention—considerably more—to the social-insurance field. He can be of great usefulness in giving technical guidance to governmental action, in determining the lines to be drawn between social and private insurance, and in conducting private insurance in the light of the present and probable future development of social insurance. Above all, he should avoid shutting himself up in his present corporate bailiwick, where he is insulated from outside and possibility disturbing currents.

It might be well to stop a moment at this point to inquire what is meant by the term *social insurance*. The "definitions" of the term that I have seen all lack the essential quality of a definition—that is *define*. Rubinow devoted an entire chapter of his book on social insurance to the "concept of social insurance" but emerged without having defined it. Mowbray intimates in a section heading of his general text that he is about to present

* Presidential address to the Casualty Actuary Society, November 20, 1942. Printed in the Society *Proceedings*, XXIX, 1.
[1] ". . . insurance other than life insurance. . . ."
[2] The Committee on Unemployment Insurance has been replaced by a Committee on Social Insurance, almost wholly inactive. (1964)

a definition, but proceeds to list the "essential features of a complete social insurance scheme." Often the term is used with no attempt at definition.

I have long cherished a rather awkward definition but one which, I submit, does *define*: Social insurance is any form of insurance in which the government goes beyond the regulation of practices and the dissemination of information. It may do so by compelling insurance, by shifting the cost, by subsidy, or by becoming itself an insurer. To the extent that it acts in any one of these directions, insurance becomes social insurance, and I should include within its scope compulsory automobile insurance, governmental schemes of war-risk insurance, governmental crop insurance, as well as the more commonly recognized workmen's compensation, unemployment, old-age, and disability insurances. While I believe that this definition properly distinguishes between private and social insurance, it includes certain governmental activities insurancewise which are not generally thought of as "social insurance" and which would be of minor interest to members of the Society. Our attention should be given primarily to those schemes of social insurance which are established or advocated to meet a broad social need, which aim to provide an adequate minimum personal income, and which are usually compulsory as to membership.

It is particularly important for the membership of this Society to note and ponder all manifestations of a conviction that private initiative, regulated by supervisory authorities, is not adequately meeting the risk problem of the public. Such a conviction has social-insurance legislation as its outlet. We should be prepared to contribute our best judgment and technical ability to social insurance where that is desirable or inevitable, and to conduct private insurance in such fashion as best to satisfy the needs not met by social insurance. In a rationally organized society the two would be complementary rather than competitive.

Social insurance, as a broad national policy, is something of a novelty in the United States, but the rest of the world has long accepted it. If you would learn how far it has been accepted, I recommend that you read *Approaches to Social Security—An International Survey*, published this year by the International Labour Office. This study indicates that "there is a strong, broad tendency to bring all persons employed in manual work and the lower ranks of salaried employees within the scope of compulsory insurance in all its branches."[3]

The British Parliament, some eighteen months ago, appointed a committee, of which Sir William Beveridge was named chairman, to draw up a

[3] Montreal, 1942, p. 35.

scheme to meet post-war security problems. The New York *Times* reported recently that he will recommend "the introduction of a comprehensive system of social insurance and the establishment of a national income minimum below which none would fall." More significant for us, there was introduced in Congress on September 9th of this year a bill,[4] providing for a broad federal social-insurance program and adding disability and hospitalization benefits to the provision already made under the Social Security Act. This bill unquestionably embodies proposals for which there is considerable support, and it, or other similar bills, will probably be given extensive consideration by Congress.

So far, casualty actuaries have had practically no part in the origination, establishment, administration, or development of social insurance, other than workmen's compensation. Life actuaries have had some part, but they have been more or less on the side lines. Social insurance has been in the hands of persons highly interested in *ends* but somewhat impatient with questions of *means*. And the actuaries, particularly the casualty actuaries, have held themselves aloof—or perhaps their interest has not been aroused.

The greater participation of the life actuaries in the discussion and practice of social insurance is at least partly to be explained by the fact that the most generally accepted development in that field is old-age and survivors insurance.[5] There are the further facts that social insurance, actual and proposed, does not threaten and may even benefit life insurance as a business, and that their experience with group insurance has developed their understanding of mass treatment of insurance problems. Granting that old-age and survivors insurance is primarily the concern of the life actuary, it seems to me that unemployment and disability insurance should be very much the concern of the casualty actuary. The hazards of both these fields are the same as, or akin to, those found in casualty insurance.

It may be thought that unemployment insurance does not lend itself to actuarial treatment, and it may be true that it will never be possible to predict losses due to unemployment with even approximate accuracy. But certainly the planning and administration of this form of social insurance would benefit from the type of analysis in which actuaries are skilled. Records should be set up so as to facilitate whatever actuarial analysis is possible, and full use should be made of statistical indications. Such analysis might eventually show how the unemployment risk can be controlled and measured.

[4] H.R. 7534.
[5] Now old-age, survivors, and disability insurance. (1964)

Social disability insurance beyond that provided by workmen's compensation has been adopted in only one state. But we shall hear more of it, and of its concomitants, medical care and hospitalization insurance, in the future, probably in the immediate future, in the form of specific legislative proposals, recommendations from high places, and urgings from a variety of sources. In fact, the first efforts to establish a federal scheme of temporary and permanent disability insurance have been made.

Here is a field in which the casualty actuary has basic material and techniques, and in which his services in analyzing proposals and in furnishing guidance could be of outstanding value. But he must understand social insurance as such, its purposes and its essential procedures, if his services are to be really useful. He is cost-minded, realistic, and no one knows as well as he what figures indicate, and how misleading or inadequate they may be. One of the greatest services he can render is to point out persistently that social insurance and private insurance, whatever they may have in common, have marked and important divergencies. As Hohaus has said, social insurance "is a new creation . . . requiring an actuarial technique that may sometimes seem rank heresy to the orthodox private insurance actuary." [6]

The private insurer and its insureds may sell, buy, continue, or renew insurance on a mutually voluntary basis—the more important social-insurance schemes are based on compulsorily assembled groups and are operated in accordance with statutory and administrative rules which largely eliminate personal judgment and volition. In the long run, in private insurance, there must be some relationship between the cost of providing protection to the individual insured and the premium charged for it—the contribution of the individual to social-insurance schemes is generally determined by other considerations. The private insurer must make its offering attractive to the buying public—the government is restricted only by the rather tenuous control of the democratic process. Preservation of precise equities for the individual insured is the ideal of private insurance— satisfaction of social needs the aim of social insurance. And where the private and therefore mortal insurer must hold solvency first of its concerns, the government need consider only its ability to collect the special or general taxes necessary to support its scheme.

And still we hear, and shall continue to hear, arguments that this or that should be part of a social-insurance scheme because it is done in private insurance.

[6] "Social Insurance in a Democracy," an address before the American Life Convention, October 7, 1942.

If it is proposed that the government furnish an insurance service which is generally needed, there are four tenable answers: that the service is entirely impracticable, that the government cannot properly furnish the service, that private initiative can furnish it to better general advantage, or that it should be furnished by the government through the agency of private insurers. In any event, the actuary should lend his special competence to the solution of whatever problems may arise.

One last word—when it is reasonably clear that social provision of insurance is desirable or inevitable, the actuary should be among the first to recognize it and to prepare for it.

14. The Lawyer and Insurance*

In asking me to address you, you have probably hoped to get something of the point of view of the large group of persons who are neither lawyers nor insurance executives, to whom insurance is a tool to be used, and who are concerned with the adaptability of that tool to its function.

One who studies insurance in the United States is confronted with a mechanism built to a rather rigid pattern and guided by traditional rules and attitudes. Citing Comte's remark that "humanity is composed of the dead and the living" of whom "the dead are by far the more numerous," Anatole France points out that our laws, our houses, our very ideas have been imposed upon us by our dead masters. "Can we revolt against them? We haven't even the time to disobey them!" So it is with insurance—the contribution of a generation to its development is meager compared with the continuing structure and methods which that generation inherits and passes on to the next.

This situation has its good points. By trial and error, insurance has evolved until it now fulfills remarkably well its prime function, that of being safe. It offers financial security equalled by no other business. By multiplying contract forms and through salesmanship it has offered and furnished a wide variety of loss coverage and incidental services to a large and increasing part of the population. By educational campaigns and by offering financial inducements it has done much to prevent loss. And it has advanced the technique of measuring probability of loss so as more equitably to distribute its burden.

The degree of these accomplishments and the manner of conducting the business varies greatly between the broad divisions of insurance, and even between individual lines. Life, fire, casualty, and marine insurance are linked together by a common purpose and a common basis of operation, but their variations of method, attitude, and achievement are so great as to defy generalization.

Consequently, it is impossible to present to you a broad unified picture of insurance as a basis for comment. It must be understood that most

* Address before the Insurance Section, American Bar Association, Cincinnati, December 19, 1945.

84

of what I may say is applicable only with qualifications to take account of the extreme diversity of the various insurance fields and of the attitudes of their practitioners.

Progress in insurance has been retarded by lack of effective criticism, due largely to ignorance of the business on the part of laymen, ignorance arising in part from the genuinely technical nature of the business and in part from the mysterious language with which it has cloaked itself. And within the business there has developed an almost religious worship of its machinery. The incentives to improvement which one finds effective in, say, the motor-car industry, buyer interest and constant self-criticism, are strangely inactive. Research as a means of locating weaknesses and improving methods has been highly developed in a few lines and all but ignored in others. And there is too much of the feeling that the institution of insurance is an end in itself instead of a tool for the service of the public.

This situation has resulted in a marked resistance to suggestions for change—in a feeling that change is dangerous, disturbing, and somewhat sacrilegious. When new ideas have shown their ugly heads they have been met too often by indifference or studied neglect; when they have become insistent, by hostility. Too seldom have they been welcomed and examined sympathetically.

At the moment the business of insurance finds itself subject to three marked pressures: broader and more intensive governmental regulation, proposals for governmentally managed insurance, and informed buyer activity.

Major governmental moves are not undertaken without some basis. Once started they may become exaggerated beyond the importance of their cause, but cause there usually is. Sooner or later insurance would probably have been declared to be interstate commerce by the Supreme Court in any event, but the present situation can be traced directly to outmoded practices which were fostered by the divided authority of the individual states. Had the business been more responsive to changing conditions, it might not have found itself challenged. Its response to the challenge is significant. First, it fought to prove that times had not changed since 1868. Second, it sought to avoid the effect of change by having itself declared exempt. Third, it is now attempting to minimize necessary change. One eloquent representative of a group of insurers summed it all up by pleading that "what we want is the *status quo* as it is now [*sic*]."

It has been realized for some time by a few minds gifted with imaginative understanding, and is now being suspected by the more "practical" (or short-sighted), that the insurance business is in the course of revolutionary change. The federal-state regulatory situation is only a symptom, though a major one, of that change. The insurance business has quite naturally developed in a competitive atmosphere as a device for extracting profits, in the form of surplus or salary, from the service of carrying risk and from other incidental services. Unless it is socialized, it will continue so to develop. But it is accepted doctrine that this business is "affected with a public interest" and is therefore subject to restraints and duties beyond those imposed by general concepts of business morality, by general law, and by the watchfulness of its clients and their representatives.

Insurance was originally sold by individual underwriters on the principle of *caveat emptor*, perhaps a reasonably satisfactory basis when insurer and insured were part of a small business community and were personally acquainted; when the contract and the perils covered were simple. But insurance has now become a quasi-public utility serving the greater part of the population in meeting a wide variety of perils instead of a few enterprisers subject to highly specialized risks.

Regulation of the future, whether state or federal (and if the states do not do a satisfactory job, it *will* be federal), should be based squarely on the principle of developing the insurance business as a financial tool for the service of the insuring public. The long-run interests of insurers should be properly conserved in the process, but adjustments to changing situations may be temporarily painful because of reluctance and tardiness in making such adjustments in the past. The elimination of indefensible practices that had been made possible by ineffective regulation or varying standards will call for major operations. Not only must organs be removed, but new ones must be created.

One of the first jobs that should be undertaken is an overhauling of statutory provisions granting powers to insurers. The present classification of insurers into life, fire-and-marine, and casualty is an historical accident —its continuance has little justification beyond the convenience of insurance executives. It is one of the principal causes of the inability of insurers to do a thorough, comprehensive job for insureds. Further divisions between lines operate in the same way, though much progress has been made in the direction of breaking down the walls.

A second job is the substitution of principles for detailed directions in the regulatory law and the creation of state insurance departments competent to apply principles. Flexible regulation applied by able officials administering well-staffed departments makes it possible to meet situations as they arise and avoids technical obstructions to progress. But unless departments are competent and independent, flexibility is dangerous; the two requirements are interdependent.

In certain fields insurers are disturbed by the imminence of governmental insurance; in others by its more remote possibility. Some forms of necessary insurance can properly be written only by the government; war damage insurance in time of war, to take a noncontroversial example. There are forms, however, now written by private insurers, or that they might write, that are the subject of controversy. For example, proposals for governmental disability insurance are constantly being made and are finding insistent support.

It may be admitted that it would be desirable for everyone to have insurance against loss of income and extra expenses incident to disability. Such insurance is being written under a wide variety of contracts by insurers of several types, but it is clear that the need for it extends far beyond its present coverage. Unquestionably, the demand induced by proposals for legislation is a challenge to private insurance. And fulminations against governmental interference, socialism, and other ideological targets are not an adequate answer. The question is how far can the demand be met and by what method can it best be met. If private insurance is the answer, then positive measures should be taken to devise means of meeting it by offering and selling coverage. If the eventual answer is to be some combination of governmental and private insurance, plans should be laid to that end. Unthinking hostility is not wise.

Until comparatively recently, insurance was generally bought blindly, even by large corporations with a reputation for efficiency. Insureds had little knowledge of insurance, and the idea of the insurance program as a part of management policy had not developed. Unless a loss occurred there was often no check on the adequacy of insurance. During the 1920's there was a faint stirring of interest in the problems of the insurance buyer. It has developed during recent years until the management of the insurance affairs of many businesses occupies the full time of a specialized "insurance (or risk) manager." National and local groups of managers are active in the study and discussion of their problems and give promise of having a real influence over the future of the business.

The lawyer has always been an important factor in insurance, for the basis of the business is the insurance contract. Every problem of the insurance business is related to that document. As types of contract have multiplied, and as each has become more complex, the work of the lawyer has increased, whether as drafter, interpreter, or advocate.

The development of governmental regulation has still further enlarged the functions of the lawyer. Insurance commissioners are largely drawn from the ranks of lawyers; the drafting of laws is a lawyer's job; insurers are constantly using the services of lawyers in determining their rights and obligations, as advisers, or as representatives before courts and other governmental bodies. The new relationship of the federal government to insurance means more work for the lawyers. There is also the academic lawyer who is student and teacher, and the lawyer turned insurance executive.

When the threat of change has become ominous, the insurance business has turned to the legal profession for advocates and negotiators. And it has had no difficulty in finding them. Consider, for example, the 1943 revision of the New York standard fire insurance policy, in fact, now a revision of the fire-insurance policies of most states, for the new form has been widely adopted. The Committee on the Revision of the Fire Insurance Policy of the National Association of Insurance Commissioners reported in 1936 that "in general the insurers are satisfied with the present policies," but that "those who are not connected with insurers [including brokers and agents] have expressed considerable sentiment in favor of revision." In 1937 one group of insurers was reported to be in favor of revision, the major group, however, showing "little interest." Finally, and reluctantly, this most influential group withdrew its opposition, and the revised policy was adopted in New York in 1942. It is not an ideal policy, but it represents a great improvement over the earlier form.

Throughout, the function of the opposition's legal department was representative rather than creative, and this in a field, that of contracts, where the legal profession might be expected to lead. This same group advertised the revised contract as one of its public benefactions.

The development of liability-insurance contracts presents a very different picture. Here lawyers have constantly pressed for improvements in language and coverage to adapt the contract to modern business and personal risks. They have encountered the unwillingness of professional risk-takers to take risks but, aided by threats of state action, they have succeeded in producing and securing the adoption of contracts which go far toward the ideal of complete and automatic coverage.

Recently the manager of an accident-and-health-insurance company writing a highly restricted contract told me that his company was proud of its claims record—that their only controversies with insureds resulted from the fact that the insured did not understand the contract. He intended this statement as a justification—it seemed to me to be a confession.

The future function of the lawyer in insurance should be along more constructive lines than has been the case in the past. If it is to be constructive, he must be more than an advocate or a counsellor whose ends are laid down by his employers. He needs to know far more than the law—he needs to understand insurance.

Lawyers who have become insurance commissioners have found it necessary not only to represent the public but to take a creative part in the development of public policy. Unlike insurance executives and the specializing insurance manager, much of the public does not know what it wants. The insurance commissioner of a state must determine what is best insurancewise for this uninformed, and numerous, segment. If he is conscientious, capable, and interested, he finds himself studying insurance, accounting, and statistics. And if he has graduated from the role of the debater employed to win cases, he may see a great light—he may learn that there are not only two sides but many sides to a question.

All of this is not to decry the role of the trial lawyer, of the advocate, but I submit that the attitude of the advocate should not be carried through to situations which require statesmanship rather than facility in argument.

Several years ago a committee of the state bar association of one of our most influential states presented a report on compulsory automobile insurance and financial responsibility laws. The majority (nineteen of the twenty-one members of the committee) stated that they had made "a thorough study . . . of proposed compulsory insurance and financial responsibility laws with reference not only to their intrinsic merit but respecting their relation to the larger problems of accident prevention." The report was quoted widely as authority in discussions and arguments on those subjects.

Analysis of the data and reasoning of this report seems to indicate that both represented acceptance of oft-repeated insurance propaganda, that figures were taken uncritically, and that the committee was quite unfamiliar with the available material on the subject. I prefer to think that these were the facts rather than that, with complete understanding of the problem, the committee was cynically making a case.

This was a situation where, as representatives of a quasi-public body, the committee should have accepted the responsibility of making the "thorough study" which it professed to have made or have merely reported "progress."

Since June, 1944, the insurance lawyer has been placed in a position where statesmanship is more than ever necessary. The South-Eastern Underwriters decision was only the culmination of a long chain of circumstances, but it was a climactic culmination. Some students of the law had foreseen it in principle; many, perhaps most, were taken by surprise—they had not realized that there *was* a federal question.

Characteristically, the first attempt to meet the problem (when it appeared that there might be a question of the result in the Supreme Court) was to send a lawyer to avert the possible consequences. The report of the hearings before the Congressional committee which considered the Baily-Van Nuys bill should be instructive to anyone who still thinks that method was wise. It is also instructive on the need for lawyers to understand insurance.

General realization seems now to be dawning on the legal profession and perhaps insurance executives that there is needed something more than drawing briefs, arguments by trial lawyers, or political deals. The insurance business and its legal representatives are faced with a complex and extensive problem of public relations, of interpretation of the law, of insurance technique, and of sound legislation to express sound policy. It is no longer a matter of a contest to be won but rather of an edifice to be created.

The fundamental fact is that insurance is an essential public service, that its only justification is its usefulness to the public. Ideally, the various agencies of the insurance business would be guided solely by the responsibility which this position implies. But we know that private individuals or organizations, left to their own devices, will be guided largely by their own short-run interests. Our system of local state regulation of insurance has been developed to control that tendency in the interest of the public.

Now comes the promise (or threat, depending on one's point of view) of intensified regulation, of federal intervention, of buying by specification, and even of governmentally operated insurance. The only sound way to meet the situation is by taking the attitude that an insurer is essentially a public instrument, and its executives public officials. They should set up, in cooperation with politically (in the better sense) elected or appointed officials a workable scheme of competition, cooperation, and regulation—all to the end that insurance shall best serve the public in meeting its risk problems. And the lawyer-statesman who understands insurance and its implications is the man to do the job.

This is not merely starry-eyed, idealistic doctrine. It may be said that human nature has not changed, that business will go on attaining its ends in much the same way as in the past. Human nature does not change, but organized expression of its desires does change. Institutions wither, and new ones succeed them. Only those survive that show ability to adapt themselves to changing circumstances.

The services of lawyers to insurance have been important—they are responsible for much that has made the insurance structure useful and safe. My plea is for broadening and intensifying their services and for recognition of the principle that, whoever pays them, they are working for the public; and that in doing so they serve the long-run best interests of their immediate employers.

"The dinosaur used to wander about the countryside well armed against the perils of his day—but it is said that when the climate changed he had no ideas." Beware of short-run practicality which often consists merely in protecting what you have. Long-run practicality involves looking into the future, forecasting trends, and suiting yourself to them. Lord Bryce once said that one should learn to view the present as though it were the past—a very practical suggestion.

15. Losses, Expenses, and Profit*

The insurance business has done itself a great disservice by creating the impression that it is highly scientific, that from its accumulated statistical data it can produce an accurate prophecy of its future losses by expert application of mathematical formulae. The public has heard much of mortality tables, statistics of experience, the law of large numbers, the theory of probability, and actuarial mathematics, mostly in praise of the wonder-working attributes of these tools in the hands of insurance technicians.

Too little has been heard of the qualifying words and phrases that are applicable to the use of the tools; of credibility, "conditions being the same," trends, emergencies, extraneous influences.

Let us look at life insurance for a moment, the field where the actuary flourishes, and toward which the inhabitants of the outer worlds of insurance and the public salaam with genuine respect. The basic reason for the extraordinary success in collecting adequate premiums for life insurance has lain in the more-or-less steady improvement in mortality over the years. But even the life insurers have had their troubles. That same "improvement" in mortality has had the opposite effect on annuity experience. And in both cases assumptions of percentages of investment return, thought to be highly conservative, have been contradicted by experience. And note that these results have largely been due to extraneous influences; the activities of the medical profession, improvement in living conditions, and the Treasury Department.

Life insurers have been the victims of at least one serious emergency that was almost completely beyond their control, the increased mortality due to the influenza epidemic of 1918–1919. It was stated by one of the leading actuaries of the period that insureds holding participating contracts probably lost approximately the amount of one annual dividend and that some insurers were rendered technically (but only temporarily) insolvent. A serious situation of their own creation was that brought about by the writing of disability-income insurance on an unsound basis, mostly under

* Address before the Annual Meeting of the National Association of Independent Insurers, Chicago, November 21, 1952.

clauses added to life-insurance contracts, but also under contracts issued independently. One of their current problems is the guarantee of income under settlement options, income which may be payable for long periods after the death of the insured, which may itself take place long after the inception of the contract.

Fortunately, the life-insurance business proper has had sufficient resources, in most cases, to absorb the deficits created by other operations, and no suggestion is made here that its difficulties endanger the security offered to insureds. It is only intended to point out, as a prelude to considering the problems of nonlife insurers, that, even in life insurance, prediction of losses is not the precise science that it is often thought to be.

If this situation is true of life insurance, where the questions of amount of loss, and whether and to whom it is payable are usually easily and definitely answered, what of lines of insurance that are subject to a multitude of causes affecting both basic perils and resultant losses? I need not, nor would I have time to, detail for this group the factors that influence the occurrence and amounts of losses. But let me remind you that among them are business conditions, the vagaries of fashion, activities of lawyers, attitudes of courts, legislative enactments, availability of materials, weather, engineering, organized pressures, political expediency, even the procreative tendencies of workers and the remarriage proclivities of widows.

The problem of recording what losses have been incurred by insurers has been pretty well solved, and the records of most of the major lines are reliable, though not always strictly up to date. Estimates of outstanding losses, though sometimes made with an eye to considerations other than those of strict accuracy, are capable of remarkably exact calculation. A considerable element of judgment and even of expediency enters into classification, but given a system of classification, the records accumulated can be, and mostly are, reliable.

The big difficulty arises in attempting to use the records as a basis for predicting future losses. Here, after gathering all pertinent experience and setting it forth in what seems to be the most revealing form, one is confronted by the question, "what does it indicate in respect of *future* losses?" The answer must be largely a matter of judgment, and judgment has a way of itself resting on the past and of being warped by bias. The bias is not necessarily that of direct financial self-interest; it may be that of position, of tradition, or of *eventual* financial self-interest.

You have been hearing of Massachusetts *ad nauseam*, but it furnishes a good example of what I have in mind. The Commissioner of Insurance calculated and promulgated 1952 rates for compulsory automobile liability insurance based on the average level of 1948, 1949, and 1950. The insurers writing such insurance in that state recommended to the Commissioner that rates for 1952 be calculated on a level reflecting losses of 1950, the latest year for which experience was available, on the ground that losses had been, and were in 1951, increasing so rapidly that earlier experience was obsolete as an indication of losses in 1952. It seems likely that, with freedom to act, they would have introduced a trend factor that would have resulted in rates considerably higher than those calculated on 1950 losses.

What were the possibilities for 1952? Losses might continue to increase, they might level off, or they might decrease. Which would be the tendency, and to what extent increases or decreases would run were matters of judgment. I expect that the contention of the insurers reflected their judgment that losses would increase, tempered by their conviction that the 1950 level was the best they could hope for. The Commissioner's rates perhaps reflected a desire to keep the increase in level to a minimum and a feeling that his position would be fortified by the use of broad experience and a traditional formula. Neither side confessed to all its motives, some of which may have been unconscious.

The insurers carried their case to the Supreme Judicial Court. That court refused to choose between the two bases. In its opinion the court said, "If the commissioner had fixed the rates on the basis of the 1950 loss data it would be difficult to say that he was wrong. But the question is not what this court would decide if it were in the position of the commissioner. . . . our inquiry here is whether the order of the commissioner was without reasonable support in the evidence. We cannot say that it was." In other words, what evidence was to be used and how to use it were matters of judgment. And the only final determinant of the correctness of the Commissioner's rates will be the 1952 experience.[1]

During the twenty-four years, 1927 to 1950, inclusive, for which the various Massachusetts commissioners have made rates, the incurred losses have exceeded the provision made for them in the rates in fourteen years, while the provision has exceeded the losses in ten. The largest percentage by which losses exceeded provision for them was 31, in 1928; the largest by which provision exceeded losses was 28.8, in 1942. The experience for the entire period shows an excess of losses over provision of 5.6 per cent.

I see no reason to change the opinion that I expressed in 1936,[2] that approval or promulgation of rates by state insurance departments carries

---

[1] The 1952 losses exceeded the provision for losses by approximately 20 per cent. (1964)
[2] *Proceedings* of the Casualty Actuarial Society, XXII, 339–341. See pages 196–198 of this volume.

with it some tendency toward inadequate rates. This situation "does not result from a desire to make or approve inadequate rates, but probably rather from a feeling that the department must be in a position to defend the rates to the insuring public (and their highly vocal political representatives). Consequently, conjectural or projection factors are ruled out—and little or no provision can be made for expected developments which are not to be repetitions of the past. If the department sponsors a set of rates, it lays *itself* as well as the rates open to attack.

"It is only natural that a department should show more hospitality to downward than upward revisions of rates and that it should feel that it must have definite evidence of insurance costs to justify its actions."

I do not have such faith in the reasonableness and ability of insurers that I should leave insurance prices entirely in their hands. I believe that any exercise of judgment in determining probable losses is subject to "some special human interest or bias." In the statement from which I have quoted I suggested the application of certain principles that, I still believe, would minimize the effect of the special human interests that affect rate making and rate regulation. The use of judgment is a necessary part of these activities; to the extent that it is necessary it should be exercised under conditions from which, as far as possible, the element of bias has been removed. Judgment will always be fallible, but it will help greatly to realize what part is played by it, and what part by mathematical and statistical processes, in the prediction of losses, which are the major factor in the making of rates.

Losses, once insurance is written, are largely outside the control of the insurer, though in some lines it may do much to persuade and assist the insured in controlling them. Expenses are the direct result of the existence of insurance and represent almost the entire cost to the public of maintaining the institution of insurance. Yet it is only recently that a determined effort has been made in the nonlife field to record with exactness and in detail expenses by nature and source. And not so long ago there had been no thought to relate provision for expenses to incidence of expense within a kind of insurance. It was assumed that expenses varied with losses. A percentage of the final rate was allowed, varying upward from the traditional 40 per cent of workmen's compensation insurance. Now variations in expense provision by size of risk are common, and the emergence of group accident and health insurance has introduced a new concept of the expense margin.

Symptomatic of the broad, unanalyzed concept of expense is the frequent contention that, if expense provision is to be reduced, an equal percentage reduction shall be applied to commissions and to other expenses, without regard to the necessity or value of the services covered by the two kinds of expense.

Present conditions are causing increases in both losses and expense, and if the expense provision remains a constant percentage, provision for expense rises as provision for losses rises. But there is an increasing tendency to question the validity of provision for expenses, as a whole and in detail. Insureds, particularly large insureds, are becoming better informed and more analytical in their approach to the composition of the premium dollar, the determination of which was so recently an esoteric rite in the hands of the high priests. Insureds will more and more want to know what they are getting for their contributions to expenses and whether what they are getting is worth the price. Justification by traditional percentages is becoming less and less effective. And taboos and slogans are not só effective in warding off competition as they once were.

It behooves insurers carefully to examine their expense structure; to know what the expense for each class of service is; to be prepared to justify expenses as being in the interest of insureds, both to insureds and their insurance-department representatives; and to these ends to study methods of adjusting expenses to service needed and rendered. Not a little is to be learned from the practices of life insurance and of the unconventional independents.

And now we come to the question of profit, or margin. I incline toward the latter word as an acknowledgment, even an assertion, of the inexactness of prophecies of losses and expenses. When actuaries construct mortality tables for practical use, they do not set down the exact number of deaths per thousand at the various ages; rather they add a margin to the observed rates of mortality. They have no illusions that mortality can be exactly predicted. So much the more do nonlife insurers need a margin to guard against the inaccuracies inherent in applying the facts of the past to the operations of the future.

That margin, of course, must be sufficient in the long run to enable a well-managed insurer to make a profit; in fact, to enable the best managed (or luckiest) insurer to make a considerable profit if rates are uniform for all insurers and based on average rather than selective data.

The general justification of profit is that it induces insurers to conduct the useful business of insurance. That profit is justified which induces insurers to continue to furnish and to develop insurance in the public interest, to take the trouble and risk. Greater profit is not justified. I am not impressed by comparisons between insurance profits and those made on butter, furniture, clothing, or in providing electricity or telephone service. The inducement needed to secure a supply of those commodities and services may be more or less than is the case in insurance, but it is not relevant.

Attempts have been made to determine a "reasonable" profit, and to support various percentages by formula, analysis, and analogy. They result in agreements, compromises, or disagreements, but these results are not evidences of any exact determination of what profits should be—no one knows. Only the interplay of countless influences will determine profit or margin, both that to be allowed for in rates and that to be realized in operation. Competition, regulation, and general economic conditions all have their effect on profits. What profits should be is a matter of judgment; what they will be is uncertain; each question is a puzzle, which, according to Webster, is "something which perplexes or embarrasses."

16. Health Insurance and
the Insured*

The insurance business has grown by a process of picking out particular causes of loss that seemed to offer a reasonable basis for prediction and to be of sufficient importance to the prospective insured to induce him to pay for protection. The spectacular and newsworthy cause has been particularly useful for purposes of insurance exploitation.

Probably this sort of development was inevitable, but it has led, in the selling and purchase of insurance, to thinking in terms of *cause of loss* rather than of *loss* itself. Hence, fire insurance, rather than loss-of-property insurance, and accident-and-sickness (or health) insurance rather than disability insurance.

Also in this marketing process, emphasis has been placed on the inconsequential and the speculative. By "inconsequential," I mean the payment of losses that are of no great moment to the insured but that seem to him to represent a return for his premium and are considered by insurers to be "good advertising." By "speculative," the accidental-death benefits in life insurance, and the double-indemnity benefits, even the death benefit, in accident insurance.

It may be taken as axiomatic that one cannot protect one's self completely against all financial loss from all perils. And there is no sound formula to determine where one should draw the line between expenditure for protection in the form of insurance and expenditures of other sorts. The fact that one must choose *what* insurance to buy and how far to go in paying premiums suggests that care should be used to buy what is most useful. And this thought leads to the question: "What principles should be followed in buying insurance," which connotes what to many is a most disagreeable process—thinking.

Life insurers are more and more emphasizing the desirability of programming, not only for the well-to-do who may properly be served by estate planning, but for the small man, particularly the one who may

* Address before the Accident and Health Meeting of the Life Insurance Agency Management Association, Chicago, March 17, 1954. Used by permission.

become a big man. In their programming activities, they attempt not only to adjust life insurance to the needs of the insured, but to apply it where it is most useful, recognizing that there are other means of meeting his needs and that life insurance should be fitted into an overall plan of protection. It is encouraging to learn that health insurers are commencing to think along similar lines.

For a person dependent on his earnings for his own support and that of others, total and permanent, even lengthy, disability is a worse financial fate than death. If a person dies, the cost of maintaining him ceases, both the normal cost and that of medical or other care. His dependents are set free to do whatever is possible to support themselves. If he is totally disabled, the cost of maintenance continues, extra costs may be incurred, and usually his family is saddled with care-taking duties. But while life insurance is generally accepted as a necessity, health insurance is either not so accepted or follows life insurance in order of interest.

This is partly, perhaps largely, due to the simplicity and the assurance of definite financial return inherent in most forms of life insurance. The insurer says, in effect: "If you pay the premium, we will pay a definite sum to your beneficiary. We cannot cancel your contract, and after a year, we cannot question its validity for any reason. And if, before death, you need money, it will be available." In addition, participating life insurers will adjust the premium to the cost of furnishing the insurance.

The small part that moral hazard plays in life insurance enables the life insurer to conduct its business on this basis. Much of the moral hazard is excluded in the original underwriting of the risk; what is left is so slight that its consequences can easily (and properly) be absorbed. There is little room in which moral hazard can operate. Death (or survival) is a pretty clear-cut event, not easily subject to counterfeiting, and certainly not to exaggeration. The payee is usually easily identifiable.

The health underwriter faces no such simple situation. He has reacted accordingly and has hedged his contracts about with exclusions, limitations, and options, usually for what seem to be sound reasons; but sometimes such provisions are ingenious rather than ingenuous. At the same time, recognizing the variety of losses that can be caused by disability, he has offered the public an increasing variety of benefits, both in the form of options and of additional coverage. Health-insurance contracts are almost infinitely variable, are written by a multitude of insurers, and lend themselves to unreasonable as well as reasonable marketing methods. They are sold by radio, by advertisements in newspapers and periodicals, by mail, and through agents and brokers. Special "nonprofit" insurers have been created to deal with certain aspects of medical and hospital care, in addition to the life insurers, specializing health insurers, casualty insurers, assessment associations, and others that have long operated in this business. To all of which must be added rumblings and proposals of governmental action.

I do not direct your attention to this tangle of hazards, interests, and methods to bring you anything new—you are already painfully aware of it. My purpose is to suggest the position of the prospective insured, especially of the insured who has recently read a popular article on the evils of health insurance or who has listened to a candidate for election whose heart bleeds for the sufferings of the common man. And when you add to all this the fact that very few persons have any conception of a logical approach to the problem of risk, or to its solution by the use of insurance, the possibility of an insured being properly covered is slight indeed.

An ideal solution of the problem of risk would be the replacement, or making good, of all loss; obviously only ideal and so far impracticable as not to be worth discussing. Since I am considering insurance, I shall confine myself to what is practicable in that field and what is advisable from the insured's point of view. And here I am further confining myself to health insurance, meaning insurance against loss due to disability, whether disability takes the form of reduced activity or of abnormal condition requiring care.

It is clear that insurance is practicable only to the extent that premiums can be collected that will cover losses, expenses, and a margin for safety or profit. It is a worthwhile social device only when the *expense* of operating the business is reasonable. Each of these statements might be made the subject of a paper—I make them only to indicate that they are basic considerations and assume that this audience requires no elaboration.

In terms of loss from disability an insured needs replacement of loss of earning power and either care or money to purchase care. And what part of this should be secured through insurance? Perhaps this question is best approached negatively. One should not insure against losses that can be borne by one's self without embarrassment or that are predictable with a fair degree of accuracy in the individual case. To the extent that insurance is taken against such losses, the part of the premium paid to cover operating expenses of the business is wasted. And the operating expense of paying small losses is, of course, disproportionate.

Another negative point—the insured should bear a part of all losses, or his coverage should be so limited as not to present too great a temptation. This point is a reflection of the unfortunate fact that complete coverage of disability losses, whether large or small, offers too much incentive to the less admirable sides of human nature, whether exhibited by insureds, doctors, or hospital managers. Complete coverage, even of losses beyond a proper deductible to eliminate small and bearable losses, would often mean such aggravation of those losses that insurance would be impracticable or at least unduly expensive. Premiums would have to be so high as to price it out of the market, or the honest and prudent insureds would be carrying the burden of losses paid to, or on account of, the other sort.

So the problem comes down to this: "How can you best furnish, and the insured purchase, coverage that is at once practicable and economical?" I believe that, in the long run, both of these ends will be most nearly accomplished by adherence to the principles I have stated.

However, principles do not automatically apply themselves. Both insurer and insured should learn to think straight and to apply their thinking. It seems to me that you have done much in developing workable non-cancellable insurance, in adopting an incontestable clause, in recognizing the deductible principle (particularly in connection with major-medical covers), in cooperating in the revision of the standard provisions, and in extending coverage beyond the too often merely palliative benefits of the past. The literature of the business and its discussions indicate that you are aware of needs, problems, and criticism, but it will not be easy to mold the business into a form consonant with principle.

And what of the insured? He responds so readily to the meretricious and is so greedy that the application of high principle might leave him cold and fail to put him in a buying mood. Further, the soundest of explanations for not paying a claim leads him to thoughts of premium money thrown away and of ungenerous or even fraudulent insurers. These characteristics of his are the reason for the sale of so much insurance that is uneconomical, and disappointing when really serious disability strikes.

The insurance business has a tremendous job of education on its hands, as do those of us who are trying to introduce some bit of practical thinking into the minds of students; education in sound insurance thinking, not merely that the insurer may be operated so as to attract premiums, settle claims fairly, and maintain solvency, but that insurance may perform the greatest possible service and not have its substance (and that of insureds) wasted on operations that consist of shifting money from one pocket to another with little genuine service.

I suggest that attainment of the following ends is highly desirable:

1. Elimination of uneconomical coverage of small losses. What is uneconomical depends on persons and circumstances; a variety of deductibles should be available. Perhaps no one loss under $25 should be covered.

2. Education of insureds to think in terms of applying available premium money efficiently in protecting themselves against serious rather than easily

bearable losses. Too often deductibles are presented as a means of reducing premiums. They might better be presented as a means of purchasing more coverage for the same premium.

3. Education of agents as advisers as well as salesmen, as service men helping the insured to get the most, not in immediate return but in protection, for his premium.

4. Reduction of expense ratios. Accomplishment of the first three ends in any degree would tend to reduce expense ratios. Direct action in rationalizing commissions to agents might diminish the total reward for mere salesmanship and increase the reward for service, even though commissions as percentages of premiums were reduced.

5. Extension of coverage to the broad mass of the public in amounts that meet their needs. The greatest weakness of private enterprise in comparison with governmental action is the inability of the former to reach as wide a group and to enforce minimum provision for need. Meeting the admitted problem, not merely by reaching numbers but by covering overall need is the best argument against governmental action. Positive accomplishment is less dramatic than noisy opposition, but more effective.

6. Application of the indemnity principle. Compensating the insured for genuine loss is the basic purpose of insurance. Promises to pay specified sums on proof of specified facts of physical condition or of undergoing specified procedures is something of a perversion of that purpose.

7. Elimination of speculative provisions. Giving a prize settlement to the insured who was injured by the collapse of the *outer* walls of a building if he was *therein* at the time of the collapse carries its own comment.

8. Elimination of exclusions. Whether exclusions are accomplished by listing as such or by an incomplete list of covered causes of disability, they represent a failure of coverage and a potent source of misunderstanding. Within the range of disability as a cause, the all-risks contract is the ideal contract.

9. Use of common understandable language both in contracts and in dealing with insureds. In other fields marked advances have been made in rewording contracts so that their intent is clearly understandable by an insured not versed in the language of insurance. Specialized groups tend to develop a jargon of their own and not to consider the misunderstanding or mystification that it conveys to the laity. "Noncancellable" carries a generally accepted meaning in the business, but may not convey the idea of "renewable" to the insured. Even the use of typically insurance words with a new meaning may be misleading. To the extent that the public

understands "coinsurance," it is as it is used in fire insurance with a practical significance quite different from that of "coinsurance" in major medical.

10. Settlement of claims as a service to the insured rather than as mere observance of the contract. This end implies employment of high-grade men instructed to make every reasonable effort to satisfy the claimant, without being lavish or condoning fraud or gross exaggeration of claims.

11. Continuous coverage. Noncancellable guaranteed-renewable insurance accomplishes this end within limits. Promotion of persistency of other types of cover works in the same direction, as does restriction to clearly justified cases of use of cancellation and refusal to renew.

I can hear the comments engendered by these suggestions— "impossible," "impractical," "academic." I should be the last to say that they could be adopted *in toto*, now or ever. I offer them as guides, as indications of what, in my opinion, the business should work toward. They are intended to lead a few to consider, first, to what extent they are worthy *as ends*, and second, to the extent that they are good, how the business may advance toward these ends. I hope that they will not arouse principally thoughts of why nothing can be done.

17. Education*

Education is being acclaimed as the solution of many of the problems of the insurance business. The organizations connected with the Insurance Institute of America are developing courses and libraries. Agents' associations are conducting short-course schools. Certification of professional standing is being offered to life-insurance agents (whose character is somehow supposed to be changed by calling them "underwriters") and is proposed for the property field.[1] Universities are adding courses both in their regular curricula and in their extension programs, often in response to the desire of agents or other insurance groups. And enthusiastic speeches and reports are spreading the gospel.

It is my first purpose to warn you against too great enthusiasm for education, too uncritical an attitude of respect for a "worthy" movement. I do so because of my concern to see education command respect in the long run as an increasingly useful activity. I do not want to see it ride the crest of a wave of popularity, only later to be succeeded by disappointment when it fails to show itself capable of miracles.

There is no magic in education. It is a useful tool for transmitting facts and ideas and for organizing facts and ideas for the service of those who take part in the educational process: instructors, students, and sponsors. It should be viewed in the same light as any other tool and be adapted carefully and critically to its purpose. It should not be treated as an end in itself and should be judged on the basis of practical accomplishment rather than of abstract worthiness.

In spite of what I have said, education suffers from a demand that it be "practical," because that demand usually takes the form of eagerness for immediate results, for the facts today that will increase the income tomorrow. It seems to me that the meeting of this demand is no part of the function of education, that, on the contrary, a really practical educational program is one that looks for results over years and decades and that promotes clear thinking rather than the mere accumulation of detailed facts.

* Address before the Fire Underwriters Association of the Pacific, San Francisco, June 4, 1941.
1 Since widely developed. (1964)

Meeting the "practical" demand is the easiest way; it pleases the audience and puts no great strain on the educator. Besides, it helps the employer to avoid the responsibility of training his own men. But it is wasteful, for it offers very little in the way of long-run service to insurance or to its practitioners. Genuinely practical education requires time, money, and an amazing amount of hard work. In the proportion that these elements are expended and carefully coordinated by competent and self-critical educators one may expect a long-run practical return from an educational program. And by "educator" I do not mean necessarily the professional educator, although I suggest that his experience and practical competence in his field could often be used to advantage.

So far I have used the term "education" as it is popularly used: to cover all sorts of efforts to instruct. But for the purpose of developing my thoughts I should like to draw somewhat arbitrary distinctions between three different methods of instruction: education, training, and apprenticeship.

I prefer to think of *education* as the effort to help persons to understand insurance and the insurance business, to gain a comprehension of its individual parts and of their functional relationship in the working whole. It is a mental process, the laying of a foundation for accurate thinking about insurance problems.

Training is the development of skill through personal instruction. It may or may not carry with it some educational value, some enhancement of the power of clear thinking. It is instruction in doing a job; it does not raise questions, but lays down definite procedures.

As an example of this distinction between education and training, take the matter of reinsurance. Education would provide a basis for discussion by presenting the facts of reinsurance practice. It would then explain the functions of reinsurance, the basis of decisions on what and how much to reinsure, where and under what terms to place reinsurance. Training would instruct in following the rules; what to do when a given advice of insurance written comes into the office, what reports to make, what records to keep. But it would have nothing to say of the reasons for this procedure.

Training may be by oral or written instruction. It may also be made a matter of apprenticeship, or more often a combination of the two methods. Apprenticeship is nonproductive practice, the handling of cases which duplicate practical work but which are only illustrative and are intended to develop skill for later practical application.

Education, training, and apprenticeship are in no sense a substitute for that part of practical experience that matures the judgment and brings knowledge to bear on actual situations. In the days when insurance and the fields related to it were simple, experience was perhaps an adequate teacher. But the extent and complexity of present-day business requires auxiliary analysis and summarization of knowledge beyond that of the specializing human being, whose own experience can cover only his special activity, and that often none too well. Instruction, in content, method, and organization, has not kept pace with this growing extent and complexity of the insurance business. It should at least be brought abreast, and I could hope to see it a bit ahead.

I am particularly concerned here with education in the restricted sense of my own definition. I shall attempt to outline for you something of its content, methods, and functions as I see them.

My idea of insurance education is that it should be primarily teaching and directing study of the language and theory of insurance to the end of inducing accurate thinking in terms of insurance. By language, I mean not merely definition of technical terms, although that is necessary, but an understanding of the significance of those terms in the broadest sense. By theory, not vaporous musings on the future but the reasoning on which insurance practices and plans are based and a critical examination of the relationship between specific practices and sound theory. I have no patience with the statement: "It is all right in theory but it won't work in practice." The theory is wrong if it won't work in practice, for theory, or reasoning, if you prefer, is the basis of all improvement in practice.

Education has a secondary function, particularly important under modern conditions, that of selection. Regardless of the stories of failures of valedictorians, success in study and success in life seem to me to be connected; both spring from superior ability. In the old days, when the president of a company was in a position to observe and evaluate all his employees, he might be expected to see ability and to reward it with advancement. But there is now less opportunity for ability to reveal itself in the highly subdivided tasks of a large insurance organization, and the executive with power to reward is far removed from the aspiring clerk. The educational process furnishes something of an index of worth and might be of major help in the selection of promising material for managerial positions.

In any practical insurance organization above the smallest there are three classes of workers: policy-making, judgment-and-knowledge using, and routine. The three overlap considerably, but a worker may, in most cases, be classified in one of these groups.

The policy-making group is small and composed of those top officers who are usually called executives. It is their job to determine the general attitude of the organization, how it is to conduct its business, what its policy is to be in respect to major questions. Above all, these men should know insurance, should think accurately, and should have ability to make and carry out decisions.

In the second group are the operating men, those for whom general policies have been set, but who require a broad equipment of knowledge and judgment to carry out the policies of the executives, while at the same time accumulating a base of information for gradual amendment of those policies. In underwriting, for example, a company will have a general policy of accepting certain classes of risk and rejecting others, of keeping its lines within certain bounds, and the underwriting staff will do the work of bringing the writing of the individual risk into conformity with that policy.

In the third group of routine workers no special knowledge or judgment is required, but skill in handling detail, accuracy, and faithfulness. When a new employee is taken on he usually enters the third class; many will never get beyond it. Those few who do will rise to the second group from which most of the executives are drawn.

Education in insurance, if it is to imply a considerable amount of instruction and study, can be of great use to those employees who have reached or have the capacity to rise to the second and first classes. For those who are to remain routine workers it will have little value. While everyone should have an opportunity to acquire an education, it should not be carried beyond the point where the individual ceases to show promise of benefiting himself and his organization.

In the three categories I have mentioned will be found home-office personnel, as well as special agents, independent agents and brokers, and in increasing numbers, insurance managers and their staffs. I believe that everyone in these groups with any prospect above a mere routine job should have a fundamental insurance education, an understanding of the language and theory of the business. How far and how intensively he should pursue his education and into what specialized paths he should turn would depend on his ability to profit.

One of the major faults of present-day insurance education is its slavish following of the division of the business into lines; it is one aspect of the impractical meeting of the "practical" demand. I would give the same *fundamental* education to every student, regardless of his probable future activity, for I feel that everyone should understand the essential unity of insurance and the relative functions of its parts, no matter what his own field may eventually prove to be. This approach would help to break down the present provincialism of thought which often refuses to apply the lessons learned in one line to the problems of another and retards the development of improved coverage.

I have frequently presented a list of topics which might be used in this functional approach. With no attempt to be exhaustive, they follow:

 I. Perils, hazards, and prevention
 II. The insurance mechanism
 III. Contracts and adjustments
 IV. Insurers (including self-insurance)
 V. Agency and brokerage
 VI. Theory of probability
 VII. Rates
 VIII. Reserves
 IX. Underwriting
 X. Insurance finance
 XI. Investments
 XII. Organization of insurers
    (a) Internal
    (b) Inter-insurer
 XIII. State regulation
 XIV. Risk management
 XV. Social insurance

In the presentation of a course of study following this outline, basic facts and illustrations would necessarily be drawn from varying lines of insurance, but the emphasis should be on the pervasive functions under each topic. Discussion of practices of individual lines should be kept subordinate to treatment of the broad insurance function.

I believe that the university, in its regular undergraduate courses, should confine itself to this type of fundamental education, possibly extending its supervision to more specialized work in cooperation with insurance groups. Organizations such as the Fire Underwriters Association of the Pacific and the agents' associations might well extend the work further along the road of specialization, but I feel that, even there, the emphasis should be on understanding rather than development of skill for immediate application. I would assign to the operating organizations the work of training their own people and of selecting them for their various tasks.

May I suggest further that no educational program can be a great success as a spare-time effort. Splendid as the beginnings of insurance education have been, and much as I respect the insurance men who have given their time to make those beginnings possible, it will be only with the undertaking of these programs by men who are primarily rather than incidentally concerned with them that they will take their proper place in the insurance world.

Let me recapitulate my suggestions. Consider education and training as a long-range practical problem. Aim at distant-future rather than immediate results. Recognize that a worthwhile program requires work, time, and money from executives, students, and educators. Confide the direction of the program to a competent person whose primary interest is in its success. Do not expect miracles. And withhold final judgment for ten years or more.

18. Risk as a Special Subject of Study*

It is unnecessary to demonstrate the pervasiveness of risk (the term is used in the sense of uncertainty) for readers of this paper. And the writer has sought elsewhere to draw a distinction between "risk that is incurred by the individual or the business concern in the hope of reward and risk that is incidental to other activities or relationships." It is this latter category of risk that seems to the writer to be worthy of special study and special courses, particularly in schools of business.

A corporation whose activities are confined to a single location invests funds in buildings, machinery, and distribution facilities. If its judgment is accurate, the operation of its plant will yield a profit; if faulty, a loss. The mere existence and ownership of its plant intact will yield no profit, though it presents the possibility of loss by partial damage or total destruction. Operation of the plant may, in addition to producing goods or services, entail liability to members of the public for damages. And the financial loss due to these incidental occurrences may cut into, or over-balance, profit; it may put the firm out of business.

Is the problem of these incidental risks (with which the remainder of this paper is concerned) sufficiently specialized and sufficiently complicated and difficult to demand specialized, first-rate managerial competence? The writer believes that it is, and business is increasingly confirming this view.

Prior to the 1930's, *risk management* appears to have been an unknown term. The function of the risk manager was only a vague concept; there is still no official of a business who, to the author's knowledge, is so designated. But, with some variations of jurisdiction, the risk manager now exists, though he may be called "insurance manager," "assistant treasurer," or what not. In fact, he has become an important part of management, although not generally one of the group known as "top management."

If the risk manager is given jurisdiction over the entire risk problem, of what will his duties consist? First, he will be concerned with determination

* From *The Journal of Insurance*, XXVI (Spring, 1959), 8–11.

and analysis of the risks to which his organization is subject; second, he will study the impact of the possible losses arising from these risks; third, he will consider and effectuate all practical prevention of loss; fourth, he will recommend or arrange financial measures to meet losses; fifth, he will keep such records, accounting and statistical, as may be serviceable in operating his department.

In fact, the complete job is sometimes split up, though not necessarily for sound organizational reasons, among two or more functionaries. To the extent that this is done it is difficult to achieve proper relationships between policies and activities that should fit closely and work together.

Worse than dividing the risk problem among individuals, each of whom is concerned with a part of it, is leaving it wholly or in large part with each division of the organization; and this for two reasons. Each division is so concerned with, and so steeped in, its primary problems that the risk problem is not sufficiently clear or compelling. One division may be so interested in storage space and efficient handling that it will pay little attention to the hazards of fire in large connected spaces or in tall stacks of material. Another, anxious to provide uninterrupted assembly lines, may disregard fire stops. Still another will avoid the enforcement of rules that might interfere with production but would prevent accidents. Second, any one division is unlikely to understand how its peculiar risk problem fits into the overall problem of the organization.

An unfortunate aspect of the development of interest in risk is that it has to such an extent proceeded from an interest in insurance. It has often not been realized that the overall problem is *risk* and that insurance is only one, though it may be the most important, contributor to solution of the problem. This has been a natural development. The early insurers covered such spectacular causes of loss as those arising from marine disasters and from fire. Later, insurance responded to the special need created by the passage of employers' liability and workmen's compensation laws which introduced a new risk of considerable potential. And so with other individual perils; either some bright insurance man developed a cover, possible insureds awoke to a danger, or selling techniques were brought effectively to bear.

But all this did not represent consideration and attempted solution of the broad problem of risk. It was only with the advent of a few risk managers that risk was attacked as a whole by persons primarily interested in it who could allocate their attention to analysis, prevention, absorption, or indemnification.

Some time ago a letter was addressed to the dean of one of the leading schools of business in the United States to ask what attention his institution gave to "insurance." (It would have been quite out of order to inquire about "risk.") His first reply suggested that such an inquiry warranted no detailed consideration. Upon being pressed he stated that he had consulted several of his faculty who were in charge of individual subjects and that in each case they considered any insurance question when it came up. One wonders whether insurance, and much less the basic problem of risk, was adequately dealt with.

Examples could be multiplied to show the illiteracy of business executives and members of business faculties in the subject of risk and insurance. The subject demands command of a special body of knowledge and of a special approach to its problems.

That inroads have been made on what was pretty general illiteracy in business is evidenced by the assignment of this specialized subject to full-time "managers" by an increasing number of corporations that are recognized for high standards of management. The following quotation, substituting "risk" for insurance and "business" for "physical plant," and inserting "needed" before "indemnification," indicates the typical attitude of present-day thinking management:[1]

> Forward-looking management has long since come to look upon insurance [risk] as a specialized field far beyond the routine purchase of policies of indemnification. The concept of assigning the functions of insurance management to an already over-burdened company official, such as the secretary, treasurer, or controller, is today just as far-fetched as would be the assigning of the legal or operating functions of the company to these same officials. Today, we thus have the full-time insurance executive heading a separate department in the corporate structure—a specialist to whom management can look for the analysis of risks to which its company's physical plant [business] is exposed, the selection of methods through which these risks may be reduced or eliminated, and the procurement of such insurance contracts as will provide [needed] indemnification in the event these risks result in financial loss.

The following three examples[2] of actual risk situations discovered by competent overall risk analysis, and of the corrective actions taken, will serve to illustrate these points:

> It was discovered that the plant of the supplier of one of the vital parts of an electronic device had no automatic-sprinkler system or other effective fire protection. The supplier was induced to equip his plant with proper protection, reducing the manufacturer's risk of business interruption and incidentally

---

[1] Liversidge, H. P., "What Management Expects from an Insurance Department," *Insurance Series* No. 98 (New York: American Management Association, 1953), p. 4.

[2] Courtesy of Henry Anderson, Insurance Manager, American Broadcasting-Paramount Theatres, Inc.

resulting in a good return to the supplier on his investment, in the form of reduced insurance rates.

During the recent newspaper strike in New York a corporation undertook to distribute its own free news sheet to its customers. Only at the last moment was it realized that it might become involved in claims for damages alleging such torts as libel or violation of copyright. Adequate insurance coverage was obtained.

One of the vital parts of an assembly was produced by the use of a complicated die, reproduction of which would require eight weeks, and only one die was in existence. Arrangements were made to build up a reserve supply of the part, and a second die was procured.

The first step in organizing risk managers for discussion of risk problems was the formation, in 1931, of the Insurance Division of the American Management Association. While membership in the Division is open to all persons interested in insurance, its *raison d'être* is the risk manager, and its activities are directed toward the solution of his problems. In 1932 Insurance Buyers of New York was organized, with members drawn entirely from the ranks of risk managers, though its name was a sad commentary on the actual functions of many such "managers." This group was reorganized as Risk Research Institute, Inc. in 1935 and made an abortive attempt to become a national organization.

A now solidly established national organization, the American Society of Insurance Management, Inc., was founded in 1950 as the National Insurance Buyers Association. While its title suggests an insurance group, its activities have been increasingly directed toward risk management. Risk[3] Research Institute was terminated, and the New York group became the New York Chapter of the National Association and later of the American Society, of which there are now eighteen chapters well scattered over the country.[4] In addition there are three unaffiliated groups. Of these twenty-one groups, three were originally formed in the 1930's; two in the 40's; and the remainder, in the 50's.

During the academic year 1956–1957, 493 colleges and universities were offering "insurance" courses in one or more main areas of instruction, of which 398 were "general or survey" courses. The total number of insurance courses of all sorts was 1,686.[5]

In addition to, and in cooperation with, academic institutions, the insurance business is carrying on extensive educational and training

[3] The unique appearance of the word "risk" in the names of any of the organizations.
[4] One of these chapters is in Montreal.
[5] Only summary figures are presented here since details and extended analyses are readily available in Ericson, William A., and Norton, John H., *College and University Courses in Insurance* (Philadelphia: S. S. Huebner Foundation for Insurance Education, 1958).

activities. Among the principal organizations are: The American Institute
for Property and Liability Underwriters, the American College of Life
Underwriters, the Society of Actuaries, the Casualty Actuarial Society,
the Insurance Company Education Directors' Society, the Institute of
Life Insurance, the Insurance Accounting and Statistical Association, the
Insurance Institute of America, and local insurance societies in various
cities. Many groups organized primarily for other purposes conduct
incidental educational activities.

These data, plus the widespread convictions of persons who have given
all or a large part of their time to the study of risk, seem to make a prima-
facie case for its treatment as a specialty. And if one considers the intricate
and independent disciplines that have developed in an effort to understand
risk and to work out means of meeting it, what started as a prima-facie
case becomes a convincing one.

There is good reason for the predominance of the word "insurance" in
the names of organizations and the titles of courses, though it often leads to
too much concern with the technique of insurance, and often those who
should be its analysts and critics become its votaries. It is mostly through
an interest in insurance that the underlying problem of risk has been
approached and that the basic ways of meeting it, with their infinite
variations, have come to be understood.

The wealth of material—language, practices, data, laws, contracts,
rules, doctrines, organizations—has bemused many a person into accumulating information and justifications into texts or lectures with little thought
of what it is all about, of taking the mass apart and putting it together again
to induce the application of reason.

One of the outstanding difficulties in the way of the educator is the
unfamiliar language and the highly abstract basis of much of the treatment
of risk and insurance. Where one would prefer to discuss ideas and take
for granted a knowledge of language and practice, it becomes necessary to
impart a factual background that looks suspiciously like training rather
than education. Even so, the importance of risk justifies the time and
effort. One who has passed through a curriculum leading to a degree
presumably indicating that he has acquired an education in business
should have experienced education in terms of risk and insurance. That
subject is a unique discipline. It is one not acquired by incidental consideration in courses in banking, marketing, finance, or industrial relations,
even though such courses may be offered by competent professionals in
those fields. For confirmation, examine the references to risk and insurance
in their text books; discuss with them the risks to which they and their
fields are subject and what principles should be applied in dealing with them.

Risk and insurance are of sufficient present and growing importance to make understanding of them essential as a part of a "business education." Acquisition of that understanding is attainable only through specialized texts and instruction, and the unique and valuable discipline so acquired has ample general educational justification.

This discussion has been an argument only for the inclusion in business curricula of specialized study of risk and insurance. As implied at the beginning, the subject, "risk," is inclusive of insurance; but the wide use of the latter term seems to make it desirable specifically to include it in course titles.

How far should a school go in developing the study of this subject? Any attempted answer to that question is beyond the scope of this paper. All that will be said here is that the same spirit should inform the treatment of an extensive insurance program that should be found throughout the school curriculum—that of education in terms of the specialized subject.

19. The Education of an Adjuster*

It seems to the writer that in a segment of business eager to describe itself as "professional," the adjuster and engineer conform most closely to the usual understanding of that term. Aside from natural endowment, there are three principal sources from which an adjuster may acquire the knowledge and skill necessary to the exercise of his profession. They are education, training, and experience.

Education, whether from books or personal instruction, is particularly adapted to building up a background of insurance theory and a comprehension of the purposes of the process of adjustment and of its interrelations with other phases of the business. It is often a lack of just such a background that makes it impossible for an adjuster to view his work in perspective, and to perform properly his function as a representative of *insurance* rather than as a technical haggler over financial items.

He needs a broad theoretical knowledge of insurance in general, and of the policy contract and its interpretation in particular, at the earliest possible stage in his development, for his work should be solidly based on that knowledge as a guide. A command of these subjects can best be attained through the educational process, since what is required is a distillation and coordinated presentation of the practical results of the labors and experience of a world of insurance men, jurists, and legislators—all those who have contributed to the gradual development of insurance principles and practices, to their present relationships with each other and with surrounding economic life. The adjuster has only one life to live and he can conserve his time and acquire *understanding* by making use of education in those things which have been reduced to principles by others, and in those departments of the business which will necessarily lie outside his personal, specialized experience.

Training, instruction in the detailed skills of his calling, is best accomplished by the apprenticeship route, by instruction on the job. No amount of description of the appearance of a bale of cotton that has lost 25 per cent of its value by fire damage is equal to an examination of the bale in cooperation with a competent superior. Inspection of a loss where arson

* From *Our Business*, June, 1940. Used by permission.

is suspected and participation in the discovery of evidence equip the apprentice with methods and perceptions which would make only a dull and probably inaccurate impression, if presented in book or lecture form.

Of *experience*, little need be said. It is, of course, the necessary basis of high ability in any field. No adjuster ever sprang full-fledged from the class-room, the study, or the training trip, or from all three combined. Its function is evident.

Given the requisite raw material, how is one to proceed to the converting of that material into an adjuster? The answer is to be found in intelligent combination of the three avenues of approach, to the end that each shall contribute that share of the work to which it is best adapted. Unfortunately, most persons seem to enjoy being partisan, and one way of showing partisanship is to argue for the virtues of practical experience and decry education, or to look to education as some sort of magical process for manufacturing mature, specialized human beings out of raw youth. Another error lies in the pressure from student and executive alike for introduction into the educational process of what they *think* is practical— imparting of detailed facts and skills—both of which are best acquired by a combination of training and experience. This latter error proceeds perhaps from a desire for quick success on the part of the student, and some slight laziness on the part of the executive.

It would be well if the three processes could go on concurrently, each performing its function of most efficiently contributing to the adjuster's development, and each coordinated with the others so as to furnish illustrative material and increase understanding. Education would occupy the largest place in the early stages, and could be continued with advantage throughout an adjuster's working life, though with decreasing emphasis. Training would be a transitional stage, with the dual purpose of furnishing a laboratory for the educational work and facts and skills for practical application. Experience would naturally develop to occupy the major place.

Any actual combination would necessarily fall short of the ideal, but an approximation of the ideal would be facilitated by treating the three methods strictly as practical tools for the attainment of a practical end. Each should be used in that spirit, without too much concession to the prejudices and personal tastes of human units. As well argue the relative superiority of saws, hammers, and planes in the work of carpentry as to discuss the equivalent claims of education, training, and practical experience. And just as a nail may be driven with a plane, so an adjuster may learn by experience many things which he could have more economically gathered vicariously.

One of the greatest difficulties in educational work is to make vivid the material presented, often in compressed and abstract form. This difficulty is particularly acute when the student has had no contact with the concrete facts to which it applies—hence the suggestion that education be combined with training and experience, where the chief difficulty is covering enough ground to acquire an accurate generalized impression.

If young men are expected to earn their wages from the very start, in terms of volume of losses adjusted, their three-fold development will be limited. Investment by insurers or adjustment organizations in education and training will be more than returned by superior efficiency in the long run.

20. College and Company Education*

In preparing this talk I have assumed that I should deal with both education and training; education as conveying and stimulating understanding, and training as preparation for specific tasks. Broadly speaking, education is the job of the college or university; training the job of the insurer.

University education is directed to two groups. The first consists of those who expect to enter the insurance business; the second, those who study insurance as part of a general business education and who, it may be supposed, will be primarily concerned with the use of insurance, by themselves or by their employers.

To my mind, much the same fundamental approach is desirable for both groups; discussion of *pure risk* (as distinguished from *speculative risk*) and of ways of meeting it, from which insurance emerges as the principal subject. Presentation of insurance becomes, for the insurance group, largely a more intensive study of the subjects presented to the general group, with some shift of emphasis. In the long run their interests are common, though human nature tends to build up divergence.

I believe that every student who specializes in insurance with a view to entering the business should have a fundamental education in the principles of risk and of all fields of insurance. Everything possible should be done to break down the lack of interest in other fields of insurance on the part of persons specializing in a particular field. This does not mean that one can have a thorough command of all fields, but one should know the language and enough of the other fields to apply their lessons to one's own field.

It is in this fundamental education that the university can best serve. The university teacher is not, or should not be, hampered unduly by the traditional divisions of the business. He can present insurance by functions, rather than by lines, and thus emphasize its basic unity, even though he must point out variations in the carrying out of the functions.

I would carry the functional approach into advanced university work,

* Address before the Annual Meeting of the Insurance Company Education Directors' Society, Skytop, Pennsylvania, May 25, 1956.

119

offering courses in which contracts are studied intensively, from their basic principles to examples from all principal lines. Similarly I would study insurers, rates and rating, reserves, underwriting, financial statements, and other subjects, dealing with functions and emphasizing basic principles as well as variations in principles and application.

The purpose of all this would be to impart and encourage understanding of insurance as such and the relative functions of its parts; so that in his later more highly specialized training and experience the student would have a balanced point of view, would attack a problem in the light of its relation to the business as a whole and not as an isolated question.

At this point, may I quote certain statements made by one of the wisest of Americans, Justice Holmes, in a talk on "The Use of Law Schools." "A law school does not undertake to teach success. . . . Education, other than self-education, lies mainly in the shaping of men's interests and aims." Similarly in the schools of business, it is best that we do not try to teach men success, but give them an understanding on which success in varying degrees may be built. I have said elsewhere that my idea of insurance education is that it should be primarily teaching and directing study of the language and theory of insurance to the end of inducing accurate thinking in terms of insurance.

By language I mean not merely definitions of technical terms, but an understanding of the significance of these terms. By theory, not musings on the future nor what Justice Holmes called "a rag-bag full of general principles," but the reasoning on which insurance practices and plans are based and a critical examination of the relationship between specific practices and sound theory.

And this is what I consider to be practical education, what would in the long run be the most useful program that the university could offer. Pressure comes from the student who wants "practical" courses today to turn into dollars tomorrow, and from the employer who seeks men equipped with skills that he can use and avoid the trouble and expense of training. Offering courses at a university in response to these pressures is a waste of time. The university should do what it is best fitted to do.

What of "company education?" The company educator is faced with the problem of dealing with a wide variety of students or trainees. Some may have had the university education in insurance that I have suggested (or a reasonable facsimile). Some will have had a university education but not in insurance. Others will have various other degrees of education. To further complicate the situation, there are those who are destined to become policy-making top executives, others who will be operating men using a high grade of knowledge and judgment but along lines laid down from above, and still others who will have routine duties and whose qualities should be those of skill, accuracy, and faithfulness.

And there is the further problem of dealing with agents and brokers who cannot be so easily classified and whose needs are vital but different.

It seems to me that the company program, to be complete, must have elements of education, training, and apprenticeship. Men and women who come to the companies are destined to occupy all three grades of eventual employment, but probably the educational department should devote its prime attention to potential policy-making and operating executives. Training and apprenticeship for routine tasks are important, but less significant.

If universities were furnishing a sufficient number of applicants for enrollment in the group of employees with prospects of success, and if universities were doing a satisfactory job of *fundamental education* in insurance, the company educator could build on the new employees' foundation. But many, and often superior, candidates will appear without earlier education in insurance, or with a less than satisfactory education. So, if the fundamental education that I have outlined as the province of the university is desirable, the company should be prepared to offer it or to stimulate their young men to get it for themselves. However, this is not the field in which the company educator can be most effective.

In the university course, it is necessary to present information as a basis for the inculcation of principles, but the informational process should convey a picture of the insurance mechanism and of its parts only to the extent essential to understanding principles and relationships.

The company educator should be primarily concerned with application, with practice, but not with a mere recital of facts and procedures. He should make clear not only what is done but why, and should prepare his students for *intelligent* activity. He has access to forms, manuals, personnel, and methods, the whole congeries of facts and procedures that are parts of the modern insurer. He is in a position to present the insurance business as an organic whole and to forward his students or trainees to their tasks as active employees with a comprehension of their work in itself and in relation to other facets that could not otherwise be gained.

This process should help to accomplish several ends: better-functioning employees, saving of time that would be spent learning by trial and error, more accurate and timely selection and grading of employees, and perhaps most important, operation of the insurance business on the basis of sound principles and with a clear understanding of its place in the economic scheme.

The assignments that I have suggested rest on my notions of an effective division of labor between the university educator and the company educator. They represent what I should consider an ideal arrangement but are subject, of course, to all the qualifications that reflect individual situations, personalities, interests, competence, and funds. I cannot hope, in a general paper, and with limited time, to do more than suggest lines of thought, but I believe that time spent in reflecting, not only on the division of labor between universities and companies, but between all segments of the educational and training process, will be well spent.

21. Reserves*

In most lines of business, including insurance, the synchronization of income and disbursements is imperfect.

Manufacturers must purchase materials and pay wages in advance of the sale of their product and must usually extend credit to purchasers. Merchants are in somewhat the same position, particularly if they take advantage of opportunities for favorable cash purchases and pay their bills promptly. To the extent that this results in a lag between outgo and income, working capital must be provided, either by accumulation of funds or by borrowing.

Insurers find themselves in a very different position. Income, in large measure, precedes the outgo which is directly related to it. In a going insurance concern there is, normally, a healthy excess of income over disbursements on account of losses and expenses during any fiscal period. But, since premiums are generally paid in advance, the insurer must always be prepared to meet the obligations in respect of which premiums have been received without depending on this normal receipt of current premiums to cover current disbursements. A company should keep itself in such a position as will enable it to meet all its obligations to the end of the term of all contracts on its books even though it should entirely cease writing new business and should thus shut off a large share of its income.

In the insurance business this end is accomplished by the setting up of *reserves* of which the two most important are the *unearned-premium reserve* and the *loss reserve*.

The unearned-premium reserve is designed specifically to adjust the finances of insurance companies to the situation created by advance payment for their services. It is built on the theory that an insurer *earns* a premium received by it in the same proportion that the period for which it has given protection under the contract bears to the total period for which the contract is to run and for which the premium was paid. For example, if a premium of $100 is paid for a contract to run two years, $25 would be earned at the end of six months, $75 remaining unearned. In practically all, if not all lines except life insurance, insurers are required by law to

* From *Journal of American Insurance*, January, 1928. Used by permission.

set up as a liability reserves based on this theory. The calculation of such reserves for the annual statement is approximate, it being assumed, in most cases, that all policies written during the preceding year have, on December 31, been on the books for six months. This assumption produces reserves sufficiently accurate for practical purposes and obviates the labor of calculating an exact reserve on each policy, resulting in a considerable expense saving.

If the payment of losses and expenses on account of contracts covering a given period proceeded *pari passu* with the release of funds from the unearned-premium reserve, the requirement of such a reserve might be sufficient to preserve a proper balance between income and outgo. But the losses and, in less measure, the expenses of insurers tend to lag behind the period covered by the contract; to such an extent, in some lines, that many years may elapse after the expiration of a contract before the losses and expenses incurred under that contract have finally been paid in full.

Examples of extreme cases of this sort are found in workmen's compensation insurance where the insurer may be liable for the payment of a life annuity to an injured workman, in certain government bonds under which losses are covered without limit on the time within which they must be discovered, in liability insurance where suits for damages may be fought for years in the courts only to end in a large verdict payable by the insurer. In fire insurance, and other lines covering loss due to the destruction of, or damage to the insured's property, there may be delay in settlement, although it is normally of short duration if a claim is not contested. Marine-insurance claims are ordinarily settled within two years of the expiration of the contract.

Examples might be multiplied and contrasts drawn between lines of insurance but in all there is the necessity of setting aside reserves for future payment of losses and loss expenses. The calculation of these reserves is one of the chief problems of the casualty and life-insurance business. There has consequently been much discussion and experimentation in this field, and much remains to be accomplished.

Basically, all reserves must find their justification in experience. To prophesy with any degree of accuracy that it will require a given amount of money to meet the future obligations of an insurer it is necessary to know, either statistically or through personal contact, what has happened in similar situations in the past; it is necessary likewise to know what will be the probable variation of conditions between the past and the future. Further, reserves must be sufficiently large to make the security of the insurer and of its insureds undoubted; but not so large as to divert funds needlessly from other purposes and create a false picture of costs.

Presented with this problem of calculating reserves, what methods may be employed for its solution? If the amount which must be paid has been determined, it will be set aside pending payment. If a claim is in controversy, it is reasonable in many lines of insurance to set aside, pending settlement, the entire amount which may become payable. In other lines, where controversy and litigation are common, there may properly be set aside an amount equal to the average payable on account of the class of claims in question. This amount will depend in some degree on the stage at which the reserve is set up. In liability insurance, for example, the longer a claim has been in litigation, the larger the probable amount that will be required finally to reach a settlement and make such payment as may be necessary. These *average values* are based on experience with similar claims in the past, due allowance being made for changes in circumstances. For example, if, on the average, it has cost in the past $1500 to bring to final settlement suits begun more than ten years prior to the date of setting up the reserve, and if the cost of conducting suits and the amount of verdicts is tending to increase, it will be necessary to set aside something more than $1500 for each suit in this stage. What this extra amount shall be is a matter of judgment guided by such data as are available.

In many cases data on past losses are so fragmentary, conditions have changed so radically, or each case is so peculiar to itself that recorded experience is unavailable even as an approximate guide for the calculation of reserves. In such cases they must be set up by *individual estimate*. This means, ordinarily, that experienced claim men will, on the basis of their personal judgment, which reflects experience in that field, estimate the probable cost of final settlement of claims. Such a method is open to wide margins of error but, in the absence of figures, it is the only one available. Experience with such estimates will, however, indicate the tendencies of individuals and of groups to over- or underestimate, tendencies which may be corrected in the final figures appearing in the statement. Individual estimates are largely relied upon in the bonding business and in the less highly developed forms of casualty insurance.

Insurance experience may be indirectly the basis of reserves via the premium rate. Suppose that premium rates have been carefully calculated and that in a given type of insurance 60 per cent of the rate has been allotted to the payment of losses and loss expenses. Suppose further that a given insurer has earned $1,000,000 in premiums for this line of insurance. If the rate is correct, $600,000 is required to pay losses and loss expenses. At any given time there will be required in the future, on account of this business, whatever amount has not already been paid out. Hence the reserve will be $600,000 minus the amount already paid. This *loss-ratio* method is applicable only where rates are held to rigid requirements and must be subject to correction for changes in conditions not foreseen when the rates were made.

There remains one method based directly on experience, and independent of personal judgment and variations in rates, the *tabular method*. On the basis of tables showing the probable happenings of the future, and derived from experience, amounts may be set aside to meet financial obligations dependent on those happenings. This method finds its best illustration in life insurance where mortality tables indicate probable future experience. On the basis of such tables the actuary calculates what amounts will probably be payable at various times, and sufficient funds, after allowance for interest and further premium payments by insured, are segregated.

Where the methods of calculation are rough or where the time element is small the interest element may be disregarded, but in calculations of reasonable accuracy or where the period for which reserves are set up make interest return an important financial factor, the reserve will, at the time of valuation, be equal to the *present value* of expected future payments, the sum which, with interest, will produce the amounts necessary to make payments when they are required. In long-term obligations, such as life-insurance contracts, not only is the interest element of importance but a variation in the assumed rate of interest may make a considerable difference in the reserve. Here, as elsewhere, a conservative rate should be chosen but not one which recognizes conservatism as an end in itself.

Reserves other than those for unearned premiums and losses are also maintained by insurers but they are of considerably less significance. Certain of these warrant mention. Reserves for *depreciation* of real estate or securities are carried to guard against overestimation of the value of such assets. *Dividend equalization* reserves provide for the maintenance of a scale of dividends, fluctuation of which might adversely affect the insurer's standing with its insureds. *Contingency* reserves are by way of preparation for unforeseen happenings; they are actually a specially labeled portion of surplus. In life insurance, the entire surplus is often so designated. Certain fire-insurance companies have, under the New York law, set up special funds (*special reserve* and *guaranty surplus*) the purpose of which is to enable them to meet otherwise fatal conflagration losses and still continue in business.[1]

Unearned-premium reserves and, in general, loss reserves are required by state laws which establish certain minima or vest the commissioner of insurance with power to prescribe. Additional reserves are voluntary. All

[1] The law was repealed, effective January 1, 1940. (1964)

reserves appear on the liability side of the annual statement and are usually the principal items to be found there. Since they are mostly required by the state, they are the principal test of an insurer's solvency. To avoid liquidation they must be offset by assets approved by the state.

If "solvency" be interpreted to mean reasonable assurance that an insurer will be able to meet its obligations, the reserves required for unearned premiums and for life insurance are, in general, extremely conservative. In the normal "running off" of the business which these reserves represent there will usually be a release of funds to surplus, since something less than the amount of total reserve will be required to meet the obligations for which it is earmarked. To a certain extent, therefore, the uninterpreted annual statement presents an untrue picture of an insurer's financial position. But fortunately the error is on the side of soundness.

In the more experimental types of insurance, and in lines subject to considerable variations, loss reserves and rates are sometimes found to be inadequate. To the extent that this is the case any technical excess in the unearned-premium reserve represents a factor of safety, and continual testing of methods and results is necessary to hold loss reserves to the accomplishment of their purpose. That insurers have such a splendid record of financial success is evidence of the ability with which this work has been done by executives and supervising officials.

A study of the development of methods for calculating reserves, and of business and governmental policy toward such liabilities makes clear the supreme necessity of continued vigilance to the end that accuracy and soundness may be accomplished. This requires constant critical analysis of reserve methods which have not proved their reliability as a basis for conservative estimates of future obligations, as well as of methods which may have overrun the requirements of safety and become unduly onerous.

22. Unearned-Premium Reserves*

Insurers generally charge for their services in advance, receiving premiums on contracts covering from one to five years' time on the inception of the contract or shortly after. As a consequence of this method of paying for insurance the insurer is in the position of owing protection and/or service to the insured in direct ratio to the unexpired term of the contract. In addition it is usual to provide in insurance contracts that they may be cancelled on the request either of the insurer or of the insured. In the event of cancellation by the insurer the same proportion of the premium must be returned to the insured as the unexpired portion of the term of the contract bears to the original term. In case of cancellation by the insured a smaller amount is due him. In order that the insurer may be able to meet its obligations to the insured in either respect, premiums become earned only to the extent that the protection or service promised has been furnished.

The pro rata portion of the premium covering the expired period of the contract is accordingly called the *earned* premium, that covering the unexpired period the *unearned* premium. In many kinds of insurance the premium becomes wholly earned in the event of a total loss and, in the event of a partial loss, earned in the proportion which the loss bears to the total amount of the contract.

It is this situation in insurance which makes a comparison of income and disbursements for a calendar year misleading as a guide to the financial results of the operations of an insurer. Much of the outgo is on account of contracts for which premiums were received during preceding years. Much of the income is made up of premiums for the contracts that will continue in force and under which losses and expenses will be paid during succeeding years.

It is the part of good management, therefore, to consider the potential obligations for the satisfaction of which premiums have been collected, and to set up a reserve on the liability side of the accounts to care for these obligations. Not only is it the part of good management, but the state

* From *Journal of American Insurance*, July, 1928. Used by permission.

insurance laws require such action. The amount so set up is the *unearned-premium reserve.*

The principal purpose of this reserve is to keep the insurer in a position of being able to meet losses and expenses on account of which premiums have been collected. Normally, in a going concern, this will be its principal function. As contracts approach and attain their dates of expiration the reserve is gradually released for this purpose. Expenses will generally be paid immediately; losses will, to some extent, depending on the type of insurance, be paid immediately. For certain types, notably liability and compensation insurance, unearned-premium reserves will be converted into loss reserves. Back of all these processes is the fundamental purpose of the financial structure of an insurer, that of enabling the meeting of obligations when due, however distant in the future the time may be.

The unearned-premium reserve may be looked upon as providing for a fund held to protect the insured, subject to call by him in case of cancellation but, in practical operation, the payment of return premiums through cancellation is less important than the meeting of losses and expenses. This reserve likewise provides for funds that can be used to reinsure in another insurer if the original insurer discontinues its business in whole or in part.

State requirements are made on the assumption that, at the time of making up the annual statement (December 31), an insurer should, in respect of each contract outstanding, have on hand the same proportion of the total premium for the contract as the unexpired term bears to the total term for which it was written. But, for convenience, unearned premiums are calculated on an approximate basis. It is assumed that policies which are written during a given year take effect, on the average, six months previous to the end of the year. In other words it is assumed that each policy is on the books six months during the year in which it is written. Consequently, on a policy written for a one-year term, one-half the premium is earned during that year, on a policy written for a two-year term, one-quarter, and so on. Following this reasoning through, it is evident that, on December 31 of the year preceding that in which the contract is to expire, it will have six months to run.

As a basis for an illustration of the application of these assumptions, suppose that a hypothetical company writes the following premiums during 1928: on one-year policies, $50,000, on two-year policies $60,000, and on three-year policies, $75,000; during 1929, on one-year policies, $60,000, on two-year policies, $80,000, and on three-year policies, $90,000. Suppose further that there are no cancellations and no losses. The unearned-premium reserve in respect of each of these items would be as follows on the dates indicated:

Year Written	Term	Premiums Written	Unearned-Premium Reserve December 31,			
			1928	1929	1930	1931
1928	1 year	$50,000	(1/2) $25,000	....	....	....
	2 years	60,000	(3/4) 45,000	(1/4) $15,000	....	....
	3 years	75,000	(5/6) 62,500	(1/2) 37,500	(1/6) $12,500	....
1929	1 year	60,000	....	(1/2) 30,000	....	....
	2 years	80,000	....	(3/4) 60,000	(1/4) 20,000	....
	3 years	90,000	....	(5/6) 75,000	(1/2) 45,000	(1/6) 15,000

While this method is sufficiently accurate for practical purposes in most cases, it does not provide an adequate measure of unearned premiums in some cases where there is a marked variation in the premium written during different parts of the year. In the year in which an insurer is formed it is usual for premiums written to increase rapidly from month to month, a much larger volume being written during the last six months of the year than during the first. Consequently contracts will not, on the average, have been in force six months on December 31, and a reserve calculated on the six months basis would be inadequate. Conversely, if a company should write less business during the last six months, the reserve set up under this method would be excessive.

Valuation of the reserve for policies written on each day of the year, while necessary for perfect accuracy, is not often required. Usually any important inaccuracy in the six-months method may be sufficiently corrected by substituting a half-month method. The assumption is made that policies written during a given month had, at the end of the month, been in force a half month. Consequently, on one-year policies, one twenty-fourth of the premium would be earned at the end of the first month, three twenty-fourths at the end of the second, and so on. In setting up a reserve on December 31, one-year policies written during December would require an unearned-premium reserve of twenty-three twenty-fourths of the premium; during November, twenty-one twenty-fourths. A period of a week may be taken instead of a month and, is, in certain extreme cases, required.

So much for the theory of the unearned-premium reserve. In practice the requirement of a full unearned-premium reserve results in the insurer setting up, as a liability, a considerably larger amount than is normally needed to meet the obligations for which it makes provision. This is due to the fact that a considerable part of the expenses are paid in advance while the reserve requirement is based on the assumption that they will be evenly distributed throughout the year. In agency companies, for example, the commission is paid by deduction and only the balance of the premium reaches the insurer. If, on a given type of insurance, the commission is 25 per cent of the premium on one-year business, a full reserve will contain an element of 25 per cent which the company has already paid out and which, presumably, will revert to surplus when the policies expire. Because of this and other prepaid items it is usually assumed, in determining the financial worth of a stock company, that there is an equity of from 30 per cent to 50 per cent in the unearned-premium reserve which would remain in the hands of the owners of the insurer on liquidation.

An insurer may find itself in the anomalous position of having written so much perfectly good business that its assets are insufficient to balance its liabilities. That portion of the unearned-premium reserve representing commissions paid in advance must be provided from surplus. If so much insurance is written that the surplus approaches exhaustion by this process, steps must be taken to curtail volume or to reinsure to the extent necessary to relieve the pressure.

Mutual insurers dealing directly with insureds present a different situation. They have certain prepaid items but a considerable part of the acquisition cost represented by commissions in other insurers is usually available for refunds to insureds, which are paid at the close of the policy year instead of at the beginning. Hence these insurers do not find it necessary to set up, out of surplus funds, a liability covering payments already made except as to the smaller prepaid items representing their acquisition cost and the other expenses incidental to putting a policy on the books.

In either case, however, the requirement of an unearned-premium reserve, calculated by the methods outlined above, is a major factor in determining the technical solvency of an insurer. If funds are insufficient to cover the reserve required and assessments fail to supply the deficiency the carrier is subject to liquidation. But since in the one case there is a large percentage of prepaid items, and in the other a similar percentage representing both prepaid items and a margin for dividends to insureds, the insurer may be perfectly well able to meet its obligations in full.

This condition leads to the query whether the standard of solvency imposed by the present reserve requirements is a proper one. If it is assumed that such a standard must be based on as exact as possible a measurement of probable disbursements the answer must be no. In other countries a precedent is found for smaller unearned-premium reserves which more closely measure the extent of the obligations for which funds will eventually be disbursed.

But it has long been an accepted theory that regulation of insurers should provide for super-safety. This reserve provides for a considerable margin for the unusual and, to that extent, serves as a surplus for contingencies.

The principal disservice of the reserve is found in its contribution to inaccurate data on the financial results of the underwriting operations of insurers. In calculating profits and in estimating the financial condition of an insurer from its annual statement, the acceptance of the full unearned-premium reserve as a liability leads to results which, in the usual case, are less favorable than the actual results. These facts are known to insurance men and to many analysts of the financial statements of insurance companies. But they are not generally known and lead at times to unfortunate conclusions.

For the purpose of determining the liquidating value of an insurer 30 per cent to 50 per cent (depending on the situation and the type of insurance) of the amount of the unearned-premium reserve should be treated as surplus. Peculiar conditions must, of course, be allowed for, but the principle is valid. In determining profits it is usual to deduct from premium income the increase in the unearned-premium reserve during the period under review. Here again a true result would be secured by deducting only that part of the reserve (50 per cent to 70 per cent) which will probably be required to meet increased obligations.

The situation may be summarized as follows: the present method of calculating the unearned-premium reserve leads to setting up as a liability a sum which is considerably larger than necessary to meet the obligations which it represents; while the liability thus set up is inaccurate, it errs on the side of safety; the acceptance of this liability as an element in the determination of the solvency or liquidating value of a carrier leads to an inaccurate picture of the financial situation of the carrier; decreases or increases in the reserve distort profits statements, increases tending to the underrating of profits and decreases to their exaggeration.

In the space here available it is impossible fully to treat the various qualifications which should be made in discussing the unearned-premium reserve as applied to particular lines of insurance. Adjustments must be made to suit the general principle, for instance, to workmen's compensation insurance, where the basis of premiums, the payroll, is estimated at the inception of the contract and is subject to adjustment by audit. Also, a reserve which is excessive if premium rates are adequate may be insufficient if rates are less than adequate. But it is believed that the statement presented covers the basic facts and principles.

23. Investments of Insurers*

Insurance contracts are written for periods varying from the twenty-four hours of the travel accident-insurance "ticket" to the life-time contracts of life insurance. In some cases, such as bonds running to the government or title insurance, the term of the contract extends indefinitely into the future. Premiums are usually due either at the inception of the contract or periodically during its life. It is the general rule that the price of insurance is payable in advance of the rendering of the service of protection, though a fixed or flexible period of credit is usual.

Losses and expenses are, in large part, distributed over the life of the contract, though in many cases, losses (and, to a less extent, expenses) are payable over a considerable period extending beyond the time of ocurrence of the event causing loss. Fire losses are usually adjusted and paid promptly; liability losses may be in the courts for years; disability pensions are often payable until the death of the payee.

Insurance, therefore, necessarily involves the accumulation of funds to meet losses. Practical experience shows that such funds must be accumulated in advance of the occurrence of losses and of incurring expenses of operation, and that additional funds must be available as security against the insufficiency of the amounts which it has been calculated will be needed for meeting losses and expenses.

In the normal course of business, it is expected that yearly cash incomes will exceed cash disbursements, in other words, that an insurer will not be obliged to dip into accumulated assets in order to meet its current obligations. Many qualifications and exceptions might be made to this statement but it indicates reasonably accurately a general characteristic of the insurance business. As a consequence of this characteristic, a large proportion of the assets, varying from about 82 per cent in the case of casualty insurers to about 95 per cent in the case of life insurers, will be invested in real estate, mortgages, stocks, bonds, and collateral loans.

Normally, such investments will be sold only when an advantageous switch from one investment to another is possible. While this statement is

* From *Journal of American Insurance*, November, 1932. Used by permission.

generally true, the probable exceptions vary considerably from one line of insurance to another. Life insurers, even in times of stress, do not expect to be obliged to sacrifice investments in order to obtain needed cash. Income from premiums, interest, dividends, and rent, as well as cash available through the maturity of bonds and other securities, should enable them to meet not only current claims but also any increased demand for policy loans. Mutual companies have a further resource in the possibility of cutting dividends to policyholders. Demands for cash due to depression or epidemic come after reasonable warning, and while they may necessitate careful planning and changes in investment policy, they would become seriously embarrassing only under the most adverse general conditions.

At the other extreme stand the bonding companies. Bad economic conditions bring dishonesty to light and result in failure to meet obligations guaranteed under surety bonds. Losses must be paid with reasonable speed, while any offsetting salvage available to the companies is indeterminate and can be realized only after a considerable lapse of time.

In general, other lines are less subject to sudden demands for large amounts of cash, but fire insurance has its conflagrations and workmen's compensation insurance its mining catastrophes.

Life insurers are sharply to be differentiated from other types in their requirement of long-term solvency. Contracts are written for life-time terms, and obligations to beneficiaries may extend over their lives. Great conservatism is necessary to assure long-continued ability to meet all obligations. Further, if a life insurer should get into financial difficulties, its policyholders could not change their insurance to other companies without considerable loss. Many would even be unable to secure insurance in other carriers because of lack of insurability. Beneficiaries would have no means of making good the loss occasioned by inability of the insurer to meet its obligations.

In other lines, contracts are written for short terms. The alert insured may be able to foresee difficulties and obtain insurance from another insurer without serious loss or inconvenience. Further, he is more likely to be carrying his insurance as a business matter and to have reasonably competent advice on the condition of his insurer. But even here, with the development of the liability and compensation lines, there is the prospect of long-continued obligations which make safety of an insurer necessary in the future as well as the present.

These differences have been urged to justify a variation in the types of investments permitted to insurers. Life insurers have for long been denied the right to invest in common stocks; only recently have they been given the restricted permission to buy conservative preferred and guaranteed stocks. Other insurers, stock and mutual, have been held to bonds issued by governmental units for the investment of an amount equal to the minimum capital required of a stock company. Beyond this amount they have been relatively free to invest as they chose.

As a consequence, insurers other than life have come in too many cases to regard themselves as conducting a combination of an insurance business and an investment-trust business. Low profits on underwriting were to be supplemented by stock-market profits. But the opinion is now pretty generally held that an insurer should stick to its last, and should write insurance on the basis of collecting premiums to cover losses and expenses, rather than for the purpose of making profitable investments. Stock companies should aim to make a margin of underwriting profits for their stockholders; mutuals should collect premiums sufficiently high to make assessments only a remote possibility. Investment of funds should be incidental to the insurance business, and not its prime function.

In accumulating funds to meet losses and expenses and to serve as a "back-log," it is not assumed that such funds will be inactive. On the contrary, they will be expected to earn their share of annual income. But the maximum of income from this source on which the management of an insurer should rely is a conservative percentage return in the form of dividends and interest. Profits from the increase in value of investments, while not to be refused when they may be realized, should not be relied upon, nor should mere paper profits blind the management to the possibility of paper losses.

In most forms of insurance, premium rates are expected to yield sufficient revenue to meet losses and expenses. But in certain cases investment income in the shape principally of interest and dividends, is counted upon to contribute to the payment of losses. In life insurance, the income from investment supplements the premiums in a marked degree, in fact, it is calculated that a certain minimum interest rate (usually 3 per cent or $3\frac{1}{2}$ per cent)[1] will be earned on the amount of the reserves, and devoted eventually to meeting claims. During the year 1931, income from interest and rent, for life insurance companies doing business in New York State, amounted to over 25 per cent of the total premium income. In certain other lines, notably disability and workmen's compensation, obligations to make payments over a considerable period involve the necessity of setting up reserves calculated on the assumption that investments will earn

[1] Now usually less than 3 per cent. (1964)

$3\frac{1}{2}$ or 4 per cent.[2] Any return from investments in excess of the assured percentages represents a gain to the insurer.

Even where no definite reliance is placed on investment earnings to meet losses and expenses, such earnings are important. During 1930 mutual fire and marine insurers doing business in New York State received investment earnings of $9,273,385, or approximately 20 per cent of the total dividends paid to policyholders. Well-managed stock fire and marine insurance companies usually keep dividends paid to stockholders well within invest- ment earnings; during 1930, United States stock insurers doing business in New York State paid out $77,137,186 in dividends or approximately 77 per cent of their total investment earnings.[3]

Insurers are, in view of what has been said, concerned with the safety, convertibility, and yield of securities. But different types of insurer, relying on investments for different purposes, properly set up different require- ments. In life insurance safety over a long period of time is of paramount importance, a high yield is desirable but never at the expense of safety, while convertibility is of least importance. The ability of the insurers to meet their obligations rests in large measure on the safety and yield of their investments. It is conceivable that it might be necessary to convert them, but highly improbable.

In fire and marine insurance safety is, of course, of great importance, but the nature of the business is such that reliance is not placed on investments to meet obligations to insureds to the same extent as in life insurance. Safety may properly be left more fully to the judgment of managements, but perhaps present restrictions could be advantageously extended, at least to cover assets equal in amount to the unearned-premium reserve. Con- vertibility is of great importance in order that such insurers may be able to meet sudden emergencies, without too great a sacrifice in disposing of assets. In other words a large share of their assets should be invested in securities for which there is a continuous demand in the market. Yield is important, but should be subordinated to other considerations.

In casualty insurance, the diversity of the business calls for a careful study of investment policy to fit the needs of each particular insurer. Lines such as bonding and credit insurance call for ready convertibility; work- men's compensation for stability of value and of earnings.

Again let it be strongly emphasized that insurer managements should keep in mind that they are primarily in the insurance business, that

---

[2] Now 2 per cent in calculating losses for rate making. (1964)

[3] From 1952 to 1958, inclusive, an average of forty-four leading stock fire and casualty insurers showed dividends to be 50 per cent of net investment income. (1964)

the purpose of insurance is to insure, and that the choice of investments should always follow the guiding principle of first making insurance more *sure*. If incidental profits accrue from investment accounts, well and good. That an investment shows possibilities of large earnings or of appreciation is not to be construed as objectionable. But it should first meet the criterion of safety, and, where necessary, convertibility, in order that investment activities may always be recognized as the tool of insurance and not an end in themselves.

24. Coinsurance*

The term coinsurance is used to designate various arrangements under which losses are shared by insurers, and also the practice of requiring an insured to bear a part of his own loss under certain conditions. It is with coinsurance in the latter sense that this article is concerned.

In marine insurance it is settled law that an insured may claim payment of loss from his insurer only in the proportion which the amount of insurance carried bears to the value of the property insured. This principle is embodied in § 81 of the Marine Insurance Act of Great Britain in the following language:

> Where the assured is insured for an amount less than the insurable value or, in the case of a valued policy, for an amount less than the policy valuation, he is deemed to be his own insurer in respect of the uninsured balance.

The rule is also followed by courts in the United States.[1] But in most, if not all, other types of insurance this principle of coinsurance is applied only when definitely required by a provision in the policy contract. The quoted rule represents 100–per cent coinsurance. If an insured has a contract covering property valued at $150,000, and insurance in the amount of $75,000, he will be paid only 50 per cent of any loss. Under a nonmarine-insurance contract the insured would receive payment of all losses in full, up to a maximum of $75,000, unless his contract contained an express provision for coinsurance.

In many branches of insurance, notably fire, it is customary to apply the coinsurance principle, although varying percentages of value are stipulated as a basis for the settlement of loss. Perhaps the best-known provision is the "80–per cent coinsurance clause"[2] under which recovery by the insured is limited to that proportion of any loss or damage that the amount of insurance bears to 80 per cent of the value of the property at the time of loss. If 80–per cent coinsurance were applied to the above example, recovery by the insured would be limited to the proportion which $75,000

* From *Journal of American Insurance*, April, 1938. Used by permission.
[1] *Vance on Insurance* (2d ed.; St. Paul: West Publishing Co., 1930), p. 79.
[2] Other clauses having the same general purpose are the "average clause," "contribution clause," "percentage coinsurance clause," "reduced rate average clause," etc.

(the amount of insurance) bears to $120,000 (80 per cent of $150,000) or 5/8 (75/120). The insurer would be liable for only $10,000 on a $16,000 loss.

Coinsurance is not applied in fire insurance to unprotected property. In some cases policies will be written with or without coinsurance, but at a lower rate with than without. Insurance on protected property is generally subject to coinsurance, with credit in the rate for percentages in excess of 80.

Certain forms of inland-marine policies carry coinsurance clauses, in some cases on a 100–per cent basis, in others on an 80–per cent basis. Coinsurance has long been applied in sprinkler leakage insurance, and discounts are allowed from the premium rate for a policy without co-insurance, varying from five per cent for one–per cent coinsurance to 89 per cent for 90–per cent coinsurance. The principle is also applied in burglary insurance and elsewhere in various degrees.

In many foreign countries the coinsurance principle is made a part of the fundamental insurance law. For example, in France, "if appraisal shows that the value of the thing insured exceeds, at the time of the casualty, the amount of insurance, the insured is considered to be his own insurer for the excess, and consequently bears a proportional part of the loss, in the absence of any agreement to the contrary."[3] In certain states of the United States, the application of coinsurance is restricted by law.[4] In most states the application of coinsurance is optional with insurers, and in some it is specifically authorized.

Coinsurance might appear to be a scheme to force insured to carry insurance beyond their desires merely for the enhancement of the income of insurers. Why should one who has insurance in the amount of $5,000 on property worth $10,000 not be indemnified for any loss to a maximum of $5,000? A popular answer to this question, which is not without validity, is provided by a second question, which might be asked by the insurer: Suppose that a loss of $5,000 or less occurs, to which half of the value does it apply, the insured's or the insurer's? The basic reason for the application of coinsurance is found in the fact that the probability of loss is greater, in many forms of insurance, in the lower than in the upper brackets of value. Losses within the first $5,000 of value of properties worth $10,000 each will in the aggregate amount to more, often much more, than those parts of losses which exceed $5,000.

Insurers regularly write contracts providing for payment of the excess

---

[3] Art. 31, Law of July 13, 1930.
[4] Florida, Iowa, Indiana, Louisiana (fire), Maine (fire), Mississippi, Tennessee, Texas. The *Insurance Almanac*, 1937.

over a given sum at a lower premium rate than is charged for those covering the initial amounts of loss. An extreme illustration of this principle is found in collision insurance on automobiles. For cars valued between $2,251 and $2,500 in New York City the premium for full-coverage collision insurance is $232; but if the insured will agree to bear himself the first $25, $50, or $100 of each loss, the premium becomes $120, $101, and $65 respectively.

Figures on the distribution of fire loss which were given in the Report of the Merritt Committee[5] are quite as cogent for purposes of illustration as when they first appeared. On a certain class of buildings the average experience per 100 fires and per $100 of value was approximately as follows:

Loss	No. of Fires	Average Loss	Total
$10 or less	82	$ 2	$164
10.01 to 20	6	14	84
20.01 to 30	3	25	75
30.01 to 40	2	35	70
40.01 to 50	1	45	45
50.01 to 60	1	55	55
60.01 to 70	1	65	65
70.01 to 80	1	75	75
80.01 to 90	1	85	85
90.01 to 100	2	99	198
		Total	$916

Assuming one fire for each 100 buildings insured, 10,000 buildings would have produced 100 fires. If each building were valued at $1,000, the total value of the property would be $10,000,000 and the loss $9,160, or $0.0916 per $100 of value. If the full value were insured the rate would be .0916.[6] But suppose that only 10 per cent of the value were insured. The insurer would then pay, per $100 of value, losses of $10 or less in full and $10 on each of the remaining losses as follows:

82 losses of $10 or less	$164
18 exceeding $10	180
Total	$344

[5] Report of the Joint Committee of the Senate and Assembly of the State of New York appointed to Investigate Corrupt Practices in connection with Legislation, and the Affairs of Insurance Companies, other than those Doing a Life Insurance Business, Albany, 1911, pp. 82 ff.

[6] This rate would provide for losses. If rates were figured on the basis of a 50–per cent loss ratio, the rate charged would be $0.18 (dropping fractions).

The losses paid on $10,000,000 of value would be $3,440; the insurance carried $1,000,000, and the rate, $0.344.

Similarly it could be shown that the rate for 80–per cent insurance would be $0.1091; the insurer would collect $8,730, and the losses payable would be $8,730. But suppose that, although the insurer assumed that insureds would take insurance to the extent of 80 per cent of value, and quoted a rate accordingly, insurance were actually taken out on each building to only 40 per cent of value. In that case the amount collected at $0.1091 per $100 of insurance would be $4,364, and the losses payable $6,730. However, if in this latter case an 80–per cent coinsurance clause were endorsed on the policy, the losses would be paid only in the proportion which the insurance carried bore to 80 per cent of the value of the property, $400/800 or 50 per cent. Settlements per $100 of value per 100 fires would be made as follows:

No.	Amount	Payments
82	$164	$82
6	84	42
3	75	37.50
2	70	35
1	45	22.50
1	55	27.50
1	65	32.50
1	75	37.50
1	85	40
2	198	80
	Total	$436.50

The application of the coinsurance clause would reduce the amount payable to $4,365, the amount paid by the insureds.[7] Had the insurer charged a rate adequate to pay $6,730, it would have collected approximately $0.17 per $100 of insurance. This example indicates the manner in which the coinsurance clause justifiably protects the insurer.

It is possible, of course, to charge a rate for insurance without the coinsurance clause which will produce premiums adequate to cover all losses, but if that is done, it means that those who carry full insurance are paying an excessive rate, and those who carry less than full insurance an inadequate rate. Where insured property is subject to fires which usually result in a large percentage of loss to value, and often in total loss, as in the case of unprotected frame buildings, the absence of the coinsurance clause does not work appreciable injustice. At the other end of the scale, the

7 $1.00 difference due to dropping two decimals.

writing of the highest grade "fire-proof" buildings in protected areas without coinsurance would be extremely inequitable. It is sometimes said that not over 15 per cent of the value of a modern "fire-proof" office building is subject to loss in any one fire, excluding conflagration losses. An owner who insured such a building for 15 per cent of its value would therefore receive in practically all cases the same payments of loss as would the owner insuring for 80 or 100 per cent.

While the examples given have been largely from the fire-insurance field, the principle is applicable wherever there is a tendency for percentages of loss to value to be concentrated in the lower brackets.

A similar situation may be observed in liability and health insurance, where coverage of small individual losses is much more expensive than coverage of losses in the upper brackets. For example, the cost of liability insurance will be increased in some cases only 15 per cent when the limits are doubled. If disability benefits under a health insurance policy begin only after the first four weeks of disability, the premium will be discounted by percentages much larger than the proportion which the four weeks bears to the maximum period during which benefits may be paid after four weeks.[8]

Since the application of the coinsurance principle is based on the situation at the time of loss, the insured who would avoid being penalized on account of insufficient insurance must be careful to maintain insurance in an amount which will at least equal the percentage specified in the coinsurance clause. With fluctuations in the value of buildings there is always a possibility that insurance which was adequate at the time of writing the policy has become inadequate at the time of loss. To obviate this possibility there has been used in some jurisdictions an "Agreed Amount" or "Guaranteed Amount" clause, under which the maintenance of a specified amount of insurance on the property would be accepted as conforming to the percentage of insurance named in the coinsurance clause. Recently this type of agreement has been used in some instances in use and occupancy (business interruption [1964]) insurance. The use of such a clause protects the insured against the penalties of the coinsurance clause. Since it is used only by agreement between the parties, it serves to put the insurer on notice that careful consideration of the percentage of insurance to value is necessary. It shifts the responsibility from insured to insurer, and may result in excessive losses for the latter if care is not taken to preserve a reasonable margin of safety, or if values increase rapidly.

While a "graded rate system" might be constructed by increasing the rate as the percentage of insurance to value decreased, it would require

[8] Coinsurance, as applied in major medical insurance follows this principle. (1964)

valuation of all risks subject to coinsurance and would not be adjusted to the value at the time of loss. Further, it would furnish a basis for controversy on every risk subject to coinsurance. Altogether it would probably be impractical although superior to a flat rate without coinsurance.

Coinsurance is sometimes justified on the ground that the fire-insurance rate is analogous to taxation. This analogy seems to the writer to be wholly fallacious. An insurance carrier sells the service of carrying risk. The value of its service is measured by the probability of loss and expense to which it subjects itself in writing insurance contracts. Coinsurance is simply a method of adjusting the value of the service to the price paid by the insured.

25. Fire Loss Adjustment*

Recent discussion of the legal status of insurance adjusters raises the question of their function in the insurance mechanism. Are they primarily insurance men or lawyers, or do they occupy a position which justifies classifying them as an independent profession? However they are classified, to what extent should their work be considered a matter of special public concern, and to what extent should it be subject to governmental regulation?

Of those who devote their full time to adjustment work there are three classes; *insurer adjusters, independent adjusters,* and *public adjusters.* Insurer adjusters are salaried employees of insurers or of cooperative adjustment organizations maintained by insurers; they represent only their employers in dealing with the public, although they may occasionally serve in inter-insurer arbitration proceedings and receive fees for their work. Independent adjusters are independent contractors who maintain their own offices, who are commissioned to adjust losses, and who charge fees for their services much as any professional man might do. They may be individuals or organized as partnerships or corporations. Ordinarily they represent only insurers. Public adjusters offer their services to claimants, charging a fee which is often a percentage of the amount collected from the insurer.

The adjustment of losses comprises three determinations: whether an insurer is liable to pay a claim under its contract; if so, how much; and to whom payment is to be made. Any activity contributing to answering these questions in an individual case is a part of the adjustment process. Many persons other than those who are, properly speaking, "adjusters" may perform, in whole or in part, the functions of an adjuster. Local agents of fire insurers are frequently authorized to adjust small losses; in other cases these same agents in effect represent the claimant in dealing with the insurer. Brokers consider the adjustment of losses on behalf of their clients a part of their normal service. Lawyers also frequently represent claimants as negotiators rather than as enforcers of strictly legal rights. In many losses, the claimant is his own adjuster.

* From *Journal of American Insurance*, August, 1938. Used by permission.

The adjuster is guided in the performance of his functions by the terms of the fire insurance contract which indicate what property is covered; when, where, and under what circumstances it is covered; what causes of loss are covered and what excepted; to whom loss is payable; how the amount of loss is payable; how the amount of loss is to be ascertained; and what rights the insurer may exercise.[1]

The procedure to be followed by an adjuster when a notice of loss has been received by the insurer has been outlined as follows:[2]

1. Inspect the scene of the loss and examine any of the insured property still to be seen.
2. Confer with the insured or his representative.
3. Examine and list the contracts.
   (a) Alphabetically by names of insurers.
   (b) With notation of agents' names.
   (c) Noting varying forms and clauses.
4. Record:
   (a) The exact name of the insured, and the names of individuals who may be members of the firm, officers of the corporation, or the individuals comprising the group.
   (b) The date, hour, and cause of the fire as stated by the insured.
   (c) The adjuster's theory of origin if he disagrees with the insured's statement.
   (d) The nature of the insured's title to or interest in the property.
   (e) Any change that may have occurred in the title or interest since the commencement of the policy.
   (f) All incumbrances on the property (these should be recorded by stating the name of the holder, the amount of the incumbrance, and the date it is due).
5. Approve, direct, or institute any work necessary to protect the property from further damage.
6. Determine whether the company is liable for the loss, and if so,
7. Prepare to discuss value and loss by
   (a) Estimating.
   (b) Inventorying.
   (c) Checking.
8. Negotiate the adjustment.
   (a) Agree on value and loss.
   (b) Apply any limitation clauses and apportion the loss.

[1] For a complete outline of the functions of the adjuster as determined by the New York standard policy, see Reed, P. B., *Adjustment of Fire Losses* (New York: McGraw-Hill Book Co., 1929), p. 3. Throughout the preparation of this article the author has made use of this treatise. Now in its second edition as *Adjustment of Property Losses* (1953). (1964)
[2] *Ibid.*, p. 10.

9. Prepare final papers and secure execution of the proof of loss, unless this is to be looked after by the insured or his representative.
10. Mail promptly to the company the final papers and report.

If, in the opinion of the adjuster, there is a possibility that a third party may be liable for the damage caused by the fire he will make whatever investigation is pertinent. An examination of this outline will show that the adjuster's work is concerned with the ascertainment of facts and an interpretation of certain of those facts in the light of the terms of the policy. The determination of whether the insurer is liable under the policy is of primary importance, the fact of liability and its possible extent being settled by the adjuster's answers, after due investigation, to the following questions:[3]

1. Has the insured named in the policy suffered a loss, and was his interest at the time of the fire that which is covered in the policy?
2. Did the fire occur during the term of the policy?
3. Is the loss a direct result of fire?
4. Is the damaged or destroyed property that described in the policy?
5. Does the claim include any property that is not covered by the policy?
   (a) Of a kind or at a location not covered?
   (b) Uninsurable?
   (c) Excepted?
6. Was the loss, or any part of it, caused by excepted hazards?
7. Is the policy valid or had it been cancelled before the loss, or voided either before or after the loss?

If the insurer is found to be liable, in whole or in part, for the loss, the problem then becomes one of ascertaining how much is to be paid. If liability is doubtful or clearly nonexistent, the adjuster may nevertheless find it desirable to collect evidence and even proceed with an estimate of the loss, protecting the insurer by carefully refraining from doing anything which might constitute a waiver of its rights or estop it from asserting its rights. In most such cases he will make a *non-waiver agreement* with the claimant under which all rights and defenses of the insurer are preserved, the claimant agreeing that any investigation or steps to ascertain the amount of the loss shall not constitute a waiver of such rights or defenses.

The first essential in the equipment of a competent adjuster is adequate knowledge of the provisions of fire-insurance contracts and of their interpretation, and an understanding of the intent of the insurer and insured in entering into a contract.

The contract and its interpretation is, of course, a legal subject, and the

[3] *Ibid.*, p. 17.

adjuster is necessarily an expert in this specialized field of the law, but knowledge adequate to his needs is readily available and may easily be mastered by one not generally schooled in the law. Documents of which he makes use, such as proofs of loss and the non-waiver agreement are standardized and ordinarily require no further legal draftsmanship. If the adjustment reaches a point of threatening court procedure, either in the direction of resisting a claim or prosecuting for fraud, the matter will be turned over to lawyers.

It is most important for the adjuster to have a clear realization of the intent of the parties, in order that he may assist in carrying out the functions of the contract as the embodiment of an intended transfer of risk. He should know when the contract is void and the limitations of its application, but he should know when to overlook technical interpretations and make payment on a loss which strictly might not be enforceable. He may be in a position to make decisions on such points himself or he may need to consult his superiors, but he should always be clear on the business, as contrasted with the legal, considerations involved.

The results of a survey conducted by Professor G. W. Goble in Champaign and Urbana, Illinois, lend support to this point.[4] He examined 538 fire-insurance policies of which 236 or 44 per cent were on properties jointly owned. Of these 236 policies, 151 or 64 per cent (28 per cent of all the policies) were void because they covered properties which were jointly owned but were insured as solely owned by the insured named in the policies, or because they were insured as owned in fee simple, but were not so owned. Properties often go for years without a fire loss and consequently with no test of the validity of the insurance, and when fire losses occur violations are frequently unnoticed or intentionally overlooked. It is highly improbable that payment would have been refused on purely technical grounds in case of loss to any of the properties whose insurance was investigated. But this situation is perhaps typical of the country at large—a considerable percentage of the insurance carried is probably technically void for one reason or another, for the fire-insurance contract is a complicated document. Further, the ownership, use, or other circumstances affecting property frequently change during the currency of a policy, without appropriate changes being made in the contract. It is the business of the adjuster to know when violation of the contract calls for denial of a claim because of its representing a situation not contemplated by the parties, and when it is properly to be considered a negligible mistake inherent in the present insurance system.

[4] *Proceedings of the Fourth Annual Meeting*, American Association of University Teachers of Insurance, December 28, 1936, p. 37.

In most cases it is readily admitted that the insurer is liable for the payment of loss. The question is: how much and to whom. Here the adjuster becomes an administrator of the company's funds and its diplomatic representative. He should protect its rights by taking proper advantage of all policy terms, such as the pro rata clause or the coinsurance clause, which reduce the amount payable. He should carefully estimate the amount of the loss in order to keep the drain on the funds at a minimum. He should cooperate in measures for protection and salvage of property. In rare cases, he should exercise options to replace, repair, rebuild, take over entire stock, or move for appraisal, if the prospects of an agreement on the amount to be paid seem too dim.

In all of this work, however, he must remember that, although it does not appear in the annual statement, an insurer's most valuable asset, and one most difficult to recover if it is lost, is the good will of the insuring public and of agents and brokers. While protecting the insurer he should be careful not to let a misguided desire to make a good record for close adjustments leave with the insured a feeling of having been cheated or sharply dealt with. He should make clear his purpose of fully indemnifying the insured in accordance with the terms of the contract, reasonably construed.

Taking the adjuster's work as a whole, by far the major part of it consists in arriving at the amount of loss by investigation, calculation, and negotiation. In general, loss on physical property is measured by the cost to replace it in its condition immediately previous to the fire. Under certain contracts covering financial losses the problem of ascertaining loss is one of accounting. The adjuster must be adequately equipped with knowledge of business procedure, of methods of estimating construction costs, of methods of protecting property from further damage, of sources of supply of commodities, of price quotations, of possibilities of salvage and disposal of damaged property, of causes and degrees of depreciation whether from use, age, or obsolescence, of premises and facilities for carrying on interrupted business. He must have an understanding of, and be able to deal with, builders, dealers, and appraisers. He must have a detective's instinct for clues and evidence, and an accountant's orderly method of classifying and listing. He must be able to distinguish and negotiate appropriately with reasonable but misinformed claimants, hostile but honest claimants, trading claimants, and grasping and unreasonable claimants. He must distinguish accidental fires and incendiary fires, damage from fire and damage from other causes, fraud and dishonesty.

Quite an order! But perhaps a sufficient indication of the peculiar combination of qualities which go to make up the competent adjuster, and to show that his is a type of work which demands a special sort of person and specialized training. He is neither lawyer, accountant, business man, detective, nor salesman, but something of all of them.

Without any attempt at precise definition, it would appear that the fire loss adjuster's position is that of the professional man as contrasted with the business man. The qualities of which one thinks as distinguishing the competent lawyer, doctor, or practicing scientist are those which go to make up the competent adjuster.

It has been suggested, notably in Missouri, that adjustment of losses is, in part at least, the practice of law, and therefore open legally only to duly licensed members of the bar.[5] It would seem that the test of whether adjustment is the "practice of law" ought reasonably to be whether compliance with the usual requirements for admission to the bar is a necessary part of the adjuster's equipment. These requirements ordinarily comprise specialized legal education and passing a comprehensive examination. Their purpose is to protect the public against incompetent handling of their legal problems.

Adjusters are generally the representatives of insurers. So far as the insurers' own interests are concerned they hardly need protection against the employment of incompetent adjusters; their requirements for authorization to adjust losses are probably of a higher standard than would be found *as to that particular work* in any governmental requirements for admission to the bar. In any event, they may be presumed to have their own interests sufficiently at heart and to be sufficiently informed to choose adjusting representatives without outside assistance.

What of the public? Should they be protected against the employment of incompetent or tricky adjusters by insurers? It would seem that their interests are sufficiently protected by the evident self-interest of insurers and by the supervisory activities of state insurance departments, which may have specific authority to hear and act on complaints against sharp practice on the part of insurers, or may bring pressure to bear even beyond the scope of specific authority.

Experience has clearly shown, however, that the public needs to be protected against the possible sharp practice or incompetence of public adjusters. These adjusters have followed tactics of the ambulance-chasing variety and have not conformed to standards which would accord with the insured's best interests. In New York, they are required to secure a certificate of authority from the Superintendent of Insurance, who may

[5] See *What is the Practice of Law in Missouri*, published by the American Mutual Alliance, February 20, 1938. The Missouri controversy had to do with casualty insurance adjustments but certain elements of it are equally applicable to fire insurance.

suspend or revoke their authority if, after due investigation, he determines that the holder of the certificate

(a) has violated any provision of the insurance law, or has violated any law in the course of his dealings as an adjuster; or (b) has made a material misstatement in the application for such certificate; or (c) has been guilty of fraudulent or dishonest practices; or (d) has demonstrated his incompetency or untrustworthiness to transact the business of a public adjuster.[6]

Many insureds are in no position to judge the competence or trustworthiness of public adjusters, especially under the emergency conditions of a fire loss. It is in accord with good governmental practice to protect them.

Governmental supervision, however, should not be adopted for its own sake; where present methods are adequate, they should be permitted to continue. It seems to the writer that general supervision of insurance practices, including adjustments, with specific regulation of public adjusters, protects the public as far as is practically possible. To require licensing of all adjusters is waste.[7] To require adjusters to be members of the bar does not cover the case. Whatever is done, there will still be competent and incompetent, honest and dishonest, adjusters, exactly as there are similar lawyers and doctors. The problem is one of bringing the standard of adjustments to the highest *practicable* level.

[6] New York Insurance Law, § 138–a.

[7] Licensing by individual states would interfere with the management of normal adjustments and would make more difficult or impossible mobilizing adjusters across state lines in cases of disasters such as conflagrations, tornadoes, and floods.

The New York law has been amended and extended to cover independent adjusters; see § 123. (1964)

26. Apportionment of Loss in Fire Insurance*

Property insured against fire is frequently covered by several contracts issued by different insurers. This situation is partially due to the limitations which individual insurers place on the amount which they will write on given risks, and partially to the fact that in the purchase of fire insurance to cover varying values and varying situations, contracts covering the same property are written at different times. It is often due to an attempt to work out a convenient arrangement of expiration dates, or to take advantage of economies in the application of rates.

Whatever the cause, an insured who experiences loss of his property frequently finds that his loss is covered by several contracts. Both he and his insurers are interested in the relative liability of the various insurers whose contracts cover the property. If the total insurance applicable is less than, or equal to, the amount of the loss, and there are no limitations on payment, the problem is a simple one; each insurer pays the full amount of its contract. If the insurance applicable under all contracts is larger than the amount of the loss, if all contracts are drawn in exactly the same terms, and if there is no clause limiting the application of the contract to the property, the loss will be paid by each insurer in proportion to the amount of its insurance. Such a settlement is in accordance with the *pro rata clause* which, in the New York Standard Fire Insurance Policy, reads as follows:

> This Company shall not be liable for a greater proportion of any loss or damage than the amount hereby insured shall bear to the whole insurance covering the property, whether valid or not and whether collectible or not.[1]

* From *Journal of American Insurance*, May, 1938. Used by permission.

[1] Under common law, if a contract of fire insurance were drawn without reference to contribution, the insured would have the right to collect from any insurer to the extent of his loss. The insurer from whom collection was made would then have the right, if he had paid more than his pro rata share of the loss, to collect the excess equitably from the other insurers. These rights are of no great interest today, since practically all insurance is written under standard contracts including the pro rata clause.

The current 1943 New York form omits "or damage" and "valid or not" and includes "against the peril involved" after the word "property." (1964)

Under these conditions the problem of apportionment of loss is a simple one. A typical solution may be stated as follows:

Property value		$50,000
Insurance		40,000
Company A	$25,000—5/8	
Company B	10,000—1/4	
Company C	5,000—1/8	
Loss		16,000
A pays 5/8	$10,000	
B pays 1/4	4,000	
C pays 1/8	2,000	

The words "whether valid or not and whether collectible or not" are intended to discourage cheap insurance, and to relieve the insurer of the consequences of bad judgment on the part of the insured, or failure to conform to the terms of any contract which he may have made. The rights of the insurer under this part of the pro rata clause will be enforced by the courts. For example, if it were found, after working out the above apportionment, that Company B was insolvent, paying only 25¢ on the dollar, the insured would collect $1,000 from B, bearing the remaining $3,000 himself. The contribution of companies A and C to the loss would not thereby be increased. Likewise, if it were found that for some reason company C's policy had been invalidated by the insured, he would have to stand the loss of $2,000.

Contracts which are precisely alike in their terms and in the description of the property (though they may differ in amount of insurance) are said to be *concurrent*. Where contracts are *non-concurrent* in the description of the property but otherwise concurrent, and where the collectible loss is not reduced by the application of coinsurance, reduced-rate-contribution, or average clauses, the problem is equitably to divide the insurance covering the variously described property. Assume, for example, the following facts:[2]

Property value:	
A	$10,000
B	15,000
C	25,000
Total	$50,000

[2] The illustrative material here used is drawn from notes prepared by the writer for courses at Columbia University and the University of California.

Insurance:

Company X on A	$ 5,000
Company Y on B	10,000
Company Z on C	15,000
Company S blanket policy on A, B, C	15,000
Total	**$45,000**

Losses:

On A	$ 6,000
On B	8,000
On C	10,000
Total	**$24,000**

Since in this case there is insurance ample to cover the loss, the insured will be entitled to full payment. The question is, how much shall each insurer pay? If the insurers agree on a method of apportionment, and none contests the validity of its policy nor withholds payment for any reason, the insured is not concerned with the method adopted. Where there is a dispute among insurers as to the method to be adopted, it is usual practice to pay the insured in full and to submit the apportionment of the amount among the insurers to arbitration. If, however, for any reason an insurer will not, or cannot, pay, the insured will be concerned to secure the adoption of a rule which will reduce that insurer's share of the loss to a minimum.

A wide variety of rules has been advanced and used in cases of this sort but "no one of them is either demonstrably sound in theory, or universally applicable in practice."[3] Solutions of the problem in accordance with three of the more widely used rules will be presented here.[4] Under the *Reading Rule* the amount of the blanket policy would be divided among the specific items of property covered in accordance with the value of the property covered. In the case cited, the amount of insurance on each item would be determined as follows:

Insurance on	A	B	C
Blanket	$3,000 (10/50 of $15,000)	$ 4,500 (15/50 of $15,000)	$ 7,500 (25/50 of $15,000)
Specific	5,000	10,000	15,000
Total	**$8,000**	**$14,500**	**$22,500**

Having determined the amount of insurance applicable to each item, the

[3] *Richards on Insurance* (3d ed.; New York: Banks Law Publishing Co., 1911), p. 442.
[4] For discussion and application of other rules, see Reed, Prentiss B., "Adjustment of Property Losses" (2d ed.; New York: McGraw-Hill Book Co., 1953), Chap. 6. (1964)

Risk and Insurance

loss payable by each insurer would be calculated in accordance with the
pro rata clause as follows (dropping cents):

Losses paid	A	B	C
Blanket	$2,250 (3/8 of $6,000)	$2,483 (45/145 of $8,000)	$ 3,333 (75/225 of $10,000)
Specific	3,750 (5/8 of 6,000)	5,517 (100/145 of 8,000)	6,667 (150/225 of 10,000)
Total	$6,000	$8,000	$10,000

Under the *Connecticut Rule*, which is a form of the *Gradual Reduction
Rule*, the full amount of the blanket insurance is made applicable to the
property on which there is the largest loss. After determining the amount
which the blanket insurer will pay on that property, the remainder of the
blanket insurance is applied to the next largest loss, and so on, until all
losses have been apportioned. Using this rule, the solution of the problem
would be as follows:

Insurance on	A	B	C
Blanket	$ 6,000 (15,000–$9,000)	$10,000 (15,000–$5,000)	$15,000 (full amount)
Specific	5,000	10,000	15,000
Total	$11,000	$20,000	$30,000
Losses paid			
Blanket	$3,273 (6/11 of $6,000)	$4,000 (10/20 of $8,000)	$ 5,000 (15/30 of $10,000)
Specific	2,727 (5/11 of $6,000)	4,000 (10/20 of $8,000)	5,000 (15/30 of $10,000)
Total	$6,000	$8,000	$10,000

In Pacific Coast territory, the companies have adopted the *Kinne Rule*,
which provides that the blanket insurance is to be divided among the
various items of property in the proportion that the loss on each bears to
the total of the losses.[5] Under this rule the following solution would result:

Insurance on	A	B	C
Blanket	$3,750 (6/24 of $15,000)	$ 5,000 (8/24 of $15,000)	$ 6,250 (10/24 of $15,000)
Specific	5,000	10,000	15,000
Total	$8,750	$15,000	$21,250
Losses paid			
Blanket	$2,571 (375/875 of $6,000)	$2,667 (5/15 of $8,000)	$2,941 (625/2125 of $10,000)
Specific	3,429 (500/875 of $6,000)	5,333 (10/15 of $8,000)	7,059 (1500/2125 of $10,000)
Total	$6,000	$8,000	$10,000

Under the Reading and Kinne Rules the blanket insurer would pay
approximately the same amount, $8,066 and $8,179 respectively, but under
the Connecticut Rule the payment would be $12,273. In general, the latter
rule would work to the disadvantage of the blanket insurance since it would
contribute to the payment of loss on the basis of larger amounts of
insurance.

[5] For a complete statement of the rule, see *ibid.*, pp. 215–219. (1964)

After long consideration (some six years), a committee of the National Board of Fire Underwriters recommended the adoption of the Kinne Rule for all cases of the type illustrated here. In the report of the committee it was stated that the result of adopting some uniform rule would "be fair and equitable and the saving of time and correspondence through the practical elimination of disputes concerning apportionments will make worth while almost any practice that is followed consistently." The Board adopted this suggestion and recommended it to the membership for application on and after February 15, 1934. The Kinne Rule is, therefore, now the official rule of the Board and is generally applied in the adjustment of losses where there are several items of property, each covered both by specific insurance, and all by the blanket policy. While there has been no official adoption of the Kinne Rule by the mutuals, it is also in general use by them.

The illustrations given have been arranged to provide for the payment of each loss in full by the insurers. But apportionment according to these rules may result in one or more items of property having allotted to them an amount of insurance insufficient to cover the loss, even though the total amount of insurance carried by the insured is sufficient to pay his losses. Under such circumstances, in order to comply with the rule that apportionment is not to be used to defeat recovery by the insured, it would be necessary to adopt a different method of apportionment, or to reapportion the insurance under the method originally adopted. The following example of such a situation, and of the solution of the problem presented by it in accordance with the Kinne Rule, is based on an article by A. W. Thornton.[6]

FACTS

Insurance—

Company A—General Merchandise		$ 5,000
Company B—General Merchandise		5,000
Company C	Boots and Shoes	2,500
	Teas and Coffees	3,000
	Hardware	2,000
	Total	$18,500

Losses—

Boots and Shoes	$ 3,000
Teas and Coffees	4,000
Hardware	8,000
Total	$15,000

[6] "Annual Report of the Proceedings of the Fire Insurance Society of San Francisco," 1910–1911, p. 11.

FIRST APPORTIONMENT OF INSURANCE

Co.	Boots and Shoes	Teas and Coffees	Hardware
A.	$1,000 (1/5 of $5,000)	$1,333.33 (4/15 of $5,000)	$2,666.67 (8/15 of $5,000)
B.	1,200 (1/5 of $6,000)	1,600.00 (4/15 of $6,000)	3,200.00 (8/15 of $6,000)
C.	2,500 (Specific)	3,000.00 (Specific)	2,000.00 (Specific)
	$4,700	$5,933.33	$7,866.67 (Insufficient)

Deficiency on Hardware = $133.33 ($8,000–$7,866.67)
$60.60 (5/11 of $133.33) to be secured from A as follows:
$25.97 (3/7 of $60.60) from Boots and Shoes
$34.63 (4/7 of $60.60) from Teas and Coffees
$72.73 (6/11 of $133.33) to be secured from B as follows:
$31.17 (3/7 of $72.73) from Boots and Shoes
$41.56 (4/7 of $72.73) from Teas and Coffees

REAPPORTIONMENT OF INSURANCE

Co.	Boots and Shoes	Teas and Coffees	Hardware
A.	$ 974.03 ($1,000–$25.97)	$1,298.70 ($1,333.33–$34.63)	$2,727.27 ($2,666.67 + $60.60)
B.	1,168.83 ($1,200–$31.17)	1,558.44 ($1,600 –$41.56)	3,272.73 ($3,200 + $72.73)
C.	2,500.00	3,000.00	2,000.00
	$4,642.86	$5,857.14	$8,000.00

At times it will be found that a blanket policy covers property on which there is no specific insurance, at the same time covering other property on which there is specific insurance. If a loss occurs which affects both sorts of property, the entire loss on the property not covered specifically will be met from the blanket policy, the remainder of the amount of that policy being treated as compound insurance on the remaining property and, contributing with the specific insurance under whatever rule may be adopted. If, however, there is a loss on an item of property covered by specific insurance and also by blanket insurance covering other items on which there is no loss, the full amount of the blanket policy will be used with the amount of the specific policy to determine the loss payable by each insurer.

In the illustrations presented above it was assumed that no coinsurance, reduced-rate-contribution, or average clause operated to reduce the amount collectible by the insured. If one of these clauses does so operate, the rule adopted must give each insurer the benefit of the clause in its contract. This result may be accomplished by using the *Limit-of-Liability Rule*, now generally adopted by the insurers. This rule provides that each insurance contract will be applicable to each item in the proportion which the limit of possible liability under the contract bears to the total of such limits. Suppose, for example, the following situation:[7]

[7] *Non-concurrent Apportionments*, Recommendations of the National Board of Fire Underwriters, January, 1934.
Since this paper was published, much broader recommendations have been adopted by a

Property value

Stock		$ 8,504.95
Machinery		19,287.72
	Total	$27,792.67

Insurance

Company A on stock		$ 3,000 (80% coinsurance)
Company B on machinery		9,000 (80% coinsurance)
Company C, blanket on stock and machinery		28,000 (90% coinsurance)
	Total	$40,000

Losses

On stock		$ 8,504.95
On machinery		8,050.00
	Total	$16,554.95

No insurer will pay more than the amount of its contract, nor more than the amount of the loss on the property covered by its contract, nor more than that proportion of the loss which the amount of its contract bears to the indicated coinsurance percentage of the value of the property covered. The lowest of these amounts is the limit of liability of each insurer. The limit of A's liability on stock is determined as follows:

Amount of insurance	$3,000.00
Limit under coinsurance clause	$3,749.83
$\dfrac{\$3,000 \text{ (insurance)}}{80 \text{ per cent of } \$8,504.95 \text{ (value)}} \times \$8,504.95 \text{ (loss)}$	
Loss on stock	$8,504.95

The smallest amount, $3,000, is the limit of A's liability. B's limit of $4,695.35 would be determined as follows:

Amount of insurance	$9,000.00
Limit under coinsurance clause	$4,695.35
$\dfrac{\$9,000 \text{ (insurance)}}{80 \text{ per cent of } \$19,287.72 \text{ (value)}} \times \$8,050 \text{ (loss)}$	
Loss on machinery	$8,050

C's limit, $16,554.95, would be determined as follows:

Amount of insurance	$28,000.00
Limit under coinsurance clause	$18,531.61
$\dfrac{\$28,000 \text{ (insurance)}}{90 \text{ per cent of } \$27,792.67 \text{ (value)}} \times \$16,554.95 \text{ (loss)}$	
Loss on stock and machinery	$16,554.95

group of organizations; see *Guiding Principles for Overlapping Insurance Coverages*, subscribed by Association of Casualty and Surety Companies, Inland Marine Underwriters Association, National Automobile Underwriters Association, National Board of Fire Underwriters, National Bureau of Casualty Underwriters, and Surety Association of America, November 1, 1963. (1964)

Losses will be paid by each company as follows:

	Limit of Liability	Loss Payable	
Company A	$ 3,000.00	$ 2,048.01	($ 3,000.00/$24,250.30 of $16,554.95)
Company B	4,695.35	3,205.37	($ 4,695.35/$24,250.30 of $16,554.95)
Company C	16,554.95	11,301.57	($16,554.95/$24,250.30 of $16,554.95)
Total	$24,250.30	$16,554.95	

By this process provision has been made for payment of the loss in full since the total of the applicable limits exceeds the total amount of the loss, and each company's limit of liability has been recognized in accordance with the terms of its contract.

The volume of disputes among companies has been to a considerable extent reduced by the general agreement on the use of the rules recommended by the National Board and by cooperative action of stock and of mutual insurers in their respective adjustment bureaus.

Careful checking of policies for concurrency both as to description of property and as to terms has done much to eliminate the cause of apportionment problems, but there will always be troublesome cases, particularly where insurance on the same property is written at different times. This difficulty is often avoided abroad by the preparation of a single contract which the various insurers subscribe.

27. The Basis of Premium Rates*

An insurance premium is a price for a promise to make good loss incurred and to provide certain incidental services. It may or may not include an allowance for profit.

Probably the most difficult problem confronting the insurer is that of fixing premium rates. The technical procedure of calculating rates is complicated; the interest of the insuring public, of agents, and of supervisory officials centers sooner or later on the price that insurers charge; and the naming of rates has come to have implications of business policy as well.

To proceed intelligently to a consideration of premium rates it must be determined what criteria they should satisfy. There are three general requirements for rates, varying in importance according to the point of view from which one attacks the problem. These requirements are: rates should be adequate; they should not be excessive; they should measure accurately the relative probability of loss of the risks to which they apply.

The first of these criteria is by far the most important. Rates should be pitched at a level sufficiently high to enable insurers to receive an adequate aggregate income, an income large enough to enable them without question to meet all demands for the payment of losses and expenses. The primary purpose of insurance is security, certainty on the part of the insured that losses and expenses to which he may be subject and which are covered by the contract of insurance will be met by the insurer; certainty on the part of the insurer that it will be able to meet its obligations in full. This requirement of security takes precedence over the nice balancing of claims for individual justice in the determination of an insurance price, the desire for cheap insurance, or the competitive urge to get business.

But the satisfaction of the criterion of adequacy should not be held to justify rates clearly excessive, nor will competition, in the normal instance, long suffer such rates to continue. It is, of course, from the point of view of the insured that it is particularly important to restrain any tendency to excessiveness, whether that quality be due to provision for unusual profits or to lack of proper economy in management.

* From *Journal of American Insurance*, February, 1928. Used by permission.

From every point of view, that of the insured, of the insurer, and of society, it is important that individual rates accurately measure relative probability of loss. The insured should know that his rate represents a just appraisal of the probable loss involved in his property or personal affairs; the insurer that, in adding an obligation to its list, it is receiving an income commensurate with that obligation; society, that each type of individual or group is bearing its own losses and expenses for, to the extent that a rate is inadequate or excessive, the insured who pay that rate are receiving from, or paying subsidy to, others.

There is no uniform basis for the quotation of rates. The units to which the rate applies are various; as $1,000 of insurance, in life insurance, $100 of insurance in fire insurance, $100 of annual payroll in compensation insurance, a motor car in automobile collision insurance, a seat in theater liability insurance. The total premium may even be the result of two different rates, each applied to a unit as is done in owners', landlords', and tenants' public liability insurance, where the units are a square foot of area and a lineal foot of frontage. The choice of a unit depends on two considerations —"first, that it shall be conveniently ascertainable, and, second, that it shall accurately reflect the scope and degree of the obligation which the insurance carrier undertakes."[1]

The selection of a practical unit for measuring the *quantity* of hazard involved in an insurance transaction is not a difficult matter. It is the measurement of the *quality* of the hazard which gives rise to problems the solution of which calls for the combined efforts of statisticians, actuaries, underwriters, and supervisory officials. The quality of hazard of a given risk depends on the *probability* of payment of losses and expenses on account of that risk. It is this intangible probability that insurers are called upon to measure, and having measured, to make the basis of the price charged for insurance. The insurer is never in the position of the manufacturer who may set a price on the basis of materials already in hand or for which contracts have been made; its price must always be based entirely on estimates. That insurance has become a stable, secure business is evidence of the accuracy with which such estimates have, in the aggregate, been made.

When an insurance rate is quoted, it applies ordinarily to a set of circumstances the results of which can, with reasonable precision, be predicted. This is done by applying the theory that what has happened in the past will, under the same circumstances, happen in the future. But this theory, in its practical application, is subject to important qualifications.

---

[1] Michelbacher, G. F., "Miscellaneous Public Liability and Property Damage Liability Insurance in the United States," *Proceedings* of the Insurance Institute of Toronto, 1925–1926, pp. 92–133. Reprinted by the National Bureau of Casualty and Surety Underwriters, n.d.

The first of these qualifications is that the insurer can conduct its business safely only by basing its operations on a sufficiently large number of cases. The evidence of what has happened in the past must be drawn from experience with a large number of units and the predicted results can be expected only if a large number is insured. The fact that one house out of two insured, burned during a given year is no evidence that half the houses insured during the succeeding year will burn, but the fact that 5,000 out of 1,000,000 insured burned during the first year is reasonable evidence that approximately 1/200 of the houses insured (if it be a very large number) will burn during the second year. The reliability of the indications of large numbers may be illustrated by repeated flipping of a coin. If a coin is flipped ten times it is extremely unlikely that it will show heads five times and tails five times though the probability of each occurring is equal. But if the coin is flipped 1,000 times one may be confident that heads and tails will each appear in close approximation to 500 times.

Another practical qualification is that the circumstances covered by the insurance for which a rate is to be made must be practically the same as those on which the prediction is based, or, if not the same, that allowance be made for changes. For example, experience may show that one in every 200 buildings of a given type burned during a given year in a certain locality. But, at the time insurance is to be written, there may have been a marked improvement in the fire-fighting equipment assigned to this locality. Or, through business changes, manufacturing processes involving increased hazards may have been brought in. In either event allowance would have to be made for such changes in circumstances.

With these principles in mind let us see how insurers actually proceed to the making of rates. In general there are two bases for the determination of rates, statistical data and judgment. Probably in no case is either the sole basis for a rate; every conceivable combination of the two is found.

A rate can be calculated with greatest accuracy when accurate data on exposure to loss and of losses realized covering a considerable period of time, a large number of cases, and definitely known circumstances which may be expected to show little or no change are available. Perhaps life insurance offers the best example of such a situation. In that business figures may be gathered covering experience with an enormous number of insured lives; a highly developed technique insures statistical accuracy; and conditions affecting the mortality of insured lives change very slowly. But even here judgment enters in considerable measure. The composition of groups of insured is largely the product of the judgment of medical examiners and of underwriters. Grouping for purposes of statistical analysis involves a degree of judgment.

At the other extreme may be placed aircraft insurance. Data on losses are almost entirely lacking and conditions of construction and operation are rapidly changing. A rate quoted on any hazard dependent on these conditions is almost entirely a matter of judgment. An insurer quoting such rates must be prepared for adverse results and must charge such results to "buying experience." But even here certain data are available; figures showing the relation of accidents to hours flown, figures on such losses as insurers may have had.

Between these extremes lie other combinations of data and judgment. For example, one finds in schedule rating for fire insurance a system of charges and credits which determines in large measure the rate to be charged for a given risk, each charge or credit representing a defect or a good point in the fire hazard of the risk. Each of these items is based on the combined judgment of a group of fire underwriters. But the level of rates for fire insurance, whether for types of risk or for the business as a whole, is determined in large measure by the profit or loss already experienced and made evident by financial data.

On occasion a rate for a certain hazard for which no statistical experience is available, may be based on a comparison with hazards which, in the judgment of the rater, are comparable with the new type, and for which experience is available. During one of the revisions of workmen's compensation insurance rates there was established a new class of risks described as "Fertilizer Dry Mixing Plants—excluding the manufacture or handling of acid, bone, and rock crushing, and the preparation of tankage." It was decided that the hazards involved in this new class were sufficiently similar to those involved in "Phosphate Works—no mining" to justify the adoption of the same rate.

In what has so far been said the writer has had in mind attempts to arrive at rates measuring the relative hazards of insured risks. Other influences likewise condition insurance rates and these deserve notice. In competition rates may be unduly cut in order to get business, the bargaining power of a given class of insured may have its effect in depressing rates, controversies with state supervisory officials may result in political compromises satisfactory to no one.

But the tendency of rating is always toward increasing accuracy of measurement of hazard, a tendency which is being promoted by continued improvement in technique and the accumulation of statistical experience. Judgment will never be eliminated but its role may be steadily decreased. And it may confidently be stated that the most useful weapon of the insurer in meeting unwarranted demands for low rates, whether from the insured, from state officials, or in the form of competitive strategy, is definite statistical evidence of insurance losses and expenses for which provision must be made in the rate. Cost accounting has enabled industrial enterprises to meet similar problems; statistical analysis is the cost accounting of insurance.

To say that statistical experience is the most desirable basis for insurance rates does not imply that judgment can be completely eliminated nor does it imply that all insurance rates may be made primarily on the basis of statistical data. There are, and probably always will be, branches of insurance which, by reason of novelty, complicated hazards, or rapidly changing conditions, will not readily lend themselves to statistical analysis. It may confidently be stated, however, that the aim of the rate maker should be the elimination of judgment and the substitution of statistical experience as a basis for rates.

28. Purchasing Insurance*

It is probable that less careful thought is devoted to the purchase of insurance, whether for business or personal ends, than to any other major financial problem. Various reasons may be assigned for this situation, though perhaps lack of general knowledge of insurance principles is most important. Because of this lack and because insurance is in a measure standardized, there is a tendency to shirk consideration of insurance problems, and to rely on the advice, too often interested, of third parties.

Specious arguments which would be of no avail in most commercial transactions are still serviceable in the hands of the insurance solicitor—his client is usually not in a position even to ask intelligent questions which will lead to a clear-cut statement of the pros and cons. Two stock insurance companies offer to take the same risk at varying rates—how is the insured to know whether the company offering the lower rate has an informed underwriting policy based on the selection of preferred risks, or is cutting rates merely to get business and endangering its safety by so doing? The agent of the one company will point out that one must always pay a good price for the best and that, since insurance is protection for the future, no chances should be taken with "cut-rate" companies. His competitor will point to the selected-risk policy of his company and its record of financial success. And probably the whole matter will be settled by an unconscious comparison of the personalities of the two agents.

Suppose a mutual offers its dividend record as an argument for its particular brand of insurance. Its stock-company competitor indicates the possibility that dividends may be reduced or discontinued, that assessments are not an impossibility. How many insureds are in a position to determine whether the prospect of savings justifies the chance involved in these possibilities? How often is a decision based on careful weighing of the merits of the case?

The question of insurers aside, how many insureds have a rational basis for purchasing or refusing to purchase the various types of cover, for securing legitimate and profitable reductions in rates, for adjusting the

* From *Journal of American Insurance*, April, 1928. Used by permission.

relative amounts of insurance and contract provisions to their own particular situations?

It is intended to imply in all these questions that the insured is generally unable properly to conceive and put into execution a practical insurance program. It may be added that he usually displays little interest in the whole subject until he has a loss which is not covered to his satisfaction. At that point his interest may become intense.

It is the purpose of this paper to indicate certain guiding principles which a prospective insured may well have in mind in purchasing insurance. It is not possible in a brief space to cover with any degree of completeness the problem of purchasing insurance—the principles suggested will be subject to qualifications and exceptions; but it is believed they will be found serviceable as a basis for intelligent thinking insurancewise.

Three solutions present themselves when one considers the problem of meeting uncertainties and perils that may result in financial loss. One may take measures to prevent the loss; one may accept the chance and the results; or one may buy insurance to make good the loss if it occurs.

Prevention is the most direct way of avoiding loss and is to be recommended to the extent that it is practical—in other words, to the extent that the cost of prevention is not a more serious problem than the chance of loss itself. The insured can make definite calculation of the practicality of prevention work by consulting the insurer which will, in many lines, quote a lower rate for insurance in consideration of the installation of preventive devices and the practice of safety work. The saving in insurance cost can then be compared with the cost of prevention. But the insured should not be content with such a comparison—there are hazards which can be met only by prevention. For example, even though a manufacturer purchased every possible sort of insurance he could not cover loss of customers to competitors during a shut-down caused by fire, or the personal inconvenience and worry incident to rebuilding his plant. Preventive work might be indicated even though insurance savings would not directly cover the cost.

Carrying one's own risk is, to a certain extent, the essence of a business or profession. The stock-market trader bears the risk of market fluctuations in the hope of profit, the lawyer devotes himself to an expensive education in the expectation of fees from clients. In neither case is insurance possible. And there are cases where insurance is procurable but not to be advised. If a business is of such a nature and extent that losses from certain causes are predictable from year to year with reasonable exactitude, those losses may be met by making direct financial provision. A large railroad system with a multitude of widely separated small stations may properly make provision for fire damage to these stations by setting up a fund from which losses will be met. Such a policy should be adopted only after a most careful analysis of the situation and should be based on demonstrable experience, not simply on a willingness to "take a chance."

We now come to the third solution of the problem, insurance. In what cases and to what extent should insurance be purchased? It may be taken as axiomatic that no individual or organization can or should purchase every available form of insurance; the drain on income would be too heavy. The first principle to observe in purchasing insurance is that *those perils should be covered which might result in serious financial embarrassment to the insured.* Such, for example, would be the peril of fire in the case of a manufacturer whose operations are concentrated in a single plant. Destruction of the plant would destroy his business. This is an extreme case, but less spectacular losses might cause serious difficulty. The breakdown of an engine, of little consequence in itself, might lead to heavy losses because of the necessity of discontinuing operations until it was repaired.

A second general principle is that *those perils should be covered which, even though the financial consequences might be borne without difficulty by the insured, are of such nature that it is profitable to purchase insurance in order to be relieved of the care and expense incidental to meeting them direct.* Of this type is the peril of breakage of plate glass. Insurance is written under a contract of replacement; the insured often desires not so much relief from the financial loss involved in the breakage as prompt and efficient repairs. Of a similar nature is the "clean-up fund" often provided by taking sufficient life insurance to meet the immediate expenses of dependents after the death of the insured.

It will be found, in many cases, that both of these principles are operative. Liability insurance offers not only protection against large verdicts but also an expert service in the investigation and settlement of claims. Steam boiler insurance, while protecting against a possibility of serious damage, is organized chiefly for inspection of boilers.

To argue against purchasing insurance on the ground of remoteness of the chance of loss is a fallacy, provided the insurance premium is accurately calculated. To be sure, as between two forms of insurance, that form which covers the more imminent variety of loss seems the more important to the insured; but he should not reject a form of insurance covering remote possibilities merely because of their remoteness, for he has no means of knowing that his is not the rare case in which the loss will take place. He should always consider what his position would be if the loss should occur to *him.*

Careful consideration of five questions will furnish the basic material necessary for adopting a sound insurance program:

1. To what losses is the business subject?
2. What are the possible financial consequences?
3. To what extent is the amount of these predictable from year to year?
4. To what extent and at what net cost may they be prevented?
5. To what extent, under what forms, and at what cost are they insurable?

In testing a program already in effect the insured should, after satisfying himself of the answers to these questions, further ask exactly what would happen if any loss should occur. Has he too much insurance there, too little here? Has he covered unimportant perils, and left important ones uncovered? Surveys which have been made of the insurance of presumably efficiently managed enterprises have shown glaring inconsistencies, lack of essential coverage, presence of non-essential coverage, and general failure to apply to insurance the same careful thought given to other business problems.

Having determined the coverage needed, the insured should see to it that it is adapted to his particular situation by the use of proper clauses, and that overlapping covers, which may give rise to arguments in the settlement of a loss, are avoided.

Determination of covers and the extent to which they are to be purchased is one of the two major problems of the insured. The other is the choice of insurers.

In choosing insurers, consider records rather than theoretical possibilities. This principle is to be applied in a broad way. It does not mean that an individual insurer, to be approved, must have a long record of successful operations. A new insurer may be manned by executives of recognized ability and be of a class which has a good record. The mere fact of its recent formation is not a sufficient reason for rejecting it. But a record of successful operation and liberal treatment of insureds is always a favorable point. Just as the insurance underwriter considers not primarily what *might* happen, but rather what, in the light of the past, will probably happen, so the insured should consider, not so much the technicalities of organization or method, as the probable results of choosing a given insurer or class of insurer as indicated by past performance. The gasoline engine has been called a mechanical monstrosity, but it works. The insured can safely be guided by results achieved by given organizations and types of organization, disregarding the technical talking points of competitive enthusiasts. Similar principles apply to the choice of agents or brokers. Here there is the additional problem of determining, in certain cases, the relative value of their services and of the savings to be made by dealing direct with the insurer.

As in the case of contracts, the insured should consider adaptability to his problem. He will find specialists among insurers and their representatives; let him select those best adapted to help him, to advise him in matters of prevention and coverage, and to settle promptly and equitably losses which may occur in *his* business.

In conclusion, let it be reiterated that the insured should devote the careful thought to an insurance program which he devotes to other important questions of policy. He should buy insurance as a financial tool to be used in avoiding the consequences of losses, and in order to prepare specifications for the tool, he should make sure exactly what those consequences may be and consider how the tool will operate if the losses occur.

29. Deductible Average*

Provision in an insurance policy contract that the insurer shall pay only losses in excess of a specified amount, which the insured himself must bear, is an application of the principle of deductible average.[1] The amount to be deducted may be expressed as a percentage of the value of the property insured, as a definite sum of money, or in various other ways. A more, generous clause embodying the same idea is that which provides that the insurer will pay in full losses which equal or exceed the specified amount. Whatever form the clause may take, if properly applied it will serve one or more of several purposes which this paper will attempt briefly to explain and to illustrate.

It is a sound principle that an insurer should not be called upon to pay losses which, in the individual case, are normal or inevitable. It is the function of insurance to provide for losses which, while they may be normal in the aggregate, are from the point of view of the insured, fortuitous. That owners of certain large risks may be well advised in insuring where their own loss experience may be expected to be relatively stable constitutes no exception to the rule. In such instances the insurer is selling service rather than insurance. The application of this principle is illustrated in credit insurance practice where the normal losses of a merchant due to bad bills are borne by him, the credit insurance company paying only losses in excess of normal. Another example is the common practice of marine insurance companies in providing for deductible average of the normal leakage of one per cent on shipments of lubricating oil in barrels.

It has been said that "over-insurance leads to fraud, full insurance to carelessness, and even partial insurance to some diminution of watchfulness."[2] Over-insurance should carefully be avoided and in some cases full insurance should likewise be denied on grounds of general policy. Such cases are found where the occurrence of loss depends in considerable measure on the care exercised by the insured. By providing for a certain

* From *The Insurance Age*, April–May, 1921. Used by permission.

[1] "Average" means "loss." The term comes from marine insurance, where the principle has its widest application. (1964)

[2] Willett, Allan H., *The Economic Theory of Risk and Insurance* (New York: Columbia University Press, 1901), p. 114.

deduction from all claims the insured is notified that he is responsible for minor losses although he is not denied protection against serious losses. Perhaps the best example of this application of deductible average is found in automobile collision insurance where policies are regularly sold providing for fifty- or one-hundred-dollar deductions at considerable concessions in rate. The difference in rate between full coverage and one-hundred-dollar deductible coverage is, in many cases, over two hundred dollars. While the avoidance of normal loss is to some degree the reason for introducing the deductible idea into this form of insurance the predominant purpose is to reduce the moral hazard and promote care on the part of the insured both in connection with his own driving and with the driving of others who may use his car. So far has the necessity of restriction of this sort become evident that many authorities oppose the granting of full-coverage collision insurance, and several companies refuse to write it.

It may fairly be said that it is uneconomic for an insurer regularly to pay losses where the cost of settlement of the loss exceeds or approaches its amount. This statement does not apply to third-party risks where a large element of the protection purchased by the insured is represented by the expenses incident to the settlement of claims. It applies rather to those lines of insurance where the losses of the property or earning power of the insured are covered. Workmen's compensation presents an excellent illustration of this idea. Here there is necessarily a considerable administrative procedure with which compliance is necessary on the part of the employer, the employee, and the insurer whenever a claim is made. By providing in the compensation law, which is a part of the insurance contract, that injuries giving rise to disability of less than a specified number of days are not compensable, a multitude of small claims is avoided. To bring all disability within the terms of the law would give rise to extra expense entirely disproportionate to the increase in benefits payable.

Another purpose served by requiring that an appreciable loss occur before payment is made by the insurer is that of preventing a considerable amount of petty fraud. It may be assumed that after a week's time has elapsed in a disability case evidence of disability or of normal condition will be quite well marked. And there are likely to be fewer attempts to simulate disability where there is no payment for a certain period. Partly for this reason the casualty insurers in their group-disability policies have adopted the idea of a brief waiting period before disability indemnity accrues.

Although perhaps not widely appreciated, policy provisions embodying the deductible-average idea may be of great service to insureds. The extent to which such provisions relieve the insurer of loss and expense should be and usually is reflected in the rate charged for varying forms of coverage. The insured with limited funds who must consider carefully his insurance costs is particularly interested in insuring against serious losses—it may in fact be more economical for him to carry himself the risk of minor losses. For example, it is generally more important for an individual to be protected without time limit against disability of more than one month than to carry protection against disability from its inception with a limit to the period for which indemnity may be received. If complete protection seems too costly, a disability contract with a waiting period of a month (or even longer) may be indicated. It may be advisable to choose this form in order to secure a weekly indemnity more nearly adequate than could be purchased under unlimited coverage. Or, as in automobile insurance, the difference between the premium for full-coverage collision insurance and for deductible coverage may be applied to raising the limits under a liability policy where there is always a possibility of very heavy loss.

It is probable that the use of this principle could be extended considerably with advantage to all parties concerned. Its extension demands more thinking on the part both of agents and of insureds than they are inclined to give, and courage on the part of insurers. There is a definite attraction in the contract that covers all losses in full and there is difficulty in convincing the insured that limitations on coverage are not devices purely for the advantage of the insurer. The "frills" which have become an almost standardized part of certain insurance contracts offer evidence of the lack of common sense with which much insurance is bought.

To insure adequately against even a majority of the risks to which one is subject is, in the usual case, financially impossible. By a judicious application of the deductible-average idea much more adequate protection might be made available. And further, the proportion of premium devoted to the payment of indemnity should show an increase and that devoted to expenses of adjustment a decrease, two developments which would contribute appreciably to emphasizing the underlying function of the business.

30. Description of Property in the Fire Insurance Contract*

The form of basic fire-insurance contracts and of the principal endorsements is standardized by law or practice in all states; interpretations by adjusters and courts have standardized their meaning. There are variations between states, more in meaning than in form, but in only a few cases are they important. The description of property in terms of its nature, location, and use is, however, still open to wide variations dependent on the skill and care of the local representative writing the policy.

Properly to describe property, careful inquiry must be made and the results of the inquiry set down in exact English. Failure to comply with these essentials leads in many cases to controversy and to failure of the contract to cover the property that the insured desired to cover. On a large share of contracts in force no claims are made, and errors or inadequacies of description are not discovered; as to many on which claims are made the parties may agree without legal action on the intended coverage even though it is not clearly stated.

The insured whose claim is denied on the ground that the property to which loss or damage has occurred is not that described in the policy may sue in a court of equity for *reformation* of the contract, or he may argue that the misdescription is the error of the insurer and that, therefore, the latter is estopped from setting it up as a defense against a claim.[1]

If the insured is to succeed in a suit for reformation, he must show that both he and the insurer intended to cover property subject to a description different from that embodied in the policy, and that the writing of the incorrect description and the acceptance of the policy so written were a mutual mistake. In most jurisdictions, the fact that the insured has not read his policy will not defeat his claim, since it is customary for such documents to be accepted and held

* From *Journal of American Insurance*, September, 1938. Used by permission.
[1] See Patterson, E. W., *Essentials of Insurance Law* (New York: McGraw-Hill Book Co., 1935), pp. 424 ff.; and *Vance on Insurance* (2d ed.; St. Paul: West Publishing Co., 1930), pp. 214 ff.

without reading.[2] If the court decides that there has been a mutual mistake it will order the contract reformed to express the true intention of the parties. If the insured shows that he correctly described his property to the representative of the insurer, who wrote an inadequate description into the policy, the insurer will be estopped from taking advantage of its own act to deny coverage. Here, also the insured is under no duty in most jurisdictions to examine the policy to determine whether its terms correspond to his understanding.

While the insured has these remedies in court he is subject to the practical necessity of presenting his evidence and arguments, and of proving his point. Even if his contention is true, he may not be able to bring satisfactory evidence to support it, and, in any event, he will be subject to delays and expense. From the insurer's point of view, it is desirable to avoid controversies, to know exactly what property is insured, and to charge a proper rate. The fact that the insured may be able to cure a misdescription by negotiation or court action, or that the insurer may defeat a claim by showing that the insured's loss was on property not described in the policy, should not make either less careful in seeing to it that the policy carries an accurate, complete description. At all times, both parties should have in mind the possibility of loss, and should so frame the description that it will be quite clear to them whether the property is covered.

Frequently the question arising in cases on description of property is the meaning of the description as written. Here there is no question of rewording the contract or of denying the insurer a defense based on its terms, but rather of determining what those terms mean.

If there is ambiguity in the description of the property insured, it will be construed liberally in favor of the insured. The question of ambiguity is for the jury to decide, remembering that in case of doubt the purpose of the contract is to provide full indemnity for the insured.

Courts are likely to be considerably more liberal in construing the description of the property than in construing printed portions of the contract. Such descriptions are usually prepared by the insurer's representative. The description will be held to apply to whatever property the parties clearly intended to insure, but the courts will not go beyond a reasonable construction of the words actually used. As Vance puts it, "The written description in the contract can be explained but not ignored."

The description of the property insured "covers not only what is specifically mentioned, but also whatever is reasonably appurtenant to it or

[2] The legal principles set forth in this article are those generally accepted; for the law in a specific jurisdiction, legal authorities should be consulted.

included in it."[3] The description of a building covers whatever would pass with the building under a deed conveying the property to another. For example, a furnace and boiler have been held to be parts of an insured house; an annex to a building has been held covered by a contract on the building. The expression "steam saw mill" has been held to include the saw machinery contained in the mill. "But the plain import of the language employed must not be disregarded."[4] The expression, "decorations to the walls and ceilings," does not include painting on outside walls. The expression "machinery used" does not include machinery kept for sale. A building "occupied as a tannery" does not include the engine and machinery within the building.

"A general understanding in the trade or a well established custom may be shown to clarify the meaning of words or terms of technical, indefinite, or doubtful import."[5] For example, evidence has been admitted to show that a policy covering a junk dealer's stock of rags and old metals covers also other material commonly held by junk dealers. In another case a stock of drugs and chemicals was held to include benzine, although the keeping of benzine was prohibited by the terms of the policy. The stock in trade of a furniture dealer has been held to cover also paints and varnish. The provision in the New York Standard Policy (lines 46–47), "any usage or custom to the contrary notwithstanding," (not in the 1943 contract [1964]) only imposes a greater burden of proof upon the insured to show that the description of property covers the material mentioned.

Additions, alterations, and repairs are frequently covered under fire-insurance contracts. The question sometimes arises as to what constitutes an addition to a building. Where the policy is on a single building any other buildings will be covered as additions if they are connected physically with the main building. In some cases buildings have been considered additions to the principal building where they have been connected in use, although they were physically separate. Where there is only one other building answering to the description of an addition, there would be little doubt that that building would be covered. In the case of a blanket policy on a group of buildings additions would mean any addition to the plant, even though the buildings were physically distinct.

Where a policy is written on stock, a fluctuating stock is covered. It is not necessary that the amount on hand at the time of loss be the same as that on hand at the time the policy was written.

The place where the insured property is located is ordinarily material to

[3] *Richards on Insurance* (3d ed.; New York: Banks Law Publishing Co., 1911), p. 288.
[4] *Ibid.*, p. 288 n.
[5] *Ibid.*, p. 289.

the contract because the rate may change with location and because insurers are accustomed to limit the amount of insurance which they will carry in any one general location. If the property is described as "located and contained" in some particular place, and the nature of the property is such that it would ordinarily be used in other places from time to time, it will be covered during the course of its customary use. The words "and not elsewhere" were added for the purpose of limiting definitely the location to the place described in the policy, even though the customary use of the property might take it elsewhere.

If the description of the property states merely that it is "located and contained" in a certain place the courts will ordinarily inquire whether its coverage in another location is material to the risk involved and whether the property described is such that the insurer should have expected it to be elsewhere in its ordinary use during the currency of the policy. If the property is of a type the use of which does not necessarily involve its being in other locations from time to time, the courts will not consider it as covered in locations other than those mentioned in the policy. Whether customarily used elsewhere or not, the words "and not elsewhere" may be taken in most cases definitely to limit the coverage of the property to the location specifically stated in the policy, although provision is made for the coverage of the property "pro rata for five days at each proper place to which any of the property shall necessarily be removed for protection from fire." This provision, which was formerly contained in the body of the policy in a more involved statement, makes definite a right resting on general principles of common law.

Definite rather than indefinite terms should be employed. Rather than describe a building merely as a "house," it should be described as a "two-story frame building with a tin roof." Its use should be specified: "as a dwelling," "as a grocery store." If the use is to be restricted to that described: "only while occupied as a dwelling." The more clear-cut a description is, the less question there can be concerning its meaning; "boot and shoe store" is better than "mercantile building," "furniture factory," than "wood-working plant." Exact street addresses should be given where possible, "25 Main Street," rather than "on Main Street"; in the country, property may be located by reference to known land marks as "on the westerly side of the road from Plympton Green to North Carver, on the south side of Colchester Pond."

Discussion of the interpretation by the courts of descriptions of insured property is instructive, and it is well for the student of fire insurance to be familiar with the legal principles applying thereto. But the chief lesson to be learned is not what the courts will say in case of ambiguity; it is that in

writing a description of the property the representative of the insurer or
of the insured should make every effort to eliminate ambiguity. The
description should clearly state the exact property to be insured in such a
way that neither insurer nor insured will have reason for conflict of
opinion. Where several properties are insured under one contract, merely
as a matter of convenience, the description of each should be clear, and
the amount of insurance and the amount of premium applicable to each
should be stated.

31. The Insurance Buyer Looks Ahead, Personal Insurance*

Since about 1930 financial security has been a matter of deep interest and the illusive and elusive goal of a high proportion of the population. A variety of instrumentalities and methods, old and new, cater to the urge for such security. Real and personal property, savings institutions, securities of private and governmental bodies, job tenure, social insurance, and private insurance—all are means to this end. Here we are concerned with programs for the purchase of insurance for personal security, insurance that has to do with chances of death, survival, and disability.

First of all, it should be clear that security is not absolute; it is relative and hopeful. One makes plans for security and intends to carry them out. On the adequacy of the plans and on the ability, whether of will or resources, to carry them out depends their fruition. And the plans, no matter how carefully laid in the light of the circumstances at the time, may be defeated by unpredictable future events.

As I proceeded with my attempt to work out some helpful comment on the buyer's problem, I became increasingly aware of two things: the greatly heightened uncertainty in every direction, and the multiplicity of considerations that may well influence any one's thinking on insurance.

Insurance is a means of concentrating financial resources where they are needed. In its highest development it represents the most economical method of meeting needs that, in the mass, are predictable, but in the particular case a matter of chance. A productive individual may be disabled and his productivity cut off in whole or in part, resulting in various needs: care and maintenance for himself, maintenance for his family, and possibly temporary bridging of the gap for his business. Death may have similar results except for care and maintenance of the individual himself. Superannuation and unemployment result in maintenance needs.

Ideally, insurance would step in and just fill the gap in resources—actually it has and will have many limitations. To the extent that it more

* Address before the First Annual University of Nebraska Insurance Institute, Lincoln, November 17, 1950.

177

than fills the gap, it is a luxury, and like the luxury of accumulating a fortune, one that is rarely practicable. Its economy, when intelligently used, comes from its adaptability to its purpose, from its ability to hold itself in reserve until a need arises and then, if the potential need has been carefully assessed, to meet it with reasonable exactness.

Perhaps another function of insurance should be mentioned. In the case of large corporations, large enough to realize within their own organizations the averages that make insurance a practicable enterprise, the insurer may serve principally as a specialist in settling claims and as an independent administrator of funds. Corporation executives may prefer to devote their full attention to their primary business and to turn over to an outside agency the settlement of employees' claims. Employees may be better served and better satisfied if the security of their benefits is independent of the fortunes of their employer.

Consideration of one's insurance problems cannot properly be divorced from that of other means of security—a program of insurance should be made to take its place in the whole security picture. But certain questions that face the buyer of insurance are of peculiar importance in that field. Assuming one's various needs for insurance benefits in case of death, survival, or disability have been accurately determined, to what general considerations should one give attention in order to develop a program that may be expected to meet these needs or at least to work in that direction?

There are two outstanding threats to any insurance program, in addition to the always present one of inadequacy of the basic financial resources necessary to pay for it. They are inflation and taxes. Both operate at both ends of the program; on the ability of the buyer to finance the program, and on the adequacy of the benefits to their purposes. Taxes reduce income. Inflation lowers the efficacy of income. Of course, some incomes may increase with inflation, but too often tardily and to a less degree.

While only a rough indication of the usefulness of the dollar in purchasing the necessities of life, the Wholesale Price Index of the Bureau of Labor Statistics is a pretty good example of fluctuations in buying power. With the level of prices in 1926 represented by 100, there was, during the nineteenth century, a variation in level from 47 in 1896 to 155 in 1814. During the twentieth century to date, the lowest level was 55 in 1901, and the highest, before 1948, 154 in 1920. Since 1940, the level has been steadily climbing, until, on October 3, 1950, it reached 169.

Many persons, intensely conscious of rising prices, are asking whether the purchase of life insurance or annuities should be undertaken or continued. This much is certain, that failure to buy or continue insurance will mean that there will be *no* protection from that source. While the value of insurance or annuity benefits may be reduced by high prices or taxes, at least one can look forward with reasonable certainty to their having *some* value.

And it should not be forgotten that earlier periods of high prices have been followed by lower prices. The index number for 1865 is 132, after which there was a decline to 59 in 1879; after that year the highest figure for the remainder of the century is 66 for 1882, and the variation from high to low only 19. The level of 154 in 1920 was followed by 65 in 1932. This is not to say that these changes will be repeated; the figures are cited only to illustrate further the uncertainty of price levels.

What the situation will be when any particular person's insurance becomes payable is in the hands of the Gods, assisted by Congress, the Politburo, and the United Nations.

It seems to me that there is only one sound hedge (and that is not absolute) against future variations in the value of the dollar, the purchase of *things* that will be useful for an indefinite period. But that hedge can cover only a part of one's needs; it does not buy butter nor pay taxes or doctors' bills.

All provision for future income is speculative, especially in terms of commodities or services. And note that, even were the purchasing power of the dollar stable over the years, there would be changes in our concept of necessities; we now demand much more in commodities and services than did our grandparents.

A cynical interpretation of all this might lead to the conclusion that provision for the future, particularly provision of fixed income, secure in amount only, is in vain. To me it means only that a buyer should make a greater effort to provide such income and give special attention to the programming of his insurance to meet his needs as precisely as possible, looking forward to revision of his plans as conditions change. There is no place for piling up amounts of insurance as resources permit, without regard to the applicability of those amounts and the method of their disbursement. Each facet of the program should be considered and reconsidered so that the premium paid will work most efficiently to achieve ends that represent the deliberate purposes of the buyer.

And the sort of thinking that leads to believing or disbelieving in types of insurance—term, ordinary life, endowment, or what not—should be exposed for what it is, the easy acceptance of doctrine by persons too ill-informed or too lazy to think. Insurance is a financial tool for accomplishing certain objectives unattainable or less well achieved otherwise; decisions as to its use should be based on practical thinking in the light of full knowledge. There is no more reason for believing or disbelieving in term insurance as contrasted with whole-life than in believing or disbelieving in a small hammer as contrasted with a large one. Each has its uses.

All of which leads to my conviction that insurance will best serve its purpose when the buyer learns to think about insurance problems. This does not mean that there needs to be widespread technical knowledge of insurance, but rather an appreciation of its purposes, an ability to formulate what the buyer needs in the field of meeting risk, a clear-headed demand for insurance that will meet his needs.

These thoughts apply to the corporate buyer of group insurance, whether life, annuity, or disability, quite as much as to the individual buying for himself. He is buying for groups of individuals who have their individual problems. Development in these fields has been hampered by the persistence of old ideas of achieving immediate competitive ends that have obscured the broad ultimate purposes of such insurance. Provision of adequate group insurance is one way of demonstrating the ability of business and other institutions to provide for the needs of their workers. Up to a point it was useful in competing for employees, but that point has long since been passed. The pension plan that provides pensions only for employees who reach the age of retirement in the employer's service is outmoded. The ideal should be a plan that provides pensions in proportion to service rendered and that does not give opportunity for defeating its ends by withdrawal rights and forfeitures. At least one employer has recognized in some degree its obligation to supplement the inadequate pensions of employees already retired.

Social-insurance schemes of various sorts have been enacted, here and abroad, covering principally superannuation, disability, medical and surgical care, and unemployment. With all their inadequacies, cumbersomeness, and maladjustments, they are evidence of a growing recognition of the risks to which man is subject and of the broad need of meeting those risks by providing money or services for those who suffer losses.

They are evidence, too, of a conviction that private initiative has not done the job that the public wants done. No amount of advertising or application of other public-relations techniques is a substitute for doing a good job. And doing a good job in the buying or otherwise furnishing of personal insurance by institutions means, again, thinking in terms of broad rather than narrow objectives—in terms of the long rather than the short run. Above all, private institutions should consider themselves as part of the general organization of the public, permitted to administer their own affairs because they contribute to the general good. Too great delay in adopting this attitude may gradually transform them into governmental units.

Until recently employers had few avenues and methods of insurance open for choice, and only workmen's compensation was compulsory. Now there are private insurers, participating and nonparticipating; state funds, exclusive and competing federal and state social-security funds; and semi-philanthropic organizations. There is a wide variety of benefit formulas and of methods of financing the costs. And while most of the plans are voluntary, employers in general have no choice but to provide workmen's compensation, federal old-age and survivors' benefits, unemployment compensation, and, in four states, nonoccupational disability benefits. In one state,[1] automobile bodily-injury liability insurance is required. Larger employers find themselves, because of union pressure or to satisfy prospective employees' inquiries, practically obliged to provide insurance benefits beyond those required by law.

Institutional buyers as well as individual buyers are under increasing necessity of practicing careful economy—they should not indulge in the shot-gun technique of covering a wide area with their expenditures for insurance in the hope that a part of them will hit the target. And the institutional buyer, even more than the individual, must consider future ability to pay for insurance. If the individual commits himself to a program that later he is unable to carry out, his readjustments are simpler, and their repercussions may be largely confined within the narrow range of himself and his family. The devising of a program of employee benefits, sound in itself and effectively dovetailing with compulsory plans, has become an intricate matter of exhaustive planning with the aid of actuaries and other consultants. Revision of the program may be an equally complicated and time-consuming process. Further, a corporation, when it embarks on a group program (whether through insurers or otherwise), has made a policy decision that it may be fatal to reverse or to narrow. A change in its program may affect its whole scheme of industrial relations, to say nothing of the possible adverse effect on the individual worker who finds himself without benefits on which he had counted but which were beyond his control.

On an employer's statesmanship in programming the voluntary benefits supplementary to those required by law and on his acumen in making the necessary insurance arrangements may depend much of the future success of his business.

By way of summary and clarification, may I suggest that:

1. Having in mind that the purpose of insurance is to meet needs that may or may not arise, the buyer's prime function is to determine those needs.
2. Insurance should be purchased as a tool to meet the need if and when it arises; on the accuracy of its adjustment to that end depends its usefulness.

[1] Now three states. (1964)

3. Although there is no sound rule to determine what amount or what percentage of one's resources should be applied to the purchase of insurance, the buyer must consider his convenience and his available resources, present and future, in arranging to meet the cost of his program.

4. The future cannot be made secure; one can only arrange a program that seems reasonably likely to meet needs as they arise—the particular needs of the individual situation.

5. Constant supervision and revision of program with changing conditions are essential to the efficient use of insurance.

6. Insurance buyers being primarily concerned with what they desire to accomplish, they should turn to experts—insurers and their representatives, actuaries and other consultants—for aid in achieving their ends through insurance. But they should always check the advice of the experts by asking themselves, first, is insurance the best means for achieving the end in view, and second, does the particular scheme of insurance and the particular insurer best serve that end.

32. Insurance and Government*

Insurance is a business which, like banking, transportation, other public utilities, and many of the professions, has been singled out for strict governmental regulation. It is said to be "affected with a public interest."

The reasons for this special interest arise, as is usual where the government has assumed a large measure of control over otherwise private affairs, out of severely practical situations. Seldom have laws been enacted or regulations promulgated as a result of foresight; they have ordinarily had as their purpose the correction of abuses or inequities already in existence. Sometimes the remedy may have been worse than the disease, but that is not to say that the disease did not require a remedy.

The New York Standard Fire Insurance Policy originated in dissatisfaction with the difficulties of adjusting losses under the terms of the conflicting policies previously in use. The strict specifications for its format resulted from the practice of printing important provisions in small type, which were brought to the attention of the insured only to explain why his loss could not be paid. Anti-coinsurance and valued-policy laws are ill-advised attempts to strike back at insurers who were more interested in collecting premiums than in paying losses. Of late years there has been a tendency gradually to convert the liability contract from a document designed only to protect the insured and his insurer to one having in large measure the function of protecting the injured claimant, who had previously been in no sense a party in interest. Rate regulation is aimed at the abuse of rating methods as competitive weapons rather than their use as a means of measuring probabilities.

But why have these practices, which surely have their counterparts in other businesses, led to so much greater a degree of control of insurance? There are a number of characteristics peculiar to the business of insurance which seem to me to have been responsible.

In the first place, the value of an insurance contract rests primarily on the ability of the insurer to meet its obligations in the future; at the time of purchase the contract is nothing more than a promise to do so. Indeed, in certain forms of insurance, such as liability, workmen's compensation, and

* First Annual Lecture on Insurance, Fenn College, Cleveland, January 19, 1942.

183

disability, the obligation may far outrun the term of the contract. In the ordinary commercial transaction, the purchaser is relatively unconcerned with the continued existence of the seller, to say nothing of his continued ability to give service or to meet other obligations. But in making an insurance contract, the insured is acting on his confidence that the insurer will not only continue in existence but will remain able to give service and meet financial obligations, that it will be an active and solvent entity. The transaction is not completed until there no longer remains a chance that the insured may call on the insurer to fulfill its contract.

Further, the insured usually pays for these intangible values in advance, and the insurer must prepare itself financially to meet incurred losses even though payment may be deferred. Pending the termination of contracts and the payment of losses, it has large funds to invest.

Some insurance contracts are written primarily for the benefit of third parties, and others inure partly or incidentally to their benefit. These parties have no part in the making of the contracts and are in a position to enforce their rights only when they accrue. The sole purpose of requiring insurance under workmen's compensation laws is to make certain that employees will receive the benefits to which they are entitled, but the choice of the insurer and the making of the insurance contract is generally in the hands of the employer. Motorists are required to take insurance to guarantee their responsibility in case of accident to others, but the injured persons are not originally parties to the insurance contract. Their rights need protection.

Most insureds are not in a position to estimate the ability of an insurer to perform its obligations, and no insured can control its future ability to perform. Insurance is a highly technical business, and accurate judgments of the condition of insurers or of the fairness of their rates or contracts are matter for experts.

The making of premium rates is not controlled, as are the prices of commodities, by costs that have been largely incurred. The insurance rate is based on probable future costs, and there is a great temptation for rate makers to be over-optimistic when competition suggests a lower rate to secure business. Rate wars have on occasion brought insurers to the point of bankruptcy.

If there were no control of the business from without, there would be many institutions which would operate soundly and fairly, but experience shows that many would not do so, to the cost of the insuring public and their beneficiaries. In Great Britain "freedom and publicity" was for long the official policy, but in recent years measures of stricter governmental control have been adopted. In this country, with its diverse commercial standards and its varying population, such a policy would be ruinous. Evidence of the changing point of view of the British government is found in the following statement of Mr. Harvie Meikle in his recent presidential address before the Insurance and Actuarial Society of Glasgow: "In the early days they [insurers] were regarded, more or less, as trading concerns whose particular interest and ultimate aim was the provision of dividends for shareholders whereas to-day we find them more in the position of large utility companies providing the public with certain social services which, but for their existence, would presumably require to be provided by the Government."

In the United States, governmental control has long been accepted as a necessary part of the insurance fabric; but there is no general agreement on the proper extent or manner of such control. On the proper objects of control, there is, however, substantial unanimity. These objects are three—solvency, fair practices, and competent service.

And the greatest of these is solvency. The ability of an insurer to meet its obligations depends on its financial condition; its financial condition depends on sound investments, accurate estimation of liabilities, and maintenance of assets adequate to cover liabilities and unforeseen contingencies. The laws of the principal insurance states have set high, even redundant, standards of solvency, and the state insurance departments have served the public well in enforcing those standards through systems of examinations, reports, regulations, and audits. Solvency of insurers is, and should be, the primary aim of governmental regulation. The setting up of security funds, the purpose of which is to pay claims to the extent of default by insolvent insurers and which are accumulated by contributions from all insurers concerned, regardless of their financial condition, is a recognition of the importance of solvency and of the social service of insurance.

Second to solvency, but an important and growing activity of legislators and insurance commissioners, is the regulation of practices that they may be fair to the insuring public and, in some measure, between insurers. Regulation of the provisions of policy contracts, of the making and application of premium rates, of adjustment methods, of advertising, all come under this head. Even here the dominant consideration of solvency is not forgotten, for in certain cases insurers are required to charge "adequate" rates, that they may receive sufficient income to cover necessary disbursements.

The state insurance departments act as experts, police, and to a certain degree as courts on behalf of the public. The purpose of regulation of practices is to eliminate unsound, unfairly discriminatory, and dishonest methods, and to secure the highest possible *quality* of protection and service from the institution of insurance.

Competence, a relatively new object of regulation, is being actively sought in the field of agency and brokerage, and to some extent in adjusting and management. Basic standards of competence are set up in qualification laws which specify education and experience requirements and give state administrative officials considerable latitude in determining by examination and otherwise whether candidates for licenses measure up to the express and implied level. Licensing of agents and brokers has, until recently, been largely a matter of fees and forms. The new requirements, now enforced in several jurisdictions, are far from onerous, and the fact that so many applicants fail to meet them is ample evidence of the ease with which incompetents (and worse) have in the past become "insurance men."

The government might conceivably take either of two extreme attitudes toward insurance; it might leave private citizens free to work in this field with no more restraint than is found in the general criminal and civil laws applicable to all lines of business activity, or it might completely socialize the insurance function, assigning it to a governmental department. It has chosen to pursue a middle course, leaving (with some exceptions) to private enterprise the initiative in offering insurance facilities and in developing them, but hedging that initiative about with safeguards for the public.

If human beings are left free to seek their own selfish ends, an unfortunately large proportion of them will do so at the expense of the public. This is particularly true if they have at their disposal a means, like insurance, which feeds on ignorance and lends itself to the machinations of trickery because its practitioners are in a position to offer proposals beyond the powers of analysis of their clients. On the other hand, complete socialization would probably stifle the individual initiative which is so great a factor in the development of insurance and which looks to the rewards of · private enterprise for its stimulus.

In recent years there has been observed an increasing demand for security and equity enforced by authority; I believe that this development will continue, with special emphasis on insurance. In meeting it I suggest that governmental regulation of insurance should be applied in accordance with the broad general principle of allowing the widest possible field for the exercise of private initiative, stimulated by reward, but subjected to restraint and guidance to make it conform to proper standards of security and equity. Left without interpretation, such a statement of principle is of little more value than other common oratorical platitudes. I propose, therefore, to break it down into certain less general, but still broad, suggestions which, it seems to me, might well serve as basic principles to be observed in formulating a regulatory program. Although I shall put them categorically, I intend them to be taken only as suggestions and as a basis for discussion. And may I remark, parenthetically, that insurance interests, in setting up and operating their various boards and bureaus, might well ponder these suggestions, for they may apply to non-governmental as well as to governmental regulation.

Legislation should set up standards rather than attempt minutely to regulate insurance, and for two reasons. First, the ability and method of legislatures are much better suited to the determination of broad policies than to the discussion and adoption of detailed rules. An objective to be attained can be understood and intelligently debated by the widely differing individuals who make up a legislative body; it can be made the subject of compromise without destroying its essential character. Second, statute law, once enacted, is difficult to change, and broad policies retain their validity over longer periods than do the rules for applying them. Let the legislature specify ends to be achieved, but leave the formulae for achieving those ends to administrative action. For example, insurers should be required to maintain assets to offset the present value of their expected losses, but the determination of values, both of assets and losses, should be left to administrative experts.

Wherever possible, without opening an inviting path to dishonesty or incompetence, and always subject to conformity to established general principles, insurance should be left free to develop new ways of serving the public. If an insurer desires to write a new line which has not been specifically authorized by law, it must, in most states, appeal to the legislature for an enabling amendment. Doubtless, the purpose of listing the kinds of insurance that insurers may write is to prevent unsound ventures or insurance which might otherwise be inimical to the public welfare. But there is just as much room for unsoundness within the confines of presently authorized lines as in novel fields, and the general public interest would be protected by forbidding the writing of insurance that is "contrary to public policy." However, care should be taken to forestall a situation such as arose in one of the leading insurance states, where the insurance commissioner was obliged under the law to license insurance carriers formed by persons whose purpose was obviously solely their own financial gain and whose methods had no connection with service to the public.

Regulation cannot completely defeat bad or dishonest management, but much can be done to protect the public from its effects. It is here that power and freedom to act are important to an insurance department. Legislation comes after the fact, but an insurance commissioner well armed with information and authority can act quickly and effectively. His most important weapon is information, both that acquired by routine reports and by special examinations. With adequate information, by the imposition of fines, by forbidding improper practices, by giving publicity to his findings, by the cancellation or refusal of licenses, and in extreme cases, by taking over insurers for liquidation or rehabilitation, he can accomplish results that would be unattainable if it were necessary to await the movement of the legislature or of the courts. Even if he has little authority to take emergency action, he is, with knowledge of the facts, in a position to exercise considerable moral pressure.

Nor is the value of complete and accurate information confined to specific cases of improper practice or of dangerous financial condition; it is the foundation of all well considered and efficient regulation. I should place the power to secure it, and the judicious exercise of that power, in the first rank of requirements for successful regulation.

While in many cases it may be desirable to make laws mandatory, to direct an insurance commissioner to act, it is often better to give him the option of acting. At times a situation can be corrected with greater effectiveness by implied or express threat of action than by inflexible and literal application of statutory rules. What provision is to be made in a particular law is a matter of judgment, but it is always important to consider whether more can be accomplished by giving the commissioner an instrument adaptable to circumstances than by handing him a rigid rule to be applied without the tempering use of his individual knowledge and wisdom.

If it is desirable to provide for flexibility in the terms of statutes, it is even more desirable for the department itself to adopt a flexible attitude. Institutions (and insurance departments and state legislatures have some of their characteristics) tend to develop traditions and to become unduly enamored of them. When they are abetted by the abhorrence of change which possesses many insurance executives, progress is pretty effectively blocked. Fortunately, there are a number of departments, and not the least influential, where progress is welcomed and even supported, without, however, urging change for its own sake. Regulation should encourage improvements in the interest of the public and should not wait for them to be forced upon its attention nor use the familiar answer to proposals that there is "no demand." It should be recognized that the remedy of yesterday may become a barrier to progress tomorrow, that measures which once protected the public may later hamper it.

In seeking equity and security, it should be remembered that the absolute is an ideal to give direction to regulatory effort. Not only are these ends but imperfectly attainable, but too great striving toward them is a possibility. The workmen's compensation insurance manual at one time contained some 1,500 classes of risk, a number that had been reached by the gradual splitting and adding of classes in an effort to recognize variations. It became unworkable to the extent of defeating its own ends, and the number of classes has been reduced by about two-thirds. A somewhat similar situation in fire-insurance rating has demonstrated the need of consolidation and simplification, toward which steps have been taken. Sometimes it is better to acquiesce in a certain degree of inequity, when the cost of achieving equity is disproportionate or where consideration makes it clear that equity is not practicable.

All of these principles must yield place to the cardinal one that the state insurance department and its head should be competent and independent of special influences. Too few of the present departments satisfy these ideals, and regulation suffers to the extent that they do not. Fortunately, the highest-grade departments are found in states having extensive insurance interests, and their laws and administration control insurance in many vital ways far beyond their borders. Governors have been known to recognize the position of insurance commissioner as one that calls for less than the usual consideration of political motives and more than usual attention to ability and judicial temperament. The staffs of departments are in some cases under civil service, which makes for a continuing reasonably able and independent force. State regulation may be said to have been a major reason for the enviable place which insurance holds in the social fabric, but there is ample room for readjustment and positive improvement.

Insurance men have been too prone to look on regulation as an objectionable interference with their immediate comfort and profit; they can do much to bring about desirable changes if they will take a long-range view of their own best interests.

33. Revision of the New York Standard Fire Insurance Policy*

Massachusetts adopted a standard fire-insurance policy in 1873, the use of which was not made compulsory. But the movement to standardize the fire-insurance policy form in each state, either by law or custom, had its effective inception with the enactment of a law in New York in 1886 directing the Superintendent of Insurance to prepare a policy "unless on or before the fifteenth day of October the New York Board of Fire Underwriters shall make and file with the Secretary of State" a policy form. The form was prepared and filed within the prescribed time and became the "old" New York Standard Fire Insurance Policy which is still required by law or ruling in fifteen states and is generally used in twelve states where no standard form is required.

This original form, while "a liberal document, judged by the standards of the time," [1] was essentially drawn to define the liability of the insurer and to protect it, as well as to afford indemnity to the insured. The fact of standardization, however, was a tremendous improvement over the chaotic and inequitable situation which had before obtained.

This form remained in force in New York until January 1, 1918, when the "new" Standard Policy went into effect. The new policy had been adopted by the National Convention of Insurance Commissioners, and although it represented the consensus of that body, it is now required by statute or ruling in only fifteen states.[2] It was more liberal than the old form, clarified certain questions, incorporated the effect of important court interpretations, and its provisions were much better arranged, but it was no revolutionary document. It leaned pretty heavily toward protection of the insurer's interests. However, it was a real improvement, and little was heard of revision until the 1930's.

The first effective attention given to the growing sentiment for revision

---

* From *Journal of American Insurance*, April, 1943. Used by permission.
[1] Rumsey, David, "The New Standard Fire Insurance Policy of the State of New York," in *The Fire Insurance Contract* (Indianapolis: Rough Notes Co., 1922), p. 41.
[2] In some with slight variations. The Massachusetts form is required in four states; two have their own special forms.

was the report, on June 12, 1936, by the Executive Committee of the National Association of Insurance Commissioners recommending that the president of the Association appoint a special committee "to study the Standard Fire Insurance Policy form heretofore approved by the Association [December, 1916] and to report its recommendations. . . ." The report was adopted, and the Committee on the Revision of the Fire Insurance Policy[3] was appointed. Its members were Louis H. Pink, of New York, Chairman; John C. Blackall, of Connecticut; John C. Ketcham, of Michigan; Owen B. Hunt, of Pennsylvania; and W. J. Dawson, of South Dakota.

The Committee made its first report at the December, 1936, meeting of the Association. They had questioned interested opinion throughout the United States and concluded that "In general the insurers are satisfied with the present policies. Those who are not connected with insurers [including producers] have expressed considerable sentiment in favor of revision and overwhelming sentiment in favor of uniformity." There was practical unanimity in recommending to the Committee adoption of the following changes:

1. Include lightning in the coverage.
2. Eliminate the clause voiding the policy for fraud because that is the common law anyway and substitute a new clause voiding the policy for a breach of warranty which caused or increased the amount of the loss or hazard.
3. Cover the hazard of destruction by civil authority to prevent spread of fire.
4. Eliminate the unconditional ownership and chattel mortgage clause and allow recovery on the policy to the extent of the proved insurable interest.
5. Eliminate the "Fall of Building" clause.
6. Lengthen the time allowed for unoccupancy to at least an ordinary vacation period.
7. Give the insured the opportunity to force the insurer to appoint an appraiser.
8. Revise the pro rata liability clause so that the policies which are void would not be included in determining the pro rata liability of each insurer.

All but Nos. 2 and 7 of these recommendations were later embodied in the revised New York Standard Policy.

At the June, 1937, meeting of the Association the Committee reported a revised form of policy which they recommended "for study," explaining that they had "revamped the present forms of policy in order to bring them up to date and make them uniform rather than a complete rewriting." Again the Committee noted "strong sentiment among the companies" against revision, and sentiment for revision among "buyers, agents and brokers, and some progressive insurance executives."

[3] The Committee is variously designated in the *Proceedings*.

At the December, 1937, meeting the Committee reported that the commissioners of twenty-three states (including Hawaii and the District of Columbia) had replied to their request for an opinion of the tentative draft, of whom thirteen believed that a revised policy was desirable and could be adopted, four were opposed, and six doubtful. Mutual insurers were reported to believe "strongly in the simplification and modernization of the policy" and stock insurers to "have shown little interest ... due, not so much to opposition to the idea of a better policy ... but to the fact that they think ... that you couldn't get it adopted by any large number of states."

By June, 1938, twenty-six commissioners favored preparation by the Committee of a "uniform fire policy of simpler form and broader coverage"; three were opposed. Twenty believed that their states would approve such a policy if it were adopted by the Association; five did not.

In December, 1938, the Committee, to which had been added Hartley D. McNairn, Superintendent of Insurance of Ontario, recommended a definitive revision of the policy form for consideration at the June, 1939, meeting of the Association, Commissioner Blackall of Connecticut dissenting. The form was a revision of the previously approved form, the Committee being of the opinion that "the re-writing of an entirely new policy" was "impractical."

At the June, 1939, meeting of the Association, the Committee (Commissioner Blackall again dissenting) recommended adoption of the revised form of policy. Superintendent Pink presented a resolution that the proposed policy "be given the general approval of this Association" and that "the Commissioners ... take steps to have the ... policy adopted in their respective states." The resolution was adopted by a vote of 16 to 11.

While the 1939 recommendation was intended as the final report of the Committee, they held further hearings and made their last report at the June, 1940, meeting of the Association, recommending "further study" by the individual commissioners.

Apparently despairing of action elsewhere, Superintendent Pink continued to press for enactment of a revised standard policy in New York. At last, in 1942, after the elimination of any substantial opposition, the legislature adopted a revised form, to go into effect July 1, 1943.

The revised policy is simpler and more liberal than its predecessor but it represents no great change in practical conditions in the fire-insurance business. A large part of the changes had formerly been accomplished by endorsement, particularly where buyers or middlemen were well informed and efficient. Provisions which might be technically violated were often waived in adjustments as a matter of liberal treatment of insureds or because of competitive conditions. However, the revised form is a distinct step forward; it regularizes, simplifies, and makes uniform, coverage and conditions which were enjoyed by many insureds, but not by all.

Throughout there are minor changes in wording which do not change the practical effect of the contract. For example, the phrase "loss or damage" in the present contract is changed to "loss" in the revised form; the expression "(ascertained with proper deductions for depreciation)" which now follows "actual cash value" in the insuring clause is dropped; the present policy will be void by its terms (as it would be at common law) in case of material concealment or misrepresentation, or of fraud or false swearing, concerning "the insurance or the subject thereof," while the revised policy specifies *willful* concealment or misrepresentation concerning these matters and the "interest of the insured." No attempt will be made here to record all such changes; in the following paragraphs only significant amendments will be explained.[4]

The outstanding changes in the revised policy are those having to do with conditions under which the contract now becomes void or is suspended, unless endorsed to the contrary, as may freely be done. The present contract provides that:

> This entire policy shall be void, unless otherwise provided by agreement in writing added hereto,
> (a) If the interest of the insured be other than unconditional and sole ownership; or
> (b) if the subject of insurance be a building on ground not owned by the insured in fee simple; or
> (c) if, with the knowledge of the insured, foreclosure proceedings be commenced or notice given of sale of any property insured hereunder by reason of any mortgage or trust deed; or
> (d) if any change, other than by the death of an insured, take place in the interest, title or possession of the subject of insurance (except change of occupants without increase of hazard); or
> (e) if this policy be assigned before a loss.

These moral-hazard conditions are eliminated in the revised form, depriving the insurer of certain defenses and making the contract an *interest* policy; i.e., it will cover whatever interest the insured may have in the property, rather than "sole and unconditional" interest only. Instead of providing that assignment before a loss will make the policy void, it is provided that assignment "shall not be valid except with the written consent" of the insurer.

---

[4] The word "amendments" is used advisedly, since the revised policy is a revised edition of the present form.

Suspension of coverage is now provided for by the following clauses:

Unless otherwise provided by agreement in writing added hereto this
Company shall not be liable for loss or damage occurring
  (a) while the insured shall have any other contract of insurance, whether
      valid or not, on property covered in whole or in part by this policy; or
  (b) while the hazard is increased by any means within the control or
      knowledge of the insured; or
  (c) while mechanics are employed in building, altering or repairing the
      described premises beyond a period of fifteen days; or
  (d) while illuminating gas or vapor is generated on the described premises;
      or while (any usage or custom to the contrary notwithstanding) there is
      kept, used or allowed on the described premises fireworks, greek fire,
      phosphorus, explosives, benzine, gasoline, naphtha or any other
      petroleum product of greater inflammability than kerosene oil, gun-
      powder exceeding twenty-five pounds, or kerosene oil exceeding five
      barrels; or
  (e) if the subject of insurance be a manufacturing establishment while
      operated in whole or in part between the hours of ten P.M. and five
      A.M., or while it ceases to be operated beyond a period of ten days; or
  (f) while a described building, whether intended for occupancy by owner or
      tenant, is vacant or unoccupied beyond a period of ten days.

Of these conditions only (b) and (f) are retained; but "ten days" in the
latter is changed to "sixty consecutive days."

The present contract suspends insurance on any property while incum-
bered, without the consent of the insurer, by a chattel mortgage, and the
insurance on any building ceases as soon as it, or "any material part" of
it, falls. These restrictions are deleted.

Hazards not now covered which will be covered under the revised form
are lightning and "acts of destruction [by order of a civil authority] at the
time of and for the purpose of preventing the spread of fire, provided the
fire did not originate from any of the perils ... specifically excluded."
The insurer is not now liable for loss

caused directly or indirectly by invasion, insurrection, riot, civil war or
commotion, or military or usurped power, or by order of any civil authority;
or by theft; or by neglect of the insured to use all reasonable means to save
and preserve the property at and after a fire or when the property is endangered
by fire in neighboring premises.

These exclusions are continued, except that "riot, civil war or commotion"
are replaced by "bombardment, rebellion, [and] revolution."[5] The

[5] Superintendent Pink, of New York, in his Preliminary Report for 1942, suggests the
following war clause for inclusion in the Standard Policy: "This company shall not be liable

exclusion of loss "by explosion or lightning" now reads "by explosion or riot," loss by ensuing fire still being covered.

The present policy excludes from coverage in any event "accounts, bills, currency, deeds, evidences of debt, money, notes or securities"; the revised policy continues these exclusions with the exception of notes. "Bullion, manuscripts, mechanical drawings, dies or patterns" are not now covered unless specifically named; this list has been reduced to "bullion or manuscripts."

Other amendments of less significance are the following: invalid insurance is no longer to be included in the amounts on the basis of which pro rata liability is determined; provision is made for the prohibition or limitation of other insurance by endorsement; the actual cash value of the property must be stated in the original inventory to be filed by the insured in case of loss; the proof of loss on a building must state "whether or not it then [at the time of loss] stood on leased ground"; appraisal may be demanded in case of disagreement as to actual cash value, and appraisers are to state the "actual cash value" in their award instead of the "sound value"; each party, insurer and insured, shall notify the other of the appraiser selected within twenty days of demand for his appointment; the policy is not valid unless countersigned by the duly authorized agent of the insurer.

The revised contract may mean that underwriters will rely more on selection of risks, and less on the protection of defenses against claims. "Whatever disadvantages arise under the new statute in the necessity of more diligent investigation by the insurer would seem to be outweighed by the advantage in protection of innocent policyholders from avoidance of their insurance on the ground of numerous technical defenses."[6] Perhaps equal advantages are reduction of detail work in planning coverage and writing policies, elimination of disputes on many points, and easier comprehension of what the fire-insurance contract really means.[7]

---

for loss or damage which may result from enemy attack, including any action taken by the military, naval or air forces of the United States in resisting enemy attack" to take up coverage where the War-Damage Corporation contract ceases to cover. Objection has been raised that such a provision would not be suited to conditions after the war and that it is not known what construction the courts will place on the war-damage contract.

6 *Columbia Law Review*, XLII, 1233.

7 The 1943 form with little or no modification is now used in all but three states. In Massachusetts, Minnesota, and Texas, the standard forms are based on, and are similar to, the New York form. (1964)

34. A Proposal for State Regulation of Rates*

The purpose of state regulation of rates is primarily protection of the insured and incidentally of the insurer through applying the criteria of adequacy, reasonableness, and nondiscrimination. The various states have shown particular concern in connection with rates for workmen's compensation, accident and health, and automobile insurance. In most states workmen's-compensation rates must be approved and accident-and-health rates must be filed, and in several states automobile rates must be either filed or approved. The great majority of the compensation states permitting private insurance of the compensation risk have laws ranging from a mere filing of rates to provisions for filing and approval. In Massachusetts, bodily-injury rates for automobile insurance, and in Texas, workmen's-compensation rates, are made by the state. In New York and in Vermont there are rating laws which undertake to apply regulation to all rates with certain defined exceptions.

It is evident that state activity in the regulation of rates is increasing. It is not the purpose here to discuss its wisdom but, assuming that rates for a particular branch of insurance are to be regulated, to inquire what method of regulation is most likely to achieve the ideal implicit in the criteria.

Without disparagement, it may be pointed out that insurance commissioners are human, that they are not unconnected with political and other local situations, and that only a minority have adequate technical training or competent advisers.

It seems clear that the greater the extent to which insurance departments are made responsible for the approval or promulgation of rates, the more likely the rates are to be inadequate. The experience with rates for automobile bodily-injury liability insurance in Massachusetts is in point—the members of this Society are familiar with it. And this situation does not result from a desire to make or approve inadequate rates, but probably rather from a feeling that the department must be in a position to defend

* From the *Proceedings* of the Casualty Actuarial Society, XXII, 339–341.

the rates to the insuring public (and their highly vocal political representatives). Consequently, conjectural or projection factors are ruled out—and little or no provision can be made for expected developments which are not to be repetitions of the past. Similarly, in matters of reasonableness or discrimination, if the department sponsors a set of rates, it lays *itself* as well as the rates open to attack.

It is only natural that a department should show more hospitality to downward than upward revisions of rates and that it should feel that it must have definite evidence of insurance costs to justify its actions.

A formula should be sought which would give a department the basis and power for effective regulation and, at the same time, put it and all interested parties in a position where correct rates are most likely to emerge from the combined private and public rate-making machinery.

The only dogmatic statement which I propose to make is that the problem is worthy of consideration. Beyond that, I propose only to advance certain tentative conclusions to serve as a basis for discussion. They will be stated categorically for the sake of simplicity.

1. A sound uniform statistical plan applicable to all insurers is the *sine qua non* of correct rates. It should be revealing in terms of the purpose for which it is designed. Such a plan should be submitted to and approved by the State.[1]

2. Rates should be made by rating bureaus representing all insurers. Deviations for individual insurers or groups of insurers should be permitted where clear justification could be shown.

3. The states should be represented by an observer in, or have access to records of, every step of the rate-making process.

4. Complete reports of experience and of the deliberations of rate-making bodies should be filed with the State, to the extent that they bear on matters of general policy.

5. Rates filed should become the official rates one month (or other reasonable period) after the filing by the bureau. They should then remain in force for a reasonable period (perhaps one year), without further revision, except possibly in the case of individual risks or classifications.

6. For a reasonable but definitely limited period after the filing of rates, they should be subject to revision by order of the state insurance department or of a board of appeals of which the insurance commissioner would be one member.

(a) Appeals to the courts should be only on questions of law.

---

1 The term "State" is here used in a general functional sense, equally applicable to individual states of the Union, or to the federal government.

7. Revision should only be made on the initiative of the insurance department, or on complaint of a party in interest, and after due hearing.

8. There should be no general public hearing on any rate filing.

9. The authority ordering revision of rates should be required to file a detailed statement of the reasons for the revision.

35. Insurance Terminology*

During recent years, persons interested in insurance have become acutely aware of problems of communication, largely raised by the hit-or-miss development of insurance terminology.

Accurate use and understanding of insurance terms are essential to sound relations among insurers, insureds, governments represented by specialized regulatory and judicial personnel, and the general public. Yet insurance terminology has followed paths of self-interest, tradition, and chance. In the United States, the situation has been particularly exasperating, since insurance has here developed along largely independent lines. The four broad classes have been fire, marine, life, and casualty. Each class has included various allied and subordinate classes, often having little or no logical relation to the principal class.

As a result, understanding among insurance men specializing in a particular class of business has been hampered, communication between specialists in different classes has been difficult, and insureds and students broadly interested in insurance have found terms thoroughly confusing.

The present writer had noted these difficulties in the course of his life-long study of insurance. They came forcibly to his attention in connection with the preparation of a brief dictionary for the Chamber of Commerce of the United States.[1] Many terms required two or more definitions, often quite unrelated.

The problem first was called formally and forcefully to the attention of the insurance world in a note in *The Journal of Insurance*, by Dr. Davis W. Gregg.[2] In that note he proposed that the American Association of University Teachers of Insurance create a committee to study insurance language and to improve it. He wrote as follows:

* From *Studi sulle Assicurazioni* (Roma: Instituto Nazionale delle Assicurazioni, 1963), pp. 477–484. Used by permission.

[1] *Dictionary of Insurance Terms* (Insurance Department, Chamber of Commerce of the United States, Washington, 1949).

[2] "A Note on Insurance Terminology," *The Journal of Insurance*, November, 1958, pp. 62–64. Dr. Gregg (President, American College of Life Underwriters, and Past President, American Association of University Teachers of Insurance) has been, and is, the principal individual critic of the terminological situation and has done most to encourage study and correction of it.

Risk and Insurance

The American Association of University Teachers of Insurance would seem to be the ideal organization to initiate a continuing study of insurance language for many reasons. In the first place, the Association, by definition, is interested in all lines of insurance. Secondly, as an organization, it can invite all segments of the insurance industry to participate without prejudice to individual interests. Thirdly, the members of the Association are those who are creating insurance literature, especially for educational use; and thus it is they who can have the greatest ultimate impact on insurance language. Finally, in a venture of scientific and scholarly nature such as this, it is logical that the Association should take the leadership.

The research will be effective only if the Committee on Insurance Terminology is truly a joint project between the Association and the various segments of the insurance industry.

The American Association of University Teachers of Insurance was formed in 1932 by a small number of teachers of insurance in American colleges and universities. It holds annual meetings, publishes its proceedings, and has interested itself in insurance studies over the years. Its membership and its activities have gradually grown until it is now recognized as the official organization of a considerable body of insurance scholars and teachers. It enjoys the respect, cooperation, and support of the insurance business and has maintained its independent standing in dealing with insurance questions. In 1961 its name was changed to American Risk and Insurance Association, but without change in its control by the academic membership.[3]

At the annual meeting of the Association in 1958 it was decided to undertake a program in insurance terminology along the lines originally proposed by Dr. Gregg. To implement the program the Commission on Insurance Terminology was appointed for the year 1959. It consisted of thirteen members, drawn from universities, insurers, and insurer organizations. Dr. Gregg was named chairman. To this commission was confided the general development and oversight of the program.

The commission announced its formation in the following terms:

> The Commission on Insurance Terminology was established in 1958 by the American Association of University Teachers of Insurance for the purpose of introducing, in an evolutionary way, greater clarity and exactness in insurance terminology. The specific objectives of the Commission are:
>
> 1. To engage in a continuing study of insurance language (words and phrases) for the purpose of evaluating the effectiveness of the language and recommending improvements where desirable.
> 2. To accumulate and publish a glossary of insurance words and phrases

[3] In the remainder of this paper each of these associations will be referred to as "the Association."

on which there is general agreement among practitioners and educators as to their meaning.

3. To develop a continuing program of information by which writers, editors, insurers, and others will have available more accurate and meaningful insurance terminology, and, through the art of gentle persuasion and assistance to those who make the insurance language, gradually bring some order out of the present chaos.

4. To cooperate with any other groups or individuals seeking to attain improvement in insurance terminology.

In order to study the terminology problem in detail and to make recommendations to the commission on matters of policy, usage, and definitions, the commission decided to appoint operating committees, each to be assigned to an appropriate sector of insurance, and to be conducted by a chairman and editor.[4]

In accordance with this plan six committees have been appointed to consider the following subjects: General Insurance, Health Insurance, Life Insurance, Pensions and Profit Sharing, Property and Liability Insurance, and Social Insurance. A coordinating group, the Committee of Editors, composed of the editors of the various committees, has been set up to make recommendations to the commission on matters that concern two or more of the operating committees and on questions of jurisdiction and form. All committees are now fully constituted and in operation. Each expects to hold two meetings per year and to deal with some questions by correspondence. The chairman of the commission and the editor of the Journal are ex officio members of all committees.

A fundamental question that has faced the commission and all committees is that of the criteria by which insurance terms should be judged. This question was first considered by the Committee on General Insurance Terminology which adopted the following criteria with the subjoined explanatory notes:

Understandability

It is desirable that a term be readily understood by anyone in interest. That perfect clarity and common understanding can always be achieved is not to be expected, but they are to be sought. Other criteria to be applied will have understandability in large part as their purpose. Accuracy of statement is perhaps the principal contribution to meeting this criterion.

Single meaning

A word having only one meaning is to be preferred to one having two or more meanings, whether in insurance alone or in more general application.

---

[4] Who might be the same person or different persons.

Functional quality

A word that clearly implies or states the function of the thing that it symbolizes is better than one that requires interpretation.

Probable breadth of acceptance

The more broadly a word will be accepted and used, the better.

Simplicity

A one-syllable word is to be preferred to a polysyllable, and a single word to a phrase.

Workability

The criterion of workability perhaps calls for satisfaction of the others, all of which are directed at practical application of words.

These criteria represent an attempt to keep in mind the interests of insurers, insureds (both the public in general and those with special interest in insurance), and public officials. No one criterion stands by itself; they are overlapping and, at times, contradictory.

These criteria were later adopted by the editors and recommended for adoption by the commission.

Each of the specializing committees has concerned itself with determination of its field of endeavor and definition of terms. The work of the Committee on Health Insurance Terminology will serve as an example.

In the United States, insurance against the consequences of disability, taken in the broad sense of any departure from normal health, is undertaken by three principal classes of insurer; life, casualty, and the specialist in this sort of insurance. The first class, life, writes it through a division of the insurer, but does not ordinarily write other forms. The second, casualty, also writes this insurance through a division, but usually writes many other forms, such as liability, workmen's compensation, burglary and theft, and miscellaneous less important forms. These insurers and the specialists offer such benefits as payment of periodic amounts in case of impaired earning capacity, hospital, physicians' or surgeons' care (either by furnishing service or reimbursing its cost), payment of fixed sums in case of designated injuries, or a variety of others.

In the past the emphasis of this insurance, known as *accident and health insurance*, has been on accidental traumatic bodily injuries, some insurers covering the consequences of such injuries only. However, contracts are written, often in combination with those covering traumatic injuries, to cover illness or disease of nontraumatic origin. Three principal reasons appear to be responsible for the relatively large volume of accident insurance and the small volume of sickness insurance; the conviction of the buying public that accidents constitute a greater danger, the lower cost of accident insurance, and the greater accuracy and ease with which losses can be adjusted.

The Committee on Health Insurance Terminology first sought a generic term to adopt and recommend as applicable to this entire field, a problem whose solution was forecast by the title given to the committee. It was early recognized that the traditional terms, "accident and health" and "accident and sickness," lacked merit. The business was becoming more and more concerned, not with particular causes of disability, but with the resulting fact of disability or departure from normal health. The choice narrowed down to *health* or *disability insurance* as a generic term to mean insurance against any consequences of impairment of physical (including mental) condition. The term "health insurance" was finally chosen, although there was support for "disability." It was recognized that the important problem was to adopt a term that would come to signify, without ambiguity, the entire field in the minds of all interested parties. Not without influence was the fact that trade associations embracing the insurers in this field had been formed and broadly accepted, notably the Health Insurance Association of America, the Health Insurance Council, and the Health Insurance Institute.

This generic term has found wide acceptance. The two outstanding textbooks in the field are titled *Health Insurance*.[5] Many insurers have revised their designation of activities in this field. Organizations, or departments of organizations, and periodicals have been renamed. The changes have generally been from "accident and health" or "accident and sickness" to "health."

Many words widely used in insurance literature and transactions fail to conform to the criteria listed above—their worst sins are in not meeting the requirements of understandability, single meaning, or functional quality. A few instances will make the point—they could be multiplied.

The words "company" and "carrier" are in wide use as synonymous with "insurer." This last word is functional; it conveys precisely what the organization or individual does and is applicable to a wide variety of forms of enterprise. Many insurers are not companies, and in some documents or discussions only careful attention to the context or interpretive knowledge indicates what the function of the company is. A company may be an insured. A carrier is primarily an agency of transportation which often is a party to an insurance contract or whose cargoes are insured. References to the carrier in a contract should be clearly distinguishable. It would be desirable to employ "insurer" wherever possible; to avoid ambiguity, and

5 Dickerson, O. D. (Homewood, Ill.: Richard D. Irwin, Inc., 1959); Faulkner, Edwin J. (New York: McGraw-Hill Book Co., Inc., 1960).

to promote understanding. Further, this word is generally used in United States statutes.

"Coinsurance" is a term generally understood in Europe and Great Britain to mean "An insurance underwritten by two or more insurers acting in concert, covering the same risk at the same time."[6] It is, or has been, used in the same sense in the United States, particularly in connection with reinsurance. But it is also used to indicate arrangements under which the insured may be obligated to share losses with the insurer. The word by itself has no clear significance.

"Claims" and "losses" are often used interchangeably to mean demands for pecuniary benefits or services, or alternatively payments of benefits or the cost of services paid or incurred in satisfaction by insurers of obligations under insurance contracts. The criteria could be satisfied by restricting "claims" to mean demands on insurers to meet such obligations; and "losses," the payments made and costs actually incurred.

One of the objects of standardization of terminology, whether by insurers or by governmental requirement, is to enable an insured to know what he is purchasing. For example, the word "noncancellable" as applied to an insurance contract is used to indicate to the insured that he is not subject to the danger of being deprived of his insurance by unilateral action of the insurer. As originally used in the health-insurance field, the insured was guaranteed continuance of his contract without change of terms for the remainder of his life or up to a specified advanced age, if he made timely payments of the originally specified premiums. The attractiveness of the term for sales purposes has led to its use with limitations to a short period or without accompaniment of a fixed premium rate. A generally recognized definition is needed to prevent these aberrations.

Many persons are misled by the common use of the expressions "by Lloyd's" and "with Lloyd's," implying that Lloyd's is an insurer. The general use of the correct expression, "at Lloyd's" or "Underwriters at Lloyd's" would indicate that the obligations under the insurance contract are not assumed by Lloyd's as such.

An example of varying meanings officially given to the same technical expression is the use of *net premiums*. In life insurance the net premium is the amount calculated, on the basis of mortality and interest, as sufficient to meet death or survival obligations to insureds or their beneficiaries. In other forms of insurance the net premiums of a given insurer are the premiums written less the total of premiums paid for reinsurance and premiums returned to insureds (other than as dividends). Which sort of

---

[6] *International Insurance Dictionary* (European Conference of Insurance Supervisory Services, 1959), p. 230.

net premium is meant is often clear from context or by virtue of the type of insurance under discussion, but it would be better if the term had a single meaning.

These are only a few examples of the confusion of current terminology. They could be multiplied. And further examples could be drawn from international sources.

The Commission on Insurance Terminology has no power to require adoption or use of its findings by the insurance business, by government, or by lexicographers. But by publicity, persuasion, and voluntary use, it is hoped that order and understanding will in some measure gradually emerge.

It is planned to bring the work of the commission to the attention of officials of insurers, actuarial societies, trade associations, government officials, risk managers of corporations, editors of books and periodicals, and writers on insurance subjects, and to enlist their cooperation both in criticizing and supporting its work and in adopting its conclusions.

What has been accomplished and what is to be hoped for?

In terms of preparation much has been accomplished. The work has been organized. Fruitful discussions have been held. A financial foundation[7] has been laid. Useful publicity has been circulated. Problems have been identified. A few terms have been defined, and usages have been recommended.

But it is to the future that the commission and its committees look. Terms and usages that have become imbedded in greater or lesser degree in the practice of insurance are not readily discarded nor amended. Significant accomplishment must be a matter for continuous work over decades and permanent interest and functioning of the commission.

Perhaps the greatest present accomplishment is the growing conviction that terminology is of major importance and that it demands the serious attention of insurance executives and students.

[7] Financing difficulties have already appeared. (1964)

Index

Accident and health insurance, 202–203
Accident and sickness insurance, 203
Accidents, motor-vehicle, 68–74
  and automobile insurance, 70
  compensation, 70–72
    and automobile insurance, 72
    compulsory insurance, 73–74
    and law of negligence, 70–71
    economic consequences, 69–71
    loss from, 69
    problems of, 69–70
Accidents, traffic (*see* Accidents, motor-vehicle)
Actuarial science, 51
Adjuster, 23
  functions, 144–148
  independent, 144
  insurer, 144
  public, 144
Adjusters, governmental regulation, 149–150
Adjustment of losses, 144–150
  contracts, 146–147
  non-waiver agreement, 146
  practice of law, 149
  (*See also* Adjusters)
Adjustment of Property Losses, 145, 153
Agency qualification, 58–59
  laws, 67
Agent, 21–22
American Association of University Teachers of Insurance, 199–200
American College of Life Underwriters, 114
American Institute for Property and Liability Underwriters, 114
American Management Association, Insurance Division, 63, 113
American Mutual Liability Insurance Company, 4

American Risk and Insurance Association, 200
American Society of Insurance Management, Inc., 63, 113
Anderson, Henry, 112
Annual Report of the Proceedings of the Fire Insurance Society of San Francisco, 155
Apportionment of loss, 151–158
  concurrency of contracts, 152–153
  Connecticut Rule, 154
  Gradual Reduction Rule, 154
  Kinne Rule, 154
  Limit-of-Liability Rule, 156–158
  Reading Rule, 153–154
Apprenticeship, 105
Approaches to Social Security—An International Survey, 80
Association of Casuality and Surety Companies, 157
Automobile insurance, compulsory, 55–56

Bankers' blanket bonds, 65
Bennett, Walter H., 66
Berger, Samuel A., 35
Beveridge, Sir William, 80
Blackall, John C., 191
Blanchard, Ralph H., 19, 44
Bryce, Lord, 66, 91
Bryson, Lyman, 1
Burning ratio, 35–37

Carrier, 203–204
Casualty Actuarial Society, 114
Committee on Unemployment Insurance, 79
Chamber of Commerce of the United States, 199
Changing Times and the Insurance Agent, 55–60

Claims, 204
Coinsurance, 138–143, 204
  agreed-amount clause, 142
  fire insurance, 138–139
  governmental regulation, 138–139
  guaranteed-amount clause, 142
  justification, 139–142
  marine insurance, 138
  Merritt Committee report, 140–141
Commission on Insurance Terminology,
  committees, 201
Commissions, 21–22
Committee on Health Insurance Terminology, 202–203
Committee to Study Compensation for
  Automobile Accidents, 72
Company, 203–204
Competition, 64–68
  boycotts, 65
  prohibitory laws, 65
Comte, Auguste, 84
Contract, 20–21, 23–24, 87–88
  all-risks, 67–68
  comprehensive, 67–68
  concurrency, 152–153
  consideration, 20
  negotiation, 21–22
    agent, 20–21
    broker, 22
    broker-agent, 22
    direct, 21
    intermediaries, 21–22
  stipulations, 20
Contract, fire insurance, description of
  property, 172–176
  ambiguity, 173–176
  New York Standard, 172, 190
  revision of, 190–195
    committee on, 88
  reformation, 172–173

The Dachis Case, 35
Dawson, W. J., 191
Dearden, Harold, 35
Deductibles, 17, 169–171
  normal losses, 169–170
Depression and insurance, 27–33
Dictionary of Insurance Terms, 199

Disbursements, of insurers, 14–15
  analysis of, 53–54

Earned premium, 128
*The Economic Theory of Risk and In-
  surance*, 169
Education, 78, 104–109, 116
  adjuster, 116–118
  classes of workers, 106–107
  courses, 113
  functional, 119–120
  functions, 106
  insurer activities, 113–114
  by lines, 107–108
  risk as special subject, 110–115
  schools, 114–115
  subjects, 108
The Employers' Liability Assurance Corporation, Ltd., 4
Equitable Life Assurance Society, 4
Ericson, William A., 113
Expenses, 95–96

Facing the Future's Risks, 1
Factory Insurance Association, 65
Factory Mutual Insurance, 42
Factory mutuals, 65
Fire hazards, 34–39
  common, 34
  moral, 34–35
    involuntary, 34–35
    voluntary, 34–35
  physical, 34
  special, 34
Fire Insurance by States, 36
Fire losses, 35
  predictability, 38–39
The Fire Raisers, 35
Fire-proof construction, 37–38
Fire-resistive construction, 37
Fire Underwriters Association of the
  Pacific, 108
France, Anatole, 84
Friendly Society in Charles-Town, 4

General average, 3
Goble, G. W., 147
Goerlich, Arthur C., 56

Governmental regulation, 10–15, 24–26,
    85–86, 183–189
competence, 13–14, 186
criteria, 186–188
federal, 85, 89–90
Great Britain, 184–185
objects of, 11–17
powers of insurers, 75–77, 187
practices, 12–13, 185–186
premium rates, 12–13, 189, 196–198
    adequacy, 196–197
    proposal for, 197–198
    reasons for, 183–184
solvency, 11–12, 185
state, 77
    insurance departments, 189
United States, 185–186
Graded rate system, 142–143
Gregg, Davis W., 199
Gross, George I., 62
*Guiding Principles of Overlapping In-
    surance Coverages*, 157

Health insurance, 98–103, 203
contracts, 99–103
group, 178, 181
programming, 177–182
    cost of living, 178–179
social, 180–181
(*See also* Accident and health insurance)
Hardin, John R., 31
Hazards, fire (*see* Fire hazards)
Hohaus, R. A., 82
Holmes, Justice O. W., 120
Hunt, Owen B., 191

Industrial Accident Prevention, 42
Inland Marine Underwriters Association,
    157
Inspector, 22–23
Institute of Life Insurance, 114
Insurance, 19
Insurance
allied lines, 19
casualty, 19
classes of, 16–17, 19
definition of, 20
and depression, 28–33
development of, 3–7

fire, 19
future of, 15–18
Great Britain, 3–4
insularity, 75–78
life, 19
marine, 19
mechanism of, 19–26
    diagram, 25
and other business, 27–28
scientific basis of, 92
United States, 3–5
Insurance Accounting and Statistical
    Association, 114
Insurance buyer (*see* Risk management)
Insurance Buyers of New York, 113
Insurance Company Education Directors'
    Society, 114
Insurance Company of North America, 4
Insurance Institute of America, 114
Insurance manager (*see* Risk manage-
    ment)
Insured's attitude, 5–10
Insurer, 203–204
International Insurance Dictionary, 204
Investments, 133–137
earnings, 135–137
by types of insurer, 134–135

Joint Committee to Sponsor the Accident
    Compensation Plan, 72

Kaplan, Abraham, 35, 62
Ketcham, John C., 191
Knight, Frank H., 1, 5

Language (*see* Terminology)
Lawyer and insurance, 84–91
Life contingencies, 19
Life-insurance experience, 92–93
Lily-Tulip Cup case, 62
Liversidge, H. P., 112
Lloyd's, 3–5, 204
The London Assurance, 4
Losses, 204
causes of 92–95
prediction of, 93–96

Manufacturers Mutual Fire Insurance
    Company, 4

McNairn, Hartley D., 192
Mechanism of insurance, 19–26
Michelbacher, G. F., 160
Motor vehicle insurance (*see* Automobile insurance)
Mowbray, Albert H., 19
The Mutual Life Insurance Company of New York, 4

National Association of Insurance Commissioners, 12, 88
  Committee on Revision of Fire Insurance Policy, 191–192
    Report of, 191–192
  Executive Committee of, 191
National Automobile Underwriters Association, 157
National Board of Fire Underwriters, 155, 156, 157
National Bureau of Casualty Underwriters, 157
National Convention of Insurance Commissioners, 190
National Insurance Buyers Association, 113
National Safety Council, 69
Net premiums, 204
New England Mutual Life Insurance Company, 4
The New Standard Fire Insurance Policy of the State of New York, 190
Noncancellable insurance, 204
Non-concurrent apportionments, 156
Norton, John H., 113

Patterson, E. W., 172
The Philadelphia Contributionship for the Insurance of Houses from Loss by Fire, 4
Pink, Louis H., 191
The Place of Conservation in Insurance, 44
Policy (*see* Contract)
Powers of insurers, 16–17, 75–77, 187
Premium rates, 12–13, 20, 159–163
  accuracy, 160–162
  criteria, 12–13, 159–160
  governmental regulation (*see* Governmental regulation, premium rates)

judgment, 161–163
statistical data, 161–163
units, 160
Premium volume, 5
Presbyterian Ministers' Fund, 4
Prevention, 3, 40–44
  Factory Mutuals, 42–43
  gains from, 42–43
  insurance and, 40–41, 43–44
  National Fire Protection Association, 43
  stock insurers, 43
Probability, 1–3, 160–163
Profits, 96–97
Programming, 8, 98–101
Public relations, 61–63
  adjuster's function, 61–63
Purchasing insurance (*see* Risk management)

The Railway Passengers Assurance Company, 4
Rates (*see* Premium rates)
Rating, merit, 41–42
  experience, 41–42
  schedule, 41–42
Ratios, 45–50
  accident and health insurance, 45–48
  automobile insurance, 48
  distribution cost, 46–48
  dividend, 50
  expense, 50
  and govenmental regulation, 49
  incurred losses—earned premiums, 45–46
  life insurance, 46–47
  loss, 45–46, 50
  paid losses—written premiums, 45–46
  premiums and inflation, 48
  profit, 48–49
  uses, 45
Reed, Prentiss, B., 145, 153
Regulation (*see* Governmental regulation)
Reinsurance, 24
Report on the Lily-Tulip Cup Case, 62
Research, 51–54
  uses, 51, 54
Reserves, 123–127
  contingency, 126

Reserves–*continued*
  depreciation, 126
  dividend equalization, 126
  governmental regulation, 126–127
  loss, 124–126
    calculation, 125–126
    estimate, 125
    interest element, 126
    loss-ratio, 125–126
    tabular, 126
  and solvency, 127
  special purpose, 126
  unearned-premium, 123–124, 128–132
    accuracy, 131–132
    calculation, 129–130
    definition, 128–129
    equity in, 131–132
    governmental regulation, 129–132
    and solvency, 131–132
Resident-agency laws, 66
Richards, George, 174
Richards on Insurance, 153, 174
Risk, 1–3, 110
Risk and insurance, 1–18
Risk management, 110–113, 164–168
  carrying own risk, 165–166
  deductibles, 169–171
  insurance, 166–167
  insurers, 164, 167–168
  prevention, 40–44, 165
  programming, 168
Risk manager, 10, 87
Risk Research Institute, Inc., 63, 113
Risk, Uncertainty and Profit, 1
Royal Exchange Assurance, 4
Rumsey, David, 190

Social insurance, 79–83, 86–87
  and the casualty actuary, 79–83
  definition, 79–80
  and the life actuary, 81

and private insurance, 82
  proposals, 80–81
  answers, 83
  purposes of, 80
Society of Actuaries, 114
Society for Equitable Assurances on Lives
  and Survivorships, 4
State regulation (*see* Governmental regulation)
Studi sulle Assicurazioni, 199
Sun Insurance Office, Ltd., 4
Supervision (*see* Governmental regulation)
Surety Association of America, 157
Survey of Accident and Health Insurance, 45

Taft, Charles, 55
Temporary National Economic Committee, 77
Terminology, 20, 199–205
  Commission on Insurance Terminology, 200–201, 205
  criteria, 201–202
  examples of terms, 203–205
  variations, 199
Thornton, A. W., 155
Training, 105, 116–117
Transportation in the United States, 77
The Travelers Insurance Company, 4

Underwriters at Lloyd's, 204
Unearned premiums (*see* Premiums, unearned)

Van Metre, T. W., 77
Vance on Insurance, 172
Vance, W. R., 172, 173

Whitney, Albert W., 44
Willett, Allan H., 169
Winant, John G., 58

CPSIA information can be obtained
at www.ICGtesting.com
Printed in the USA
LVHW091530040121
675656LV00005B/53